The Price of Power

Inside Ireland's Crisis Coalition

PAT LEAHY

PENGUIN BOOKS

PENGUIN BOOKS

Published by the Penguin Group

Penguin Books Ltd, 80 Strand, London WC2R ORL, England

Penguin Group (USA) Inc., 375 Hudson Street, New York, New York 10014, USA

Penguin Group (Canada), 90 Eglinton Avenue East, Suite 700, Toronto, Ontario, Canada M4P 2Y3
(a division of Pearson Penguin Canada Inc.)

Penguin Ireland, 25 St Stephen's Green, Dublin 2, Ireland
(a division of Penguin Books Ltd)

Penguin Group (Australia), 707 Collins Street, Melbourne, Victoria 3008, Australia
(a division of Pearson Australia Group Pty Ltd)

Penguin Books India Pvt Ltd, 11 Community Centre,
Panchsheel Park, New Delhi – 110 017, India

Penguin Group (NZ), 67 Apollo Drive, Rosedale, Auckland 0632, New Zealand
(a division of Pearson New Zealand Ltd)

Penguin Books (South Africa) (Pty) Ltd, Block D, Rosebank Office Park,
181 Jan Smuts Avenue, Parktown North, Gauteng 2193, South Africa

Penguin Books Ltd, Registered Offices: 80 Strand, London WC2R ORL, England

www.penguin.com

First published by Penguin Ireland 2013
Published in Penguin Books 2014

001

Typeset by Palimpsest Book Production Limited, Falkirk, Stirlingshire
Printed in Great Britain by Clays Ltd, St Ives plc

ISBN: 978-0-241-95782-0

www.greenpenguin.co.uk

Contents

Introduction

He would face greater challenges and accomplish more significant feats as leader of his country, but few of Enda Kenny's later achievements would attract such immediate enthusiasm and whole-hearted approval as his first public act on his first full day as Taoiseach. He walked to work.

Broadcast reports swooned over the new Taoiseach's astonishing deed. An evening news bulletin marvelled that he had walked 'unaided' into the office. 'All in all, a good start, then,' was the summary on another bulletin. It was the same in the newspapers. One commentator said he heard people say all the time that Kenny was 'such a refreshing change . . . [his] boyish enthusiasm for the job is what is lifting the weight' – the weight in question being the crushing effects of debt and recession on their lives. A second wondered if there was 'a touch of the Ronald Reagans' about him. Enda Kenny, said another, was 'leading the way'. Yet another wrote that his walk up Merrion Street 'signalled a new era'. A week after Kenny was elected Taoiseach one of the country's most influential columnists wrote that 'the walk to work with a smile on his face has lifted people's spirits.' The fascination with the walk to work endured long afterwards and beyond the Irish media. Even *Time* magazine, which, to the inexpressible delight of his staff, featured the Taoiseach as its cover story in a 2012 edition, marvelled at this daily perambulation.

It *was* true that Kenny's pedestrian commute demonstrated some sort of a connection with ordinary people and – more importantly – a determination to maintain that connection. But the remarkable level of admiration Kenny received for his walk told another, perhaps more significant story. Sometimes journalists are unwitting weathervanes for the public mood – what the media chooses to report, and how it does so, conveys greater and deeper truths than simply the facts presented to the public. So it was with the lionizing of the Taoiseach's morning march. People desperately wanted a government they could believe in, or at least not despair of. After a bewilderingly rapid collapse – from undreamt-of wealth and prosperity, to economic depression, debt, unemployment and emigration – the Irish people were crying out for relief, for leadership and for real hope that things would get better. They wanted the new government to succeed. Perhaps for this reason, nobody dwelled on the fact that the main reason Enda Kenny walked to work was that he lived in an apartment around the corner from Government Buildings. It is 711 yards from the front door of his apartment block on Fenian Street to the gate of the Department of the Taoiseach on Merrion Street. He always walked to work.

Kenny did not speak in the Dáil on that first day. There was no sitting because he had to attend a European summit in Brussels, his schedule a signpost to the changing structure of national leadership, but also to the immediate pressures that faced the new government. Within hours, he would have to resist strong-arming by the leaders of France and Germany on Ireland's corporation tax arrangements. But the previous day he had spoken in the Dáil, to accept his nomination for Taoiseach. In the emotional imagery-laden language he often deployed for major speeches, Kenny described the Ireland whose leadership he had just assumed:

'People are frightened of losing their homes. Parents are rendered speechless at the sight of their children boarding planes to countries where spring is autumn and our today is their tomorrow. Employers are traumatized by laying off staff and shutting down businesses. Workers pray for invisibility as they queue for the dole. Families worry that the neighbours might see the St Vincent de Paul calling to their door and dread the postman dropping bills like stealth bombs into the hall.'

Describing it was one thing. Fixing it was another. On a few unseasonably warm days in the spring of 2011, the new Taoiseach did make a bright start to his premiership. But leading his government to success would be more difficult and a lot more complicated than schlepping up Merrion Street of a morning. And there would be more than a few stumbles along the way.

The incoming administration's biggest decision was not a decision at all. At no stage, either before taking office, or after they had entered government, did the key figures in Fine Gael or Labour – either separately or together – discuss the possibility, in any serious or actionable way, of walking away from the plan they had inherited. The bailout, EU/IMF/ECB Troika supervision, the banking debt and the accumulation of national debt were the defining features of the economic and political landscape presided over by the new government. Its leaders did not conceive of a departure from the existing roadmap.

The framework of the coalition's economic policy was therefore set by two documents formulated months before it assumed office – the four-year national recovery plan drawn up by Brian Lenihan and his officials, and the original memorandum of agreement between his government and the Troika. There were many significant amendments to them, to be sure. But were the former finance minister still with us, it is likely he would approve of much or most of what the coalition has done. In this and in much else, the mission the new government set itself was to fix the country's broken economy and political systems, not to completely reinvent them.

When the country was last dug out of a fiscal hole in the late 1980s, political wits joked – but they were only half joking – that the country at last had what it had always wanted: a Fianna Fáil government implementing Fine Gael policies. Now that had been turned on its head. The country had a Fine Gael-led government implementing the policies bequeathed to it by its Fianna Fáil predecessor. The place of Labour in this would be one of the recurring and troublesome themes of the coalition and remains an unresolved question.

Fine Gael and Labour did not accept the Troika terms because they were led by crypto-Fianna Fáilers. They did so because the country was running out of money. Says one of the architects of the government's policy, '"Do we stick with the bailout?" It was never really discussed. Why? Because the state had no cash! And because our banking system was leaking deposits. We needed cash and if someone else was prepared to give us €18 billion every year, then we would have considered it. But it was never really a debate.'

Two and a half years later, Eamon Gilmore recalled this in a speech to a Labour Youth conference in Cork. 'When we came into government, I remember very clearly being told that the country had five months' money left. We formed the government in March – that meant that we could have kept the schools open until the holidays begin, but, come September, there would have been no money to pay for them. We had enough money to pay for schools, for hospitals, for pensions and wages for only five months.'

It would become one of the building blocks of Labour's political rhetoric. But it was true; there was no gainsaying it. And it explains why the possibility of defaulting on Ireland's sovereign debt – or that element of it assumed from the banks – was not considered by the incoming government. According to the people involved, the default urged by many quarters was such an unrealistic option it was never on the agenda. There would be several confrontations with Ireland's lenders about the terms of the arrangement. But the principle of the arrangement was never in question.

Was there another way? There is always another way. But no course of action is without cost, despite what many of those clamouring for default claimed. 'Increased poverty, reduced services, a long-standing scar on the financial psyche of the population and political casualties are the common denominators of the short term after a default or crisis,' wrote the editors of the book *What If Ireland Defaults?* in 2012.

The prophet of the bust, Professor Morgan Kelly of UCD, was one of the honest advocates for default. He acknowledged that in the event of a default, 'We would immediately reduce government spending by about one third to balance our budget. We would have no choice because we would be unable to borrow.' As an economic proposition, this is extreme; as a political programme, it is a non-starter. Between 2009 and 2011, gross spending was reduced by €6 billion, a scything that resulted in the massacre of Fianna Fáil candidates in the general election. Kelly's prescription would have seen the coalition cut spending by some €19 billion immediately.

In a world where economic and political certainties were being destroyed, the principals of the coalition knew that the cataclysm such a sudden balancing of the national finances would represent could not be ruled out. But no Irish government was likely to choose it voluntarily. Michael Noonan put it another way. He told his staff: People have too much to lose.

Having made the choice to accept the programme devised by their predecessors, though resolving to work to change aspects of it from within, the task facing Kenny and his government in the spring of 2011 was overwhelmingly a political one. With the economic path decided, the question was the coalition's capacity to follow it. It would soon become clear that with Troika officials breathing down their necks, ministers' room for manoeuvre was greatly limited. What they had to do was maintain public acceptance and social cohesion while the harsh economic medicine stipulated in the bailout programme took its course.

There was some early encouragement for their efforts. A couple of weeks after the government took office, one of Kenny's most senior aides met a potential investor in Irish bonds. The aide went to the meeting armed with spreadsheets, debt projections and economic forecasts. But when he met international fund manager Michael Hasenstab, the conversation was all about politics. Hasenstab could do the numbers himself. He wanted to judge the political capacity and will of the new administration. He would later buy some €10 billion of Irish government debt.

But economics is not an exact science. Even if the coalition was to bring the public finances under control, it had no guarantee that this would fix the crisis in the wider economy, much less produce a political and electoral dividend. If anything, the opposite was the case, as Labour would find out in a by-election two years later. After its candidate was trounced in Meath East in March 2013, Labour minister Pat Rabbitte explained the predicament in his customary pithy way: 'Falling bond yields butter no parsnips.'

Since taking office, the coalition has reduced gross spending by some €3 billion. The resulting political pain has been immense. The problem is not unique to the Irish government. All over Europe, governments have struggled with the same dilemma: how to implement the economic policies they believe are necessary, while maintaining popular legitimacy and credibility. And all over Europe they have paid the price.

By summer 2013 Enda Kenny was being spat at during protests against his government's economic policies, and accused of being a murderer for his legislation on abortion. His government and his party had plummeted in popularity, and his main and historic rivals in Fianna Fáil had performed an astonishing resuscitation in the opinion polls. His government had presided over a continuance of unpopular austerity policies – loading further taxes on workers, cutting welfare benefits, reducing public spending on health and education. Huge numbers of people believed the coalition had 'broken their promises', the government's own research showed. Demonstrators outside Eamon Gilmore's constituency office shouted at him that he had 'betrayed James Connolly'. A yawning budget deficit had been closed somewhat, but remained unsustainably high, running in 2013 at almost a billion euros a month. The pain of the burdens imposed on the population was clear and evident; the benefits promised seemed elusive and uncertain. The public finances had been stabilized and set on the path to recovery, but it was a treacherous route, bordered by economic uncertainty on one side and political unpopularity on the other. Governing in the age of austerity was a brutal experience.

Kenny's coalition – the 'national government' hailed in those early days when his walk to work was still a thing to be marvelled at – had creaked and tottered on occasion, and his Labour Party partners were increasingly bruised by the demands made on them. Labour had watched a procession of its elected representatives – ministers, TDs, senators, councillors and an MEP – resign the party whip in disgust, disappointment or despair. Each coruscating resignation speech inflicted new wounds on the leadership and made it more difficult for the foot-soldiers who remained. The party's principal response was to heap derision on the departed, and to insist things would get better, for the country and the party. It was part aspira-tion, part analysis. The party's greatest fear for itself was that the recovery of the country's fortunes – for which it had sacrificed his-toric levels of public support – would leave it behind; that either no political dividend would materialize from an economic recovery, or that when it did, it would all go to Fine Gael. It was a sensible fear.

It may not have seemed like it, but by the time Pat Rabbitte was bemoaning the inability of bond yields to butter parsnips, the government was already successful – at least by the measure of willingness of investors to lend money to the state, the stark measure that had brought about the bailout in the first place. Simply put, yields measure the markets' views; and for the exchequer, high yields are bad, low yields are good. In the early months of the coalition, the yield on Irish bonds climbed as high as 13 per cent at a time when the equivalent German bonds were yielding 2.7 per cent. When the voters of Meath East were delivering their unfavourable verdict on Labour's candidate, Irish ten-year yields had fallen to about 3.5 per cent. (Once upon a time, not too long ago, only the specialists in government, and the political community that orbits it, knew what bond yields were; now, it seems, everybody knows.)

As Rabbitte understood only too well, without falling bond yields there would be no butter, and no parsnips either. But his comments following the Meath East debacle were not simply an example of a grumpy minister bemoaning the electorate's ignorance and ingrati-tude. Rabbitte's understanding of politics is more sophisticated than that. He knew that Labour's unpopularity, and the associated jitters in its parliamentary party, undermined the political capacity of the party leadership and therefore of the government as a whole. And that restricted its freedom to act. This would become a central theme of the middle phase of the coalition's life.

By its mid-term point, the coalition had found that the price of power was a heavy one. Yet, the first part of the task the coalition had set for itself – to steady the country's financial situation and regain economic sovereignty after the bailout – had been achieved or nearly achieved. But the second – to profoundly reform the politics of

Ireland – is much more uncertain. It would be difficult to say with any conviction that the nature of politics in Ireland is much different now to what it was when Enda Kenny became Taoiseach. Is government better than the last years of a disastrous Fianna Fáil-led administration? Certainly. But are our politics profoundly different? Hardly. That remains, at best, a work in progress.

Some government insiders, frustrated by the pace of reform, believe this is one of the chief reasons for the government's unpopularity: the rhetoric of profound change in our politics has not been matched by delivery. In 2011 Enda Kenny and Eamon Gilmore diagnosed that the political system had failed, and promised to change it. In office, they have certainly tried to change the system for the better – but also to preserve it. To many voters, this sounds like a retreat.

The promise of change is potent at election time. The trouble is always: change to what? When Gilmore and Kenny promised change in 2011, many people heard the promise of a change from the discredited politics of the Ahern era. However, to Kenny and Gilmore, the real change was the replacement of the government. To them, this was self-evidently a change for the better. And so it was for the public, temporarily. But the public had either been led or chosen to believe that a more fundamental change to politics was in the offing, and before the new government's first year had elapsed, trust and confidence in it had taken a battering. Their parties' opinion poll numbers, as they usually do, would soon reflect that.

Both published and private research showed the broken promises theme looms large in voters' minds. As it does in the minds of many government backbenchers. One frustrated TD told me, 'We promised people a new politics. We haven't given it to them.' Indeed, as it ages, the coalition seems to exhibit more of the characteristics of its predecessors, rather than fewer. The controversies – entirely of their own making – faced by James Reilly and Alan Shatter would not have been out of place in any Fianna Fáil government since Haughey. This tendency represents as much a threat to the coalition's re-election prospects as the economic straitjacket that will confine future governments of whatever stripe.

Ireland's crisis coalition has packed much incident and drama into its short half-life. The journey from the fraught negotiations on the Programme for Government – when negotiators gawped in disbelief as officials stumbled through bleak descriptions of the state of the nation – to the summer of 2013, when the coalition busily planned for an early budget and a bailout exit, is the story of this book.

This is a biography of this government, but an unfinished one. It is the story so far – a story of low politics and high ambition, of human frailty and of selfless sacrifice, of ambition fulfilled and frustrated. It is a tale of very high stakes; of failures of nerve and grace under pressure, of choices made, unmade and fudged. It is a very human story, centred around a relatively small group of people, whose choices and actions, successes and failures, greatly affect the daily lives of their fellow citizens and the fortunes of their country, and will perhaps for decades to come.

If Tony Blair practised 'sofa government' from his study, this coalition practises 'Sycamore government' – the real decisions are taken not in the cabinet room, but across the quadrangle of Government Buildings in the Sycamore Room, the location for the weekly meetings of the Economic Management Council. The EMC – comprising Taoiseach, Tánaiste and the two finance ministers, Michael Noonan and Brendan Howlin, supported by their most important aides and officials – is an inner cabinet where almost all significant decisions are made. Its foundation constitutes the biggest structural change in cabinet government in the history of the state. Some of the advisers and civil servants around the table in the Sycamore Room are in many ways more powerful than most cabinet members.

The relationships between the four members of the EMC and their senior staff are central to the functioning of the coalition. Enda Kenny's partnership with Eamon Gilmore is unlikely – they are different animals; opposites in many ways. Yet, though they are not personally close, they have forged a solid bond at the heart of government. Michael Noonan and Brendan Howlin have formed an axis across the twin finance departments that is at the very core of the deals and compromises on which a government such as this stands or falls. Theirs is a different relationship to that of Kenny and Gilmore

– they have moments of discord and disagreement, born of the fact they are in the frontline of the natural differences on tax and spending that might be expected between parties of the centre-right and centre-left – but it is similarly crucial to the coalition.

In addition to the politicians in the EMC, two further sets of relationships are vital to the operation of the government. Andrew McDowell, Enda Kenny's chief economic adviser, and Colm O'Reardon, who fulfils the same role for Eamon Gilmore, form an indispensable bond in agreeing policy at the heart of the government. Mark Kennelly and Mark Garrett, chiefs of staff to the two leaders, are *consiglieri* – trouble-shooters and problem-solvers for their bosses; their role is to manage the politics of coalition government. Like all powerful non-elected advisers, these four are routinely the subject of fierce complaint and bitter resentment from elected politicians, both TDs and ministers. It does not worry them; they have the absolute trust of their masters.

Of the two leaders, it is Kenny who has had the happier time of it in government, settling into the role of Taoiseach with a comfort that has amazed the many former detractors in his party and beyond. He has proved, even through the moral and political maelstrom of the abortion issue, a steady and canny manager of his own party. It is impossible to find anyone in Fine Gael who believes the party did not make the right choice when it decided against sacking him in favour of Richard Bruton. But the weaknesses that prompted his party to challenge him less than a year before he became Taoiseach are real and they have not disappeared. Though he is more confident with the detail of domestic and economic policy, he still struggles occasionally. While he has shown the bearing of a leader of the nation in some Dáil performances – particularly when he declared himself 'a Taoiseach who happens to be a Catholic, not a Catholic Taoiseach' (to much media swooning) – at times he is prone to desperate waffle. The largely positive personal press he has received has not dwelt on the fact he has sometimes said terribly silly things. His assertion to a press conference that the Seanad should be abolished because it failed to criticize the policies of the Celtic Tiger period is not an analysis that stands up to much interrogation.

The response to this among Kenny's staff has been to protect him as much as possible from media encounters. He does few full-length searching interviews. For many years his detractors have belittled his intellect, and, while this is a serious underestimation, it is true that he is no intellectual. Like most Irish politicians, he is a pragmatist: policy is a plan to him, not a working out of how the forces of government, administration and society interplay. He is not naturally at home with thinking about policy in a broader sense. Sometimes this can leave him seriously disadvantaged. In one text exchange with a senior government adviser, I teased that he had been mad to leave his previously well-paid employment to work in government, especially as he was not getting his way on some policy matter. He replied: 'The bit in meetings where Enda runs out of road with the speaking note and has to fend for himself, so to speak, is worth all that despair.'

More than intellect or charisma, a politician's most important quality is judgement. As the British political commentator Janan Ganesh has said, this is best informed by a politician's animal instinct, his sense of smell. Bertie Ahern was the master at it, displaying an awareness of the electorate's needs and tolerances that won him three elections. Kenny's is not as acute, but it is pretty good and pretty consistent. He operates much of the time on instinct. Mostly that instinct is conservative. Often his inclination is to do nothing, to let events take their course until the decision required somehow manifests itself. Yet this instinctive politician leads a party whose every policy position is carefully researched and calibrated with an eye on the public mood. No party has used as much voter research, through focus groups and polling, as Kenny's Fine Gael.

Before Enda Kenny got lucky at winning elections, he was lucky at not winning them. His two great strokes of luck were to lose elections – the leadership contest against Michael Noonan in 2001 and the general election of 2007. Had he beaten Noonan for the leadership, he would have been crushed by Bertie Ahern a year later. Had he won the general election in 2007, the boom would have turned to bust just as surely as it did under the hapless Brian Cowen, and Fianna Fáil would have said, We handed you the best economy in the world and look what you did. After that, Fine Gael and Labour would not have been let near government for a generation.

For Eamon Gilmore, this may be Labour's fate anyway. If our strategy works, one aide explained to me early in the administration's life, and the economy and the country recover, then we'll probably be re-elected. If it doesn't we'll all have bigger problems than the Labour Party's poll numbers. This is not quite right. It is quite possible that the economy recovers and the country emerges from its state of crisis, but that Labour garners little or no credit for it – only blame for the unpopular policies it implemented along the way.

Gilmore's load in government has been heavier than Kenny's, and the difference seems written in the two men's faces – Kenny's pre-ternaturally youthful countenance is almost permanently unruffled, while Gilmore's brow seems equally constantly furrowed. Labour's instincts – and a goodly chunk of its party members – rebel against the harsh austerity measures that the government has implemented. But if so, Gilmore is not blameless – to win seats at the last election he made promises that he would not and could not keep in government. And while his party has not been as unpopular as some of its members think, government is becoming harder and harder for it. His personal ratings have plummeted. One of his colleagues, who knows him best, reflected wryly on how his once huge popularity had been replaced by equally enormous unpopularity: 'I thought both positions were rather unfair to him.' There is some truth to it.

The restlessness of Gilmore's party has been one of the recurring stories of the coalition's early years. Much of it has been visible; some of it has not. And all the while, behind the scenes, a simmering rivalry with his deputy leader Joan Burton threatens to boil over and cause someone serious injury.

The first phase of this government has been about crisis management. The next will have to see the coalition set out a more distinctive political vision, a new direction, a plan for a post-bailout world. Those at the heart of government say nothing could be harder than facing the reality of governing a state whose financial viability, even with the bailout funds, was balanced precariously at the edge of a cliff. But they know that the second half of their term will be fraught with more political pitfalls, trickier and more complicated than the first. And they will, like all politicians, think more and more about elections as these approach. The purpose of this book is to offer a bare and real account of those first days, before they are forgotten, ignored, mythologized, or wilfully misrepresented in the pursuit of political goals.

When first discussing this project with people, I was conscious that, by definition, it would be a tale without an ending – or at least without a satisfactory one. Yet the magnitude of the crisis faced by the country and its government, and the scale of the decisions faced and taken by the government in those early years, seemed worthy of chronicling in their own right, while events were still relatively fresh in the protagonists' memories, and before they could be reinterpreted in the light of future events – especially elections. The essence of the book is therefore narrative, rather than analytical; I seek to tell the story of what happened, rather than pass judgement upon it. Some measure of judgement and analysis is unavoidable, of course; but in the main, readers can make up their own minds about the people who govern them.

What I have tried to do is tell the story as seen from the inside, rather than from the outside. There are always two political realities: the one presented to the public, and the one that takes place behind the scenes. It is the latter that has always fascinated me, and that I have tried to write about. It never ceases to amaze me how much the true inside story sometimes contradicts the published reports (including my own) when it eventually becomes clear. Often, though not always, the fault for this lies with the government; the cult of secrecy is strong in Irish governance. Sometimes there are good reasons for this; often not. I have always tried to tell the stories of politics and politicians as they really are. Very often that is more complex than one of knaves, fools and heroes.

Even over such a relatively short period, it would be impossible to chronicle every act of the government. What I have tried to do instead is to concentrate on events that have a longer-term signifi-cance for the coalition, and for the country, and to describe these events in as much detail as I can manage. I have chosen events that not only have an import in and of themselves, but that also tell us something about the nature of the government. The book is as such arranged in a series of roughly chronological episodes. The narrative begins not when the coalition takes office, but rather with the heave against Enda Kenny in the early summer of 2010. I have chosen this jumping-off point because I believe it is impossible to properly understand Enda Kenny as Taoiseach without understanding the challenge to him – or more importantly, his overcoming of that challenge – that the heave represented. Its echoes continue to reverberate.

I am indebted to the people in government and around it who spoke to me of their experiences. This book is the product of over one hundred interviews and many hundreds of conversations with people at all levels of politics. As I did when writing my first book *Showtime*, an account of Bertie Ahern's years in office, I conducted all such conversations on an off-the-record basis, agreeing that I would not identify the source of information or accounts of events. Some readers may find this frustrating or unsatisfactory. I believe it is justified by the frankness which it has encouraged. Ultimately it is a matter of trust between author and readers; and readers can judge that for themselves. For my part, it means that some people who otherwise would be constrained have spoken openly and truthfully about their experience of government, even when those accounts are sometimes uncomfortable. There already exist voluminous records of the government's and of individual politicians' attributed thoughts about their deeds and achievements in office. It is not the purpose of this book to add to these.

A large number of very busy people have cooperated in the writing of the book. They did so, I am sure, for a variety of reasons. What they all shared was a belief that theirs was a story that should be told, that the citizens of Ireland should have an account of what their government did during the greatest crisis to face the country in its history. I am grateful to all of them. I know I have trespassed many times on their goodwill and patience. In return I can only say that I have told the story of this government as honestly and fairly as I can.

Most of the book is a product of these interviews, which were conducted specifically for this project, and of the many hundreds of follow-up queries that they generated. Of course, given the nature of the day job, it also draws on my work for the *Sunday Business Post*, while some elements of the account of the 2011 general election rely upon interviews conducted while writing a chapter for the latest in that invaluable part of the canon of political writing in this country, the 2011 edition of the How Ireland Voted series. Some material in the early chapters concerning the collapse of Brian Cowen's government draws upon interviews I conducted for a two-part RTÉ television documentary, *Crisis: Inside the Cowen Government*, in 2011. I am also indebted to my fellow political correspondents in Leinster House for their tireless and comprehensive reporting, especially since the changing nature of my duties at the newspaper since I undertook this project has meant that I have had less time to spend around Kildare Street.

As before, I have quoted conversations where I have a reliable record of them, either from the participants, from people who witnessed them, or from people who were given an account of them. A small number rely on contemporaneous reports, both my own and others. Where I have occasionally described what people were thinking, it is because I have a convincing report of it, either from the people themselves or from people to whom they expressed those thoughts. I am afraid that some conversations are conducted in the private argot of political life, and that can involve liberal measures of profanity. I have included this simply to give as truthful an account as I can. I apologize in advance to readers who are offended.

I am grateful to Michael McLoughlin at Penguin, whose enthusiasm, belief and judgement I trust and admire. By publishing a series of books in recent years, Michael has done more than most to explain to the Irish people what has happened in their own country; I am proud to have been a part of that process. Patricia Deevy has again been a superb editor – wise in little things and large, exacting, sympathetic and Stakhanovite in her dedication to the book. Cliff Taylor, editor of the *Sunday Business Post*, has been tolerant of occasional absences and understanding of the workload that I took upon myself. My colleagues and friends at the newspaper have come through a difficult time with their good humour and belief in the importance of quality journalism intact. Long may it so remain; I am grateful to all of them. My parents, Seamus and Kay Leahy, gave me an early familiarity with the written word and a belief in doing worthwhile things well that has informed my life and my work. My sister Caitriona has been one of the project's greatest supporters in a variety of ways. She corrected proofs of the book, with assistance from my father, when she had many other demands on her time. The rest of my family in Clonmel and the vast horde of the MacKenzies in Dublin have been supportive and sympathetic throughout. Barbara MacKenzie and Yvonne Keating have often seen more of my children than their father has, while Stephen MacKenzie also provided a quiet space for writing, a priceless facility unavailable in a happy but incessantly noisy home. My friends have been tolerant, encouraging and un-interested where appropriate. I apologize to all for disappearing for extended periods and I am grateful to them – especially to Peter MacDonagh and Martin Mackin – for their continued counsel, friendship and stimulation.

Circumstances at the newspaper meant that it was impossible to take extended periods of leave, so this book was written in the evenings and at weekends over the last two years. As she did during the writing of *Showtime*, my wife Nicola created time and space for me to research and write by assuming almost entirely to herself the care of our children, and also again added to their number during the process. She encouraged and sustained me throughout in every way. For all this, and for so very much else, I am grateful beyond words. This book is dedicated to her.

The heave

Enda Kenny was eating his steak. The ground-floor interior of McGrattan's restaurant, on a laneway opposite Government Buildings, is gloomy, with little natural light, and perhaps for that reason it is often visited by politicians. They can eat their steaks in peace.

There would be little peace for Kenny on this occasion. On a balmy evening in early June 2010, the Oireachtas press gallery was having its summer drinks party in the bar at the rear of the restaurant, so as the political correspondents arrived in ones and twos, they passed Kenny's table. Many stopped to say hello. Kenny, as is his wont, had a word for them all.

The Fine Gael leader is by nature an extremely good-humoured and gregarious man, even by the standards of politicians, a breed used to having their steak dinners interrupted. But now he seemed jaded and preoccupied. He smiled and greeted and punched arms and sent over a round of drinks as usual – but he looked grim and ashen, as if some terrible news had just been broken to him.

That's exactly what had happened. Soon the drinking journalists' phones began to beep and hum with the same news that had so deflated the leader of the opposition. The *Irish Times* was publishing an opinion poll the following morning, and the results were dreadful for Fine Gael – and for its leader. By 8.30 p.m. the numbers were beginning to fly about: bad news travels fast. They were confirmed on RTÉ's *Nine O'Clock News*. Fine Gael's support had dropped by four points to 28 per cent, the party's lowest poll rating in the *Irish Times*/MRBI series since the financial crisis dawned in 2008; it was also the first time since the crisis that it had dipped below the psychologically important 30 per cent mark. Fianna Fáil support had collapsed, and the country had tripped into economic freefall, yet, in the three years since the general election of 2007, Fine Gael had managed to add just a single point to its ratings. Worse, the poll showed that Labour had overtaken Fine Gael, and now stood at 32 per cent, a record high and the first time the party had ever led the field in such a poll. Kenny's personal ratings were even more damaging: his already weak standing with the public had deteriorated further, with a sharp seven-point drop to 24 per cent, his lowest results in the series since having become party leader in 2002. There was no bright side to it. One senior party figure texted, 'It's a fucking disaster.'

The alacrity with which politicians dismiss opinion polls in public is only matched by the intensity with which they obsess over them in private. It's an iron law of politics that whenever you hear a politician saying that he doesn't pay any attention to opinion polls, he's lying. Though, in fairness, nobody was saying that about this poll.

Less than an hour later, Richard Bruton, the party's deputy leader and finance spokesman, kept a scheduled appearance on RTÉ's *Prime Time* programme to discuss the recent reports on Ireland's banking collapse, published the previous day. He must have known what was coming. 'Do you, Richard Bruton, have confidence in your leader?' Miriam O'Callaghan asked him. 'It's not about me . . .' he parried. 'I'm just as much in the dock in terms of Fine Gael's failings. We're in the dock. We have to look at our whole performance as a party.' This wasn't going to wash with O'Callaghan, and Bruton knew it. 'It's a straight yes or no,' she said simply. 'It's not about me,' tried Bruton again.

It was Thursday, so most TDs had left Leinster House and were back in their constituencies. Some were watching. One frontbencher thought: Fucking hell! Those that weren't watching quickly heard about it.

Bruton left RTÉ and travelled across South Dublin to the TV3 studios, where he was appearing on Vincent Browne's late-night programme. Browne's show is, to put it mildly, unpredictable for the politicians who appear on it, but Bruton's intellectual self-confidence and mastery of policy detail have always put him at his ease during his appearances. Browne often seems to be able to smell a politician's fear, but Bruton wasn't afraid of him that night. Indeed, the mood in the studio was at times jocular. Bruton himself – his phone had been going non-stop since the *Prime Time* comments – seemed almost giddy. He dodged around the inevitable question, seeming to row back a bit, but only a bit, offering a watery endorsement of all Kenny had done for the party, but never expressing outright confidence in his party leader. Browne came at it another way: did he have leadership ambitions? 'In the swag bag of every corporal is a lieutenant's baton,' he tittered. Fine Gael TDs all over the country texted and phoned one another frantically. The typical question was: 'What's going on?' For those who had been anticipating a challenge to Kenny for months but had no forewarning of Bruton's extraordinary comments, the question was active, rather than passive. The young Dublin TD Lucinda Creighton, who had become hugely frustrated by Kenny's leadership, spoke to her fellow young turks Simon Coveney and Leo Varadkar. Her question was simple: 'What the fuck are we going to do now?'

The following day, Friday, was a maelstrom of rumour, spin, speculation and plotting. Journalists pestered Fine Gaelers of every rank and hue to find out if there really was a heave afoot against Kenny's leadership and, if so, who was on which side. Many let their phones ring out and didn't return messages. There was nothing to be gained by admitting they hadn't a clue what was going on. Some were trying to make things happen; others were trying to prevent them. Kenny and Bruton were attending different social events: Kenny was in Cork, where party grandee Peter Barry was being made an Honorary Freeman of the city, while Bruton was in Dublin, attending the wedding of Jennifer Carroll, the party's legal adviser, and Hugo MacNeill, the former Irish rugby international and now managing director of Goldman Sachs. There was an incessant stream of phone calls to the Fine Gael guests at both events.

In many ways Richard Bruton is not a politician at all. He has a mastery of policy detail that puts experts to shame. Indeed, his policy wonkery has often aroused suspicion and occasionally derision in Irish political debate, where most participants prefer to deal in broad strokes and generalities. This engagement with detail has sometimes combined with his natural caution to make him painfully slow in reaching decisions. When he was last in government in the mid 1990s, his office was known as 'the black hole': when something went in there, it never came out. This was harsh, but not entirely unfair.

Now Bruton was facing a decision, the defining decision of his political career. The *Irish Times*'s front-page headline that day had trumpeted: 'Labour now the biggest party in State for first time, poll shows'. Even allowing the headline writers a lot of latitude in interpreting the poll's findings, this was laying it on a bit thick. There was ample evidence in other polls and in Fine Gael's own research to show that, while Labour was on a surge, asserting that it was now the most popular party was certainly open to question. Claiming it was the 'biggest' party was just nuts. But the story was out, and Fine Gael was in a panic about it.

There had been rumblings about Kenny's leadership forever. The rumblings became rumours of a coup four months earlier, when George Lee resigned his seat in a blaze of negative publicity. Lee's brief political career was a lesson in misadventure. It had seemed like a masterstroke for Fine Gael when the RTÉ economics editor had showed up to run for the party in a by-election in Dublin South, but after a mere nine months Lee had resigned from the Dáil, complaining of his frustration at having 'virtually no influence' on Fine Gael's economic policy. It was a fundamental misunderstanding of what the party had wanted from him. Fine Gael already had people to make economic policy; what it didn't have were enough household names whom the voters liked and trusted.

Nothing came of the rumblings against Kenny after Lee's departure, partly because no one would give Lee the satisfaction. But the reasons for the unhappiness with the leader were still there. Bruton and others had despaired of Kenny's performance in media outings and in the Dáil over the recent months, and the poll offered evidence that the public was seeing the same things. As Fianna Fáil imploded, the topography of Irish politics was being reordered. Maybe Labour really could overtake Fine Gael. Bruton knew, like everyone else who had read a focus group report or knocked on the doors, that there was huge public resistance to Kenny. For one thing, voters had difficulty seeing him as a Taoiseach. The deputy leader was sure the frontbench would back a change.

And yet Bruton remembered the heaves against his brother John – during which Enda Kenny had stayed steadfastly loyal – and how the toxic legacy of a family at war had poisoned the party for a decade and more. Kenny had promoted him, depended on him, deferred to him. Bruton knew it would be a painful betrayal. Kenny's allies – his strongman Phil Hogan especially – would want him to fight, Bruton expected. But surely he would see the inevitability of defeat and just resign? Bruton mingled easily with the lawyers and investment bankers and rugby heroes and future government ministers at the black-tie reception in Carroll and MacNeill's Killiney home, pondering the inescapable question that now faced him. Sometimes caution and delay are the best course in politics; but bold action is more often conspicuously rewarded. If not now, when? Bruton knew the time for waiting and considering was nearly over.

Phil Hogan was way ahead of him. Ever since the party's outbreak of the heebie-jeebies after George Lee's departure, Hogan had figured this day would come. He knew that there was a gathering group of dissidents, he knew Bruton would be their champion – if they could get him to run – and he figured that the period before the summer was the time of maximum danger. As Fine Gael TDs publicly acknowledged the need for the leader to up his game in the wake of Lee's exit, Hogan spoke to the party's health spokesman, James Reilly, and to the chief whip, Paul Kehoe. They began to confer regularly, speculating on the state of play within the dissidents and drawing up rough lists of the loyal, the disloyal and what might be the crucial swing votes in the middle. From March they began canvassing gently and locking down votes. Maybe it might never come, Kenny hoped. Hogan thought otherwise.

When the *Irish Times* poll detonated, Hogan was in London for a Fine Gael golf fundraiser, but his political antennae started twitching furiously. When he heard Bruton's comments, he called Kehoe and Reilly. 'Start checking these guys,' he said, listing out the TDs and senators that they had identified as potential waverers. Hogan would fight furiously for Kenny. But he knew he was also fighting for his own political career. If Bruton won, he was finished. Later he went through the names with Kenny again. On the Friday, Hogan could feel the momentum gathering for Bruton and knew that there would be pressure on Kenny to resign and avoid a damaging internal battle. But he assured Kenny that they would have the numbers. 'Now you're not going to do anything stupid, are you?' he asked from London. Kenny replied instantly: 'I will like fuck.' Satisfied, Hogan ran through his numbers. He reckoned he had a majority on the first night.

The first requirement in politics is that you have to be able to count. But Bruton was reluctant to begin the messy business of totting up heads and canvassing. He first wanted to speak to Kenny. The two had a number of telephone conversations on the Saturday, in which Kenny appealed to Bruton to back down and issue a public declaration of support for his leadership for the Sunday newspapers. But Bruton had made his mind up. There was no going back.

Bruton began to phone frontbench members, starting with those he knew were disillusioned with Kenny's performance as leader: Brian Hayes, Billy Timmins, Denis Naughten. But Hayes and the others were worried about the crazy lack of preparation for such a serious undertaking and had already discussed letting Bruton off and just sitting on their hands. They reasoned that Kenny would be so damaged by a Bruton challenge that he could be taken out later by someone else. But Bruton would be hugely damaged as well, they knew; and there was no real alternative to him in the public's mind as a leader of Fine Gael: it was too soon for any of their generation. So if it was going to happen, they felt they had to begin canvassing hard among the backbenchers immediately. Bruton wouldn't let them. He wanted to talk to the frontbench first and secure their support. If a majority of his frontbench told Kenny that he had to go, Bruton reasoned, surely he had to go? Eugene Regan, an influential senator, called him and advised that he needed to start ringing the backbenchers. 'No,' Bruton replied, 'we'll deal with it on Tuesday at the frontbench meeting. They'll see that a change is inevitable.' 'But what if they don't?' Regan asked. 'They will,' Bruton answered.

Kenny returned to Dublin on Sunday morning, and met with Bruton. It was a difficult encounter for both men, but neither would alter his position from that of the previous day. Meanwhile, the Sunday newspapers were full of stories about the heave. Unnamed sources predicted that Kenny would have to resign at Tuesday's frontbench meeting, when it became clear that he no longer enjoyed his senior colleagues' support. There were public declarations of backing for the leader from Hogan, Kehoe, Reilly, Alan Shatter, Jimmy Deenihan, Michael Ring, Charlie Flanagan and Frances Fitzgerald, but the rest of the frontbench – all ten of them – stayed silent. Everyone drew the obvious conclusions from the silence. Despite having failed either to canvass or to lock down votes, the dissidents believed the momentum was unstoppable now. One opponent wondered: Does anyone seriously believe he can lead Fine Gael with Richard Bruton on the backbenches?

But Bruton was turning out to be a hopeless candidate. He had no campaign manager, no media strategy, no message, no head counters, no strongarm men, no foot soldiers. Brian Hayes and the others struggled to pull the Bruton campaign together. But it wasn't really a campaign; it was more a point of view.

Meanwhile, the Kenny camp, with Hogan and Paul Kehoe making the running, was targeting not just the TDs but, crucially, the fifteen senators and four MEPs. They all had votes too. This would turn out to be a decisive move.

On Monday, Kenny seized the initiative and sacked Bruton as finance spokesman and deputy leader. It was a bold and provocative move; there would be no compromise, no easy way out for everyone. You were either with the leader, or against him. Battle had been joined. To his staff, Kenny appeared both resolute but also genuinely saddened by the affair. He constantly told them two things. First, he was going to win. And, second, that it was a terrible tragedy for Bruton himself. 'This is a terrible mistake,' he told one of his most senior aides. 'This isn't what Richard wants. This isn't his fault. He's been pushed into it by a bunch of thugs.' Bruton himself was taken aback by Kenny's move. He rang Brian Hayes, who was in his car. 'Kenny has just sacked me!' he said incredulously, and started giggling. Canvassing and briefing continued all day, and that evening Bruton again went to the RTÉ studios, where, on the *Frontline* programme, he was interrogated by Pat Kenny about his leadership plans. But he waffled, lacking a clear message about just why he wanted to be leader and what Fine Gael under him would do. His only backup at RTÉ was his son, a politics student at Dublin City University. It didn't look much like an unstoppable machine.

Tuesday is when TDs from the country make their way back to Dublin for the Dáil's afternoon sitting. The dissidents on the front-bench – Varadkar, Michael Creed, Olivia Mitchell, Naughten, Fergus O'Dowd, Hayes as well as Bruton himself – had arranged to meet at 7.30 a.m. in the Green Isle Hotel on the outskirts of Dublin to plan their approach to that morning's crunch frontbench meeting, when they hoped to force Kenny to resign. Olwyn Enright, the social protection spokeswoman, who was also among the rebels, took part in the meeting by speakerphone. But someone had tipped off RTÉ reporter Valerie Cox, who duly turned up and confronted the TDs as they were about to leave. Panic ensued, with several of the group literally making a run for it to avoid Cox and a photographer, jumping into their cars and speeding off. Cox reported in live to *Today with Pat Kenny* on the farce.

Simon Coveney – thought to be among the rebels but not present at the meeting – was immediately fingered as the source of the leak and became the subject of hysterical suspicions about a 'double agent' in the ranks of the rebels. In fact, Coveney *had* been in contact with Phil Hogan. Such contacts between two opposing camps are not that unusual in political contests of this nature, especially when both sides have a shared interest in avoiding mutually assured destruction. But Coveney also had another agenda. He believed that he could possibly be a compromise candidate for the leadership, acceptable to both camps – an idea that was assiduously being put about by the Cork TD Jim O'Keeffe. Hogan thought it was 'hilarious' but entertained the idea in order to glean information about which TDs might be playing both sides. Unbeknownst to Coveney, Phil Hogan was also in contact with Brian Hayes. 'He [Coveney] told me he was the only candidate who could unite the party,' Hogan told Hayes. Neither man shared that view. Coveney eventually voted against Kenny.

A few hours after the Green Isle getaway, at 11 a.m. on Tuesday, the frontbenchers filed into the Fine Gael party room on the fourth floor of Leinster House, a smallish room dominated by a large table.

Kenny laid into them for twenty minutes. He would be tabling a motion of confidence in his leadership on Thursday. And he would win, he told them, and appoint a new frontbench. They should all consider themselves sacked immediately. He gathered up his papers and swept from the room, followed by Hogan and Kehoe. Billy Timmins made after them, and had an angry confrontation outside with Kenny. The rest of the frontbench remained, many of them shell-shocked at the unexpected turn of events.

The contest now entered its final, bitter phase. The rebels conferred quickly and decided to march out on to the Leinster House plinth in order to explain their case publicly to the media. Conscious of the emerging perception that the anti-Kenny camp was the private school boys – or 'The Cappuccino Plotters', as they were dubbed by some commentators – they agreed that the Roscommon TD Denis Naughten (though cappuccino is widely available throughout Roscommon) would be their spokesman. 'We are putting our careers on the line in what we believe is the best interests of this country and in the best interests of the Fine Gael,' he said. Naughten had agonized more than most about joining the attempted coup against his fellow West of Ireland man, and he would be the subject of some fury from Kenny supporters for his decision. As events turned out, he was exactly right about putting his career on the line. But another career was about to be resurrected.

Kenny had reached out to Michael Noonan, who had languished on the backbenches since his leadership of the party had ended so disastrously in the election of 2002. Noonan had been a brooding presence on the backbenches since his leadership ended – 'I'm in Siberia,' he used to tell people – but he made occasional forays into public debate. He was the first TD in Leinster House publicly to voice fears that the 2008 crisis in the Irish banks was a crisis of solvency, rather than liquidity, as both government and banks claimed at the time. Two weeks before the heave he gave an emotional interview to Pat Kenny on RTÉ's *Frontline* show, telling of his struggles to care for his wife, who was suffering from Alzheimer's disease, which aroused great public sympathy.

Politics sometimes sees remarkable second acts, and one was

commencing now. Kenny called his predecessor, and then went to
see him in his office. Neither man has ever revealed what was said,
though both have denied a deal was made. Others think differently.
The facts are these: Kenny won an extremely tight election in which
every single vote counted. And then he made Noonan his finance
spokesman. Bruton's supporters had been sure that Noonan was on
their side. When they saw the headline in the *Irish Times* after the
heave, they thought again. It read: 'Noonan says he is willing to serve
on frontbench for Kenny'.

Why were the rebels so sure of Noonan's support? Because for
months he had been a sort of intellectual hub for their criticisms and
doubts about Kenny's leadership. Noonan has been in Leinster House
since 1981, and he likes the company and conviviality of other politicians. He often gravitated towards the members' bar in the evenings,
where he and a group of pals, including Jim O'Keeffe and Tom Hayes,
would talk politics. In 2009 and the first half of 2010 he was also a
regular in Buswells Hotel on Wednesday evenings, where the begin-
nings of an anti-Kenny camp were assembling. Most had little against
Kenny personally, but they were increasingly coming to believe that
he would never be Taoiseach. Brian Hayes was there often, Timmins,
Naughten, Creighton usually and others – Coveney, Varadkar – occasionally. 'We've no leadership, our policy priorities are wrong, nobody
knows what we're doing,' Noonan told them. 'We're going to miss
the biggest opportunity ever.' The group became tighter in the
months after George Lee's departure. Hayes and Timmins reviewed
polling data that underscored Kenny's weakness with the public. At
the March party conference in Killarney, the group left the Great
Southern Hotel and went across the road to another hotel in ones and
twos – several after being rounded up by Noonan – to talk among
themselves about what could, or should, be done. It was obvious that
Bruton was the alternative as leader. But the biggest problem, some of
them thought presciently, 'might be Richard himself'.

As a former leader, Noonan was entitled to keep his own counsel
and to stay out of the debate. 'I know how I'm voting,' he told the
press, 'but I'm keeping it to myself.' Nobody questioned him further.
On the day before the vote, I bumped into him in the early evening as

he was leaving Leinster House, on the Merrion Square side. There's a longish walk from the door of Leinster House to the gate on to the street, and we walked together and chatted. I asked him how he thought the vote would go the following day. 'The only thing you can be sure of is that nobody knows how it will go. And do you know why?' he said. 'Why?' I asked. He grinned mischievously and answered in that unmistakable broad Limerick drawl. 'Because politicians,' he said, 'are fucking liars.'

If there was a deal with Noonan, it wasn't the only one. Phil Hogan and Paul Kehoe were the dealmakers-in-chief. John Perry, Shane McEntee and Dinny McGinley were promised jobs in a Fine Gael administration. So was Lucinda Creighton, who went public with the offer. 'Nonsense,' said Phil Hogan, 'that's a lie.' The two detested one another. The final two days were about the hand-to-hand fighting that usually decides such contests. Other TDs were promised no running mates in their constituencies, a promise that was so obviously going to be broken that nobody should have taken it seriously. Paul Kehoe was deputed to secure Terence Flanagan's vote and promised him no running mate. People who have never spoken to me before are suddenly my best friend, Flanagan said to people. But he still promised Kenny his vote. Shortly before the subsequent general election, Flanagan was informed by headquarters that he would have to take a running mate. No way, he said, I've been promised. Well, things change, he was told. This is politics. Flanagan said that if a running mate was imposed, he would go public with the broken promise and run as an independent. Investigations revealed that he was actually serious. Others weren't so lucky. Tom Sheahan in Kerry South received a similar promise of a free run. Things changed: a running mate appeared and Sheahan lost his seat. Dublin South Central deputy Catherine Byrne told people that she had been promised a job for her husband, who was unemployed. All sorts of deals were cut. One of the victims was Ciaran Conlon, Kenny's loyal communications director, who was moved sideways in the post-heave reorganization of the backroom staff. Conlon had been a brilliant servant of Kenny's and few doubted his ability; however, in the process of executing his duties he had crossed many of the party's TDs and made plenty of enemies. The volume of complaints from TDs about 'unelected advisers' had increased in recent months. Often the job of such people is to do or say things to TDs that the leader can't or doesn't want to. It's part of the job description, but there's a price to be paid for it eventually. Kenny knew that he 'needed to fix things with the parliamentary party'. Now some of the TDs wanted him out, and Kenny needed their votes. Conlon was somebody's price.

A number of TDs did what politicians often do: they waited to see which way the wind would blow. Some held out to see what offers would come in the door. Others went looking for them. Fine Gael was probably going to be in government after the next election; there would be spoils of victory. Some TDs publicly changed their minds. Charlie Flanagan, the party's justice spokesman, issued a statement over the weekend calling for Bruton to pull back from his challenge. 'This is not the time for internal strife that will undoubtedly leave serious wounds and long-term scars,' he pleaded. 'Enda Kenny is the leader of Fine Gael and he has my full support.' Later, Kenny was going through his list of waverers with Phil Hogan. 'Charlie Flanagan,' said Hogan. 'Ah, he'll be all right,' said Kenny. 'He will in his bollocks,' Hogan replied. On Wednesday, Flanagan said he would be voting for Richard Bruton.

But by the time the fateful parliamentary party meeting began on Thursday, 17 June, the wind was flagging in the rebels' sails. One of their leaders sat in the Leinster House restaurant asking journalists who they thought was going to win. The political correspondents thought, Well, that doesn't sound terribly confident. One dissident observed morosely of his colleagues, 'They all just gave up on the morning.' Phil Hogan, meanwhile, was bullishly insisting that Kenny would not just win, he would win well.

Kenny's tactic of putting down the motion himself meant that, under the rules of the meeting, he got to speak first and last. Both speeches held the room, though that was perhaps to be expected. He had rehearsed his speech carefully and plucked at their emotions as much as anything else. At one stage, Kenny held up his phone, saying he had a text message from his son: 'Dad, they don't deserve you.' Timmins held up his phone, saying, 'Hey, there's no signal in here!'

There was roaring and shouting and weeping and the beating of chests. The rebels sat amazed as people who had complained for years about Kenny got up and castigated them for their treachery. The MEP Mairead McGuinness had complained to several of the leading rebels about 'how terrible' the leadership was; only a few weeks before she had asked a group of TDs in Brussels what they were going to do about Kenny. 'He's a disaster!' she told them. Now she came into the meeting and 'lectured us for being manipulated by the media' and for their careerism. 'They all want to be leader,' she said of the rebels. Jim Higgins, the MEP who had been a constituency running mate of Kenny in Mayo, attacked the rebels, singling out Simon Coveney in particular. Several of the rebels, who had been subjected to Higgins's regular complaints about Kenny – he bore a particular grudge about having been denied the job of Leas-Chathaoirleach of the Senate in 2002 – found it 'stomach-churning'. 'Ah look,' one of the leading rebels reflected afterwards, 'nobody's mind was changed by the speeches.'

Summing up, Kenny castigated the plotters, one by one. To John Paul Phelan, the young Carlow–Kilkenny senator who had justified his vote against Kenny on the grounds that he could not find a single member in his constituency who wanted Enda as leader (Phil Hogan sat glowering at him), Kenny said he would turn up at his selection convention the following week and find him one. To Leo Varadkar, who had floated the idea of Kenny as a future minister for foreign affairs (originally an offer by Bruton), he said, 'Leo, I'm sorry, I cannot have a situation where you go on television and offer me the job of foreign affairs minister.' Kenny spoke about past leaders of the party whom it had dumped in panic and now eulogized. His final words were: 'When I win this vote, I'll go on to be Taoiseach.' The room rose in a standing ovation.

Two tellers were nominated, chairman Pádraic McCormack and Dublin Central senator Paschal Donohoe. The votes were counted quickly, checked and rechecked. Then McCormack announced the result: Kenny had carried the day. His supporters erupted, some of them in tears. Phil Hogan stood grinning broadly in triumph. The rebels slumped in their seats 'totally deflated'.

There was a bit of yahooing outside from a group of Mayo county councillors who had come up to Dublin to support Kenny, but the handlers frantically tried to put a lid on it. Kenny emerged on to the plinth grinning broadly, amid the traditional scrummaging by TDs and senators trying to get into the shot with him. Kenny and his supporters were euphoric. 'We move on from here as a completely united party,' he told reporters. Poor Richard Bruton was summoned to the front of the maul, and a beaming Enda clasped his hand awkwardly as the TDs cheered. It was excruciating for Bruton, the final humiliation. Around the edges, the dissidents loitered, several almost speechless. Most believed that if they had organized themselves properly, they would have won. Now their careers were at the mercy of the man whose leadership skills they had so derided.

In contravention of party procedures, the margin of victory was kept secret and has been much debated. The figure circulating on the day was 38–32, meaning that just four people could have changed the result. Later, there was an attempt by Kenny's spinners to put about the notion that the margin had been wider, perhaps ten or even fourteen votes, though few believed it, not least because they only mentioned it when it was pointed out that a margin of six votes meant that Kenny had certainly not won a majority of his own TDs (the senators and MEPs were overwhelmingly on his side). The rebels believe it might have been four votes, or even two. Whatever the exact result, history records only one fact: Enda Kenny had faced his toughest ever challenge and he was victorious. When he had been expected to wilt, he had shown his mettle. He was, in the phrase of the day – flogged to within an inch of his life by spinners, winners and excited supporters – 'the Man of Steel'. 'By the time the next election comes,' wrote Noel Whelan perceptively in the *Irish Times*, 'the minutiae of this week's heave will be forgotten, but the fact that Kenny was tough and saw off the challenge will be remembered.' The Man of Steel doctrine was now official.

The Bruton heave, and Kenny's successful and aggressive counter-offensive, was perhaps the most important episode in his long road to becoming leader of his country. It transformed him from an often ineffectual opposition leader to the head of a party preparing determinedly and thoroughly for office, a Taoiseach-in-waiting. You cannot understand Enda Kenny as Taoiseach without understanding the cathartic effect of the heave on him, say several of the people closest to him. He went into the heave as 'Indakinny', in the belittling epithet of the *Irish Times*'s sketch-writer Miriam Lord, and came out of it as the Man of Steel. That might have been overdoing it a bit, but he was certainly a man and a politician transformed by the heave. If a leader's character is a better guide to how he will perform in a crisis than any amount of policy, Kenny had surely passed a vital test on the path to his destiny. It was, agree virtually all those closest to him in politics, the making of the Taoiseach.

He clearly could have lost the vote had Bruton been a better candidate or run a better campaign. Indeed, had Bruton run an even vaguely competent campaign, the result might have been different. As it was, a majority of Kenny's TDs almost certainly voted against him; he was saved by the senators, whose seats he promised to abolish, and the MEPs. The what-ifs of history torment the losers, but they also often show the true nature of the choices that were made, and the consequences that flowed from them. The present coalition – if it existed at all – would have been a very different government under Richard Bruton. Few of even Kenny's staunchest opponents then believe now that it would be a better government under Bruton.

In politics, sometimes elections in themselves become part of the qualification process for leadership. The attempted coup and the confidence vote in Kenny in June 2010 demonstrated both for his friends and for his foes that there was a stubborn, iron will in him, allied to a ruthlessness that his sunny exterior belied. It also revealed how prepared he was to let others fight dirty on his behalf if needed. Perhaps most of all, it showed Kenny's most underrated quality: an even temperament, which gave him a priceless calm under fire. Victory did not take away the shortcomings that had led to the rebellion in the first place, nor the voters' nervousness about them; but it showed that they were balanced with qualities that the rebels had misjudged and certainly underestimated.

A number of direct consequences from the heave would come to work to Fine Gael's advantage. An internal reorganization of

Kenny's staff would vastly improve its operations; communications, internal and external, became sharper and simpler. Noonan's addition to the frontbench gave finance and economic policy a political edge it had lacked under Bruton. Everything became focused on preparations for the general election.

Things did not turn around immediately. In the aftermath of the heave, Labour was exultant and Fianna Fáil unable to contain its amusement. Both had got exactly the result they wanted: a fractured Fine Gael, with Bruton's credibility destroyed and Kenny (who they continued to deride, now more than ever) still at the helm. Subsequent polls were to show that the public remained unimpressed by Kenny, and there were many who continued to believe that he would never be Taoiseach. But the question wasn't so much would Kenny win the election for Fine Gael; it was whether he would lose it. It was clear by then that Fianna Fáil could not possibly hope to be part of a new government. Whatever Fine Gael's troubles, the Fianna Fáil–Green government was collapsing; if that wasn't immediately apparent, it was because the collapse was happening in slow-motion. Some thought the government's disintegration would accelerate. But nobody anticipated what was about to occur.

2

Gilmore for Taoiseach

The noise from the conference hall in the Hotel Kilkenny was rising and rising. Alex White's warm-up for his party leader was raising the temperature. White, a senator, barrister, former RTÉ producer and soon-to-be candidate for the leafy expanses of Dublin South, was in many ways a typical middle-class metropolitan Labourite, but he knew where the conference's erogenous zones were, and the audience roared their approval at his jibes at the Fianna Fáil–Green government. Naturally, they reserved a special spleen for their left-wing competitors. Eamon Gilmore was in an adjacent room as the applause and cheers thundered through the walls. His aides came in for a final few words. He could hear the crowd was warmed up for him. But they wanted to tell him something else, too. 'There's a gang out there from Labour Youth,' they told him with ten minutes to go before his televised address to the Labour Party conference. 'They're waving posters with GILMORE FOR TAOISEACH on them.'

'Okay,' said Gilmore. He sounded a bit unsure.

'Don't let them put you off.'

'Okay.'

In government you can do things; in opposition you can only talk. For the leader of the second opposition party, who has to fight for anything beyond the most meagre media rations, an event like the party conference is especially important. It's the leader's one opportunity in the year to speak at length, unmediated, directly to the public. In the autumn of 2008, as people tuned in to the economic and political affairs of the country, sensing that what politicians decided was soon going to play a much bigger part in their lives, Gilmore had used the Dáil to elbow his way into the public consciousness. Now, on a Saturday night in early December 2008, he appeared on their television screens all guns blazing in anger at the misgovernment of the country, talking action, optimism and plans for a brighter future. It was maybe the most important speech he had ever delivered, and he nailed it. As his TDs did the traditional Irish politicians' lunge to get into the television pictures on conclusion of the speech, the Labour Youth cheerleaders waved their GILMORE FOR TAOISEACH banners until their arms ached. An idea had been planted.

The Gilmore for Taoiseach motif became a party staple over the course of the following two years. On the face of it, it was a straight-forward attempt to promote the party leader, to place Gilmore on a par with Brian Cowen and Enda Kenny, and to make the next election a proper three-way contest. But it was also a direct dig at Kenny. Everyone who conducted polling research and focus groups, every-one who knocked on doors to remind their constituents who they were, knew that in the public's mind there was a problem with Ken-ny's becoming Taoiseach. Labour, in particular, was acutely aware of this. The party had fought the 2007 general election shackled to the notion of Kenny as Taoiseach and had a bitter memory of it, blaming public resistance to Kenny for their failure to win seats. 'Our non-performance in 2007 had a lot to do with Enda and the idea of him as Taoiseach,' one of the architects of the campaign told me. There were a couple of obvious holes in that argument – for a start, Kenny hadn't prevented his own party from winning an extra twenty seats – though it's true that the Fine Gael alliance did little for Labour in the end. Whatever the exact make-up of the 2007 result, the conven-tional wisdom among the Labour leadership now was that Kenny was a liability and Labour could profit by contrasting him with Gil-more. Labour's efforts were pretty transparent, and Fine Gael could see what its opposition rivals were at, but Labour didn't much care that they could.

When news of the heave against Kenny broke in June 2010, Labour's reaction was the same as Fianna Fáil's: amusement, curiosity and satisfaction. Some senior figures privately interpreted it as an outworking of Fine Gael's 'Big House' superiority complex – which they loosely and dismissively defined as the larger party's sense that it was entitled to be the leader of any non-Fianna Fáil government. 'Labour are ahead so there's something wrong – we have to change the leader,' was how one Labour person described it. There was always a wing of the Labour Party that was a lot more comfortable with Fianna Fáil than with Fine Gael, with which it felt class differences in a way that it didn't with Fianna Fáil. Labour recognized the reality that government with Fianna Fáil could never be contemplated in the current circumstances. But that didn't mean the party was falling in love with Fine Gael either; if anything, its determination to assert Labour's identity was sharpened.

Opinion was divided not only about the likely outcome of the heave but also about what might be the most advantageous result for Labour. Some senior figures thought that the best thing for Labour would be to have Kenny win by a small margin and remain *in situ* damaged, and without the assistance of Richard Bruton. The public had already made up its mind about Kenny, they thought, and would be unlikely to change it. They felt that had to work to their advantage. Others, who remembered Bruton's low-key role in the Rainbow government of the mid 1990s, reckoned that he would be a hard sell to the Irish people and so hoped he would win. 'We didn't see Richard Bruton as a strong leader. He wasn't a threat,' said one senior figure. 'He should have been an adviser,' said one adviser. Collectively, however, the Labour leadership saw the Fine Gael heave as 'a win-win'. The process could only damage their opposition rivals, and either outcome would be satisfactory.

Privately, the Labour leadership didn't actually believe the *Irish Times* poll that precipitated the move against Kenny, reckoning that, while it was correct in showing a trend of rising support for their party, it overstated Labour's support by concluding that it was now the 'biggest party'. 'We never thought the ratings were permanent but they gave us the chance to be one of the three contenders, not the also-rans,' says one senior figure.

Despite the reservations they had about that one poll – whatever its seismic effects in Fine Gael – taken with all the other polls, it offered conclusive evidence that Labour was on a steady upward march. The regular Red C/*Sunday Business Post* polls had also showed jumps in support for Labour, while Fianna Fáil withered and Fine Gael had settled in the low thirties. Labour was the party with momentum.

The surge had also been turbo-charged by Gilmore's high-octane performances in the Dáil and in the media, where he totally eclipsed Kenny as the spokesman for an Ireland that was increasingly angry. Gilmore had turned into a brilliant Dáil performer and succeeded in articulating the feelings that many voters had about the deteriorating economic situation, and especially about the Fianna Fáil–Green government's perceived mixture of haplessness and helplessness: incomprehension, disbelief and, then, a rising fury. He tortured Cowen in the Dáil, culminating in his accusation that if Cowen had known the extent of the difficulties at Anglo Irish Bank before he first guaranteed and then nationalized it, then that was an act of 'economic treason'. Words are weapons in politics, and Cowen visibly reeled from the blow. It was an iconic moment.

The public may not usually take much notice of what happens on the floor of the Dáil, but the political correspondents do. Evening-news bulletins regularly featured Gilmore's zingers from the day's exchanges, while newspapers contrasted the Labour leader's punchy indictments of the coalition with Enda Kenny's windy and often ineffectual attacks. Gilmore's righteous and articulate indignation made for great opposition politics, and the sense began to grow that 'Gilmore for Taoiseach' might turn out to be more than a slogan. Party handlers continuously told themselves not to get carried away; but even at the very top that was easier said than done. 'Opinion polls are such that we would win a seat in every constituency. That's 43 for a start. There are constituencies where we are stronger and where we can win more than one,' Gilmore told the *Irish Times* in an interview that summer. In election-planning meetings, Labour began to adjust its expectations and its assumptions. It would clearly need more candidates.

As the party climbed in the polls and the prospect of Gilmore for Taoiseach started to gain weight, Labour began to face accusations that it had 'no policies'. Though Labour spokespeople immediately characterized this to interviewers as a 'Fianna Fáil attack', it was just as often heard coming from Fine Gaelers. In any case, it was good old political knockabout. Labour had policies coming out of its ears:

forty-five policy documents and thirty-five private members' bills since 2007. But the accusation wasn't without foundation entirely: Labour had produced plenty of policies, but what it hadn't done was take hard fiscal positions. Pressed by Harry McGee in that *Irish Times* interview, Gilmore ruled out property tax and water charges but declined to say where he would raise revenue. It was too early to say where many savings could be made, he said. Sure it was.

The truth was Labour was committed to reaching demanding budgetary targets but reluctant to say how it would get there. The charge that Labour's popularity was built on populist attacks and no policies began to stick a little, and it was thrown around in more and more broadcast interviews. Some commentary suggested that this both annoyed and concerned Labour, which was rubbish: Labour was simply being criticized for being too successful in the polls. As one senior figure said to me at the time, that's a problem he would be content to deal with every day.

Happy and all as they were to be criticized on the grounds of their success, some of the cannier heads in the Labour backroom discerned that something had changed about Fine Gael's message. It had. Mark Mortell, a long-time party supporter, activist and one of the sharpest communications brains in the country, had moved from a position of offering advice when asked to an almost full-time role on Kenny's staff.

Mortell had been on the end of a phone for Fine Gael for years. A former party activist, councillor, adviser, mover and shaker, and appointee to a number of the most important state boards, he ran an arm of the FleishmanHillard public relations and lobbying giant in Dublin. He had been allied to Kenny's leadership for several years and played an important role in the 2007 general election campaign, after which he returned to his work in the private sector. Now, with an election on the horizon and the party having flagellated itself publicly on the leadership issue, Mortell was persuaded to come to Kenny's aid again. Work also began on a blueprint for the election – which Fine Gael leadership believed could happen at any time – under a fourteen-strong group chaired by Frank Flannery. This detailed document, containing a message plan and strategy for the campaign, backed by detailed voter research, was ready in the autumn.

Even before taking up the post officially in the autumn, Mortell was playing a substantial role behind the scenes. Some people in political communications are good at crafting sharp messages; others are good at longer-term strategy. Mortell is good at both. Pretty soon, the party started to sound a little livelier, especially on finance matters. But the different tone of the communications was only the visible – or audible – part of a wider reorganization of the Fine Gael leader's key staff. As had been agreed at the time of the heave, Ciaran Conlon, the party's press secretary, was moved to election planning. Most jobs in politics just have an inherent lifespan, and Conlon's as press secretary had reached its natural end. 'There's a cycle. He was on the downward part of it,' summarized one senior party figure. He was replaced by his deputy, Feargal Purcell, a former army officer who had joined Fine Gael's press room in 2008, though Mortell remained the key strategic and tactical authority. Andrew McDowell, who had been the principal adviser on economic and financial matters until then, was given overall control of formulating policy in the run-up to the election. 'Andrew is now running policy,' Kenny told people. Conlon's exit also increased the power of Mark Kennelly, Kenny's 'chef de cabinet', or chief-of-staff. Some wondered if Kennelly had had a hand in Conlon's move; in any event, he soon formed a vital nexus with Mortell in Kenny's office. They were in some ways an odd pair. Mortell is urbane, clubbable and unflappable, a product of Blackrock College, a member of the Fitzwilliam Lawn Tennis Club. Though from Bray in County Wicklow, there is an unmistakable metropolitan mien about him. Kennelly, a Kerryman, is described by one of those closest to him as 'inscrutable, energetic, paranoid . . . very bright and utterly committed to the leadership'. He would become indispensable to Kenny, and a powerful presence in government. When I asked one of his colleagues to define his subsequent role in Government Buildings, he answered that Kennelly was in charge of the next twenty-four hours – but he was in charge of *everything* in the next twenty-four hours. He would be lampooned in political circles for his habit of appearing in photos and television pictures beside the Taoiseach, but this actually underscored how close he was to his principal, and how much clout he wielded. Mortell, on the other hand, was a largely invisible presence. Whereas Mortell's CV includes stints at blue-chip companies such as Mars, Guinness and Bank of Ireland, Kennelly has been in the political world since leaving university, working for a succession of Fine Gael politicians, including the last three leaders of the party. Together they refashioned Fine Gael's political capacities with one goal in mind: beating Labour in the general election.

That Labour, not Fianna Fáil, would be Fine Gael's chief opponent was one of the key strategic insights that the election planners reached that summer. In a way, it was simply the obvious conclusion based on the poll numbers and on the transformed political context. Even Fianna Fáilers were saying privately – and, as the election neared, some were saying it publicly – that the party needed a spell in opposition. Yet for Fine Gael to focus on Labour, rather than on Fianna Fáil, still required a transformation of the mindset with which Fine Gael had approached every general election since the 1930s. Politicians often give out that the public has no memory; they, by contrast, have elephantine memories, and so do the parties they represent. It required an effort of will and imagination to shift focus to Labour.

'When they ring you and ask if you will serve, say "yes",' Michael Noonan told Brian Hayes quietly. It was the night Enda Kenny beat back Richard Bruton's challenge, and Hayes, the sergeant-major of the rebel platoon, was contemplating his life-to-come in the political gulag. He had been in politics for almost all of his adult life, and the future had been filled with promise. No longer. 'They're not going to ring me,' he replied. 'I'm finished.' Noonan knew more than most that political fortunes ebb and flow. 'When they ring,' he soothed, 'say "yes".'

But they didn't ring. Hayes didn't really think they would. He didn't go and plead, like some did. He didn't even particularly sit by the phone. He just looked forward to the summer holidays.

Before anyone got away on any holidays, Kenny appointed a new frontbench. A mixture of youth and experience, gushed the *Irish Times*, though really it was a mixture of a large number of Kenny's supporters and a small number of the cowed former rebels. As expected and promised, Michael Noonan was the new finance spokesman, while another old warhorse, Seán Barrett, became foreign affairs spokesman. Richard Bruton was forgiven and made enterprise spokesman. Kenny's forgiveness might not have been complete, but it was genuine. He had been less angry at his former deputy than at some of the other rebels. In any case, Bruton was too heavyweight for Kenny to leave him out, and it was such an obvious gesture of bridge-building that even if Kenny had loathed Bruton – which he didn't – he would probably still have appointed him. In fact, within days of the heave, Kenny had dispatched McDowell to have lunch with Bruton. 'How can I get him back?' Kenny wondered. 'Work on him.'

Simon Coveney and Leo Varadkar, two of the younger rebels, were also reprieved, as were Charlie Flanagan and Fergus O'Dowd; Hayes, Michael Creed, Denis Naughten and several others were not. James Reilly was made deputy leader; Phil Hogan director of elections. At the press conference in the Merrion Hotel, the reprieved rebels looked by turns happy and a bit sheepish. Across the road in Leinster House, the unreprieved ones seethed.

One of them, the outspoken Dublin TD Lucinda Creighton, went to the MacGill Summer School in Glenties, County Donegal, and launched a scathing attack on her own party. Despite the relaxed and social appearance of the event, MacGill is the leading forum for self-examination and self-criticism by the country's political class and by those who study and commentate on it. Creighton had travelled the road from Dublin over the Donegal mountains with a serious purpose. She was spikily critical of Fine Gael's corporate fundraising, linking it to the 'cute hoor politics which has defined and tainted Irish public life like an incurable cancer'. As Creighton intended, her speech and the accompanying interviews – which had been prompted by a *Sunday Independent* story about property developers attending a Fine Gael golf classic in the K Club – caused a huge ruckus. When Kenny was doorstepped about her excoriating speech, he stuck to professions of ignorance: hadn't heard it, hadn't seen it, didn't know what the fuss was about, couldn't comment on something he hadn't read, he stonewalled. Asked about the Ronald Quinlan *Sunday Independent* story that prompted it, he affected not to have 'bought or read that paper for three years'. The reporters thought: Ah, would you come off it!

But it wasn't so much Kenny whom Creighton was targeting with her comments – though it was hardly a secret that she had no great regard for her leader – as Phil Hogan, with whom she had clashed bitterly during the heave. In fact, the relevant parts of her speech had been pretty much a description of how she viewed Hogan – her reference to 'cute hoor politics' echoed charges that had circulated around the time of the heave. Everyone knew she was talking about Hogan, and Hogan knew it too. As it happened, he was also at MacGill that day to deliver a speech on Fine Gael's proposed political reforms. MacGill is heavy on policy and debate – evening debates frequently run until 11 p.m. or later – but most people spend some time in the bar as well, and that night the two Fine Gael TDs stood at opposite ends of the room in the Highland Hotel. Neither was very complimentary about the other. Creighton's comments would later lead to a High Court libel action by the developer Michael O'Flynn, which was settled by way of an apology, with Creighton agreeing to pay some of O'Flynn's costs.

Not all the divisions in Fine Gael would be tidily overcome. But some of them would. Later that summer, Brian Hayes was summoned to meet Frank Flannery in the plush lobby of the Westbury Hotel, off Grafton Street. 'We'd like to give you a job,' Flannery told him after the chit-chat over the coffees in the china cups. Junior finance spokesman. The late unpleasantness was 'all behind them', he purred. Hayes would be Noonan's right-hand man, and after the election, who knows? Two months earlier Hayes's career lay in ruins; here was a way back, maybe. Hayes knew he was on probation, but he accepted. The pair parted in good humour. Before he left, Flannery told him, 'Enda Kenny is in political heaven right now.'

But Mortell was keenly aware that, despite the outward signs of unity, the parliamentary party remained riven by the animosities that had been generated by the heave. At its September think-in he emphasized the importance of getting beyond it. Running through the general election planning, he told them frankly, 'If you don't do this together, you are fucked. United you might succeed, but divided you will definitely fail.' Divisions were largely subsumed by the momentum of the approaching election. But they never disappeared entirely.

It was one of Taoiseach Brian Cowen's mistakes – half born of long observation from the comforting and comfortable seats on the government side of the House, and half born of arrogance – not to take Enda Kenny seriously. As Kenny strained every sinew to up his game after the heave, Cowen belittled him in the Dáil, mocking the 'strong new persona of the new leader of Fine Gael', to his own backbenchers' delight. But Michael Noonan wasn't so easy to dismiss.

Noonan had been Fine Gael's most unsuccessful leader in its history, a hotly contested achievement in a party that was itself the perennial runner-up of Irish politics. He'd had the misfortune to come up against Bertie Ahern not just when Ahern was at the height of his powers but when he'd had sufficient exchequer resources at his disposal to give effect to almost any policy he wanted. And Ahern was clear about what he wanted: he wanted to win elections, he wanted to stay in power. So in the first six months of the election year 2002, when he'd gone toe to toe with Michael Noonan, Ahern's government increased spending by 22 per cent over the previous year. It was difficult getting the system even to accommodate this much extra money. Fianna Fáil was so far ahead of Fine Gael politically, organizationally and in every other way that it was always going to win. The tsunami of money that Charlie McCreevy threw at the country in advance of the election meant that Noonan had never had a prayer.

Yet for all that was ranged against him, Noonan was still a poor leader. Unsure whether to let his naturally aggressive instincts take their course or to tone down his attacks in the face of the contagious emollience of Bertie Ahern, he ended up doing both and neither properly. The more he talked, the more he seemed at odds with the country he was talking to. Nothing went right for him. The custard pie that landed on his snout during the election campaign kind of summed it all up. Visibly shocked on election night at the scale of his defeat, Noonan immediately resigned as leader, and so ended, it seemed, a career in national frontline politics that had flared brightly at its outset, but had ultimately disappointed. Even after he took over the chair of the public accounts committee in 2004, Noonan remained a distant figure around Leinster House and a marginal presence in national politics.

There were personal as well as political reasons for this. He had a triple heart bypass operation in late 2007. And his home life had changed beyond recognition. Noonan's wife Florence had developed Alzheimer's disease in the late 1990s, and her condition had begun to deteriorate seriously in the mid 2000s. Noonan found himself spending more and more of his time caring for her in what was steadily becoming a difficult and distressing situation. Eventually, Noonan and his family opted for full-time care in a nursing home in Limerick. In May of 2010 Noonan was ready to tell the story in the hope, he said, that other people in similar circumstances would realize that they were not alone. In a compelling interview with Pat Kenny on the *Frontline* television programme, Noonan spoke openly and emotionally of the experience of caring for his wife and of realizing that he could not manage on his own any more. As he broke down into tears and struggled to compose himself, the grief for the wife he had already lost seemed to erupt from him in great waves. 'The first morning I was showering her . . . she fell and I couldn't catch her and . . . she was lying on the floor.' He hunched in his seat, and wept.

It was probably the first the public had seen of Noonan since he was leader of Fine Gael. But this was a different man. Life and age soften most men, but in Irishmen of Noonan's generation, who entered grandparenthood at the time that he did, the effect is especially pronounced. The extended families that they now presided over were a world away from the dutiful but authoritarian upbringings many remembered from their own childhoods. Their world was not as tough a place as it had once been, and nor were they. Noonan had changed, and the public could see that.

None of which meant that Noonan still wasn't able to deliver hard-nosed political attacks. He was, and often appeared to have lost none of his relish for it. In a *Morning Ireland* encounter with Fianna

Fáil's justice minister Dermot Ahern, someone with a reputation as a heavyweight slugger (of which he was quite proud), Noonan displayed the same pugnacity as of old. Taunted for not having declared his hand in the Fine Gael heave, Noonan responded, 'Isn't Dermot Ahern a nasty little man who keeps making personal comments about me?' Oh, said the Fianna Fáil handlers, the public won't like that, no, they won't, it's the old Michael Noonan, and we know how that one ended up, don't we? They couldn't have been more wrong. The public had changed their minds about a lot of things, and they were now developing quite an appetite for hearing opposition politicians smack Fianna Fáil around. For Fine Gaelers, many of whom shared Noonan's view of Dermot Ahern, this sort of thing was fantastically encouraging. The press, always panting for a new angle, responded with a flurry of 'The Bruiser is Back' profiles. That was only part of the story, but it was an important part. And the press was right in its summary: something pretty important had changed.

To the senior staff, Noonan was a bit of an unknown quantity. He hadn't participated in the politics or policy-making at all, and now, all of a sudden, he was at the very heart of the party's machine. He was notoriously difficult to read, especially for people of a younger generation, and most of the young turks around Kenny were two political generations removed from Noonan. Some of them found him slightly intimidating.

The day after his appointment to the finance brief, Noonan asked Andrew McDowell to come to his office. His long-time adviser and assistant Mary Kenny was there, and McDowell knew that Noonan relied heavily on her advice. As McDowell spoke, Kenny nodded every now and then, which he took as a good sign. Noonan himself was clear about what he wanted: a clearer narrative and a sharper political message. He thought the party's policy platform under Richard Bruton had been too detailed and not sharp enough, leaving it open to political attack. Labour's success in the polls was evidence of this, he thought. 'This is unnecessary,' he said. 'Fianna Fáil would never do this in opposition.' He didn't have any problem with the substance of Fine Gael policy in most instances: he just wanted it presented more simply and more sharply.

The staff immediately recognized that he was a different animal to Bruton. They saw him weighing up decisions and statements politically. Can I sell this? Could it come back to bite me? One of them thought the difference was that with Bruton, policy-making was an intellectual exercise undertaken in order to discover the right thing to do. With Noonan it was a political process. Can I attack the government without cornering myself? He was horrified that, despite the economic state of the country, Fianna Fáil was still managing to attack Fine Gael for being irresponsible. This staple of political debate continued right up to the time Brian Lenihan was negotiating with the Troika in the autumn of 2010.

There was one particular aspect of policy where Noonan wanted Fine Gael to take a softer line. Richard Bruton's 'good bank/bad bank' plans would have required some bondholders to be 'burned', a metaphor with which everyone would soon become so familiar. Noonan was a lot more cautious, probably because he knew it wouldn't be so straightforward when Fine Gael was in government. One staffer remembers how they gradually stepped away from the hard, unilateral line integral to the 'good bank/bad bank' strategy. The establishment of NAMA had more or less put paid to Bruton's plans anyway, but Noonan was still determined not to give any unnecessary hostages to fortune. They used to say, 'We will burn bondholders and impose losses,' but the staff noticed that they were now adding, 'As long as Europe agrees.' A few of them thought: He's fudging it. He would continue to fudge it right up to the very last minute when, as finance minister, he had to make a decision on it.

Though it seems ludicrous in the knowledge of what happened subsequently, many people in Fine Gael, Labour and the rest of the political establishment in the summer of 2010 expected some sort of a Fianna Fáil resurgence before the next election had to be fought. A combination of factors drove this fear. Fine Gael and Labour had been fighting Fianna Fáil for every seat, for every vote – and usually losing – for so long that they found it difficult to comprehend the scale of the paradigm shift that was under way. Fianna Fáil had always been on top, driven above all by the desire to gain and to retain power.

It was only rational to expect that it would not give up power without the mother and father of all battles. And the narrative in Fianna Fáil circles, which influenced parts of the media and therefore opposition thinking, was that the Taoiseach must someday soon contrive a more effective communications strategy – or at least a less disastrous one. Surely he would not go on ignoring the need to talk to the country?

There was also a sense in some quarters that an economic recovery of sorts was taking hold and that this would inevitably bring a political dividend. Following the party's poor performance in the June opinion poll, the *Irish Times* editorial writer thought that it might have hit rock bottom: 'Fianna Fáil's bad showing in this opinion poll could mark a low point for the party ... Acceptance of the Croke Park deal by a majority of public sector unions represents a considerable achievement. Public sentiment in economic recovery [*sic*] is gradually improving.' The paper's political editor, Stephen Collins, noted that sniping between Fine Gael and Labour had 'opened the door for a Fianna Fáil recovery'. Collins was by no means the only one to believe it was possible. And, at a more basic level, Fine Gael and Labour – and nearly everybody else – just didn't appreciate how bad things actually were.

3

The hangover

'Probably to my future cost,' Fianna Fáil junior minister Martin Mansergh told the Dáil, 'I hold a Burkean view of the duties of a deputy, in that he or she owes constituents not just his or her industry, but his or her judgement.' Fianna Fáil had always been inordinately proud of Mansergh; but the idiosyncratic media performances of this public school- and Oxford-educated Protestant Republican since coming to high office in his own right had not generated a similar following among the public. Possibly this was because, despite his exotic background, Mansergh was as die-hard a Fianna Fáiler as has ever been wrought in the more conventional forges of cumann activism and local politics, and the market for die-hard Fianna Fáilers was contracting fast in the summer of 2010. But if he was loyal, he was not typical; few of his colleagues shared Mansergh's views on the 'Burkean' role of a TD, assuming, that is, he meant Edmund, and not Ray. This was evidenced by, for example, their voting through the anti-stag hunting legislation on which Mansergh was speaking that afternoon in late June, despite the widely acknowledged (including by themselves) fact that they were almost universally opposed to it. Indeed, several of them stood up in the Dáil and denounced the legislation, before voting for it.

This was the neurotic state of the government in its final summer. TDs knew that the terrible judgement of the voters awaited them (though they had no idea just how merciless it would be), but scrambled to avoid it. Like a prisoner on death row, they knew the fate of the administration, but sought desperately to postpone it at any cost. Despite their growing disdain for the Green Party, they had to accede to its demands. Fine Gael may have done its best to hand its opponents a stick to beat it with when it launched a civil war against itself, but it was only in the ha'penny place compared to the government.

With the disintegration of the public finances gathering pace in the summer of 2010, with unemployment skyrocketing towards 450,000, and with young people fleeing the country in their thousands, the Fianna Fáil–Green coalition gathered what was left of its political forces and went to war on that great threat to the public weal: stag hunting in County Meath.

Of course, it was a Green Party bill, part of the price John Gormley and his colleagues had wrung from Fianna Fáil for the Greens' continued support the previous autumn, when the Programme for Government between the two parties, first agreed after the 2007 general election, was renegotiated. 'Renegotiation' was a polite term for what had happened; in actual fact, it was more akin to a shakedown, in the course of which the Greens had simply raised their price for staying in government. With Fianna Fáil fearing a heavy defeat in the event of a general election (though clearly it would have been nothing as bad as the cataclysm that would subsequently befall the party), Cowen felt he had no choice but to accept the Greens' new terms. They included an end to stag hunting – which, though a great annoyance to the Greens, was carried on by only one hunt, the Ward Union, in Meath – and new restrictions on dog breeding. They were desperate gestures to appease the grassroots of the Greens, which saw the dream of government turning into a nightmare before its eyes. In fairness to the Greens, they never attempted to disguise their motivation in presenting these measures. They would later learn the folly of governing for your grassroots: you run the risk of keeping them at the expense of your voters.

In a funny sort of way, the Greens' willingness to lose their seats was always one of their great strengths in government. It gave them the courage to do difficult and unpopular things that they thought were right. Of course, just because the Greens thought something was right didn't mean that it was. Their political purity sometimes also made them unwilling to listen to what other people thought. So, in another way, it was also one of their greatest weaknesses.

Labour opposed the bill, a move which reeked of opportunism, even by the standards of opposition in Leinster House. Tired of being tormented by Labour, the Greens were disgusted by this hypocrisy.

'Deputy Gilmore is a complete and utter coward,' John Gormley spat during a bad-tempered debate on the bill in the Dáil. 'The man does not stand for anything.' Gormley himself sounded like a man on the edge. He quoted Hansard reports from an 1825 debate in the House of Commons on bear-baiting and bull-baiting. He attacked the opposition for representing 'an uncivilised mindset . . . people who do not have an ounce of compassion'.

The official record of the Dáil records the close of the second-stage debate:

> DEPUTY JOHN GORMLEY: As for the Labour Party this is a shameful evening for it. I commend the bill to the House.
> (*Interruptions*)
> QUESTION PUT: The Dáil divided: Tá, 73; Níl, 69.

Four votes – two TDs. Having lost Michael Lowry and Jackie Healy-Rae, the coalition survived only with support from independents Maureen O'Sullivan and Finian McGrath, who normally voted against the government. Fianna Fáil TD Mattie McGrath would soon resign the whip ('in despair'). The numbers were now getting too tight for comfort; the slow-motion disintegration of the government was beginning to accelerate. For the public looking in, it was beyond comprehension that the political energies of the government were being spent on stag hunting and dog breeding. It was as if they were governing for the satirists. Addressing himself to the stag hunting issue, outspoken Green deputy Paul Gogarty asked the Dáil's presiding chairman, 'Is the word "bullshit" proscribed under standing orders?' It is, he was told.

To many looking in, that was a pity. It seemed an appropriate description of proceedings.

Often great events seem inevitable in hindsight, and we are left wondering why nobody saw what was coming. But historical review compresses events and makes causality plain in a way that it never was to those who experienced those events at first hand. History sorts the significant from the insignificant by forgetting the latter. Perhaps in retrospect the imminence of a government collapse – and a rout of

Fianna Fáil – should have been clear. Yet, at the time, for anyone who underestimated the economic hole the country was in and the extent to which Fianna Fáil was rotting from the inside out, some sort of a Fianna Fáil fightback was a reasonable surmise. Perhaps better information and analysis would have revealed the government's troubles and the inevitability of an election and a new government. But nobody could have expected the extent to which the party which had dominated Irish politics since the early 1930s would almost destroy itself. And the destruction was led from the very top.

It was against this background that Fianna Fáil gathered in the Ardilaun Hotel in Galway in mid September for its annual parliamentary party 'think-in'. The think-ins were part policy seminar, part morale booster, part media opportunity and part drinking session. Unlike ard fheiseanna, the boys and girls went stag – no wives or husbands. Usually there was a big dinner and a speech after a long day's windbagging, and then a night's craic in the bar. Some of them went to bed early. Others stayed up half the night. For journalists, it was a useful opportunity to talk informally to ministers and TDs. That – and a natural proclivity for socializing – meant many of the press corps tended to be among the late nighters at these events. So was Brian Cowen.

The events of the night were later painstakingly and lovingly re-created in dozens of media reports over the subsequent days. Three things are certain: one, it was a long night; two, Cowen entertained people in the early hours with a series of anecdotes, impressions and a song ('Whisht up, this is a classic,' the *Daily Mail* reported him saying, before he sang 'The Lakes of Pontchartrain' at 3 a.m.); and three, nobody seemed to think there was anything especially scandalous about it that night. The trouble would only start in the morning.

Those who serve senior politicians as political aides or advisers or as part of their civil service private office say that they vary in their levels of neediness. Some are demanding; others easy. Some of them have to be 'mammied' completely; others are relatively self-sufficient. Some demand detailed preparation for interviews; others are content to wing it. Civil service gossip, though generally discreet on the question of his drinking, had long regarded Brian Cowen as needing a lot of attention. He was not generally disliked, and some officials were tremendously loyal to him. Among those who worked closely with him, he was at least as well liked – and probably more so – as his predecessor, Bertie Ahern. But he was sometimes hard work. Many ministers can get themselves up and started in the morning; Cowen required assistance. All sorts of stories circulated about how he had needed the help of officials. Whatever about that, he often had to be woken up and warmed up and given a cup of tea before interviews. Eoghan Ó Neachtain, his press secretary, and Nick Reddy, his private secretary, used to go into his hotel room and make him a cup of tea. This was not necessarily related to any drinking the night before; they would do it whether Cowen had had an early night or not. But it was obviously more necessary when he had been in the bar until 3 a.m.

Because it was a party event, Ó Neachtain did not travel to Galway; instead, the party's new press director, Pat McParland, had his first outing in charge of Cowen's media relations. To call it a baptism of fire hardly does it justice. But other members of Cowen's Government Buildings staff were in Galway, most notably Joe Lennon, his principal adviser. Lennon was the subject of much fingerpointing afterwards, though others wondered if he could really be held responsible for Cowen's failure to get up in time. What did they expect Lennon to do: haul the Taoiseach out of the bed and get him dressed? The truth is that his advisers didn't bang on Cowen's door because he had got away with this sort of thing so many times before.

Not this time. Cowen eventually straggled into the breakfast room – where the interviews with the party leaders are traditionally held by *Morning Ireland*, complete with the clatter of cutlery and crockery in the background – a few minutes late and just before the interview was due to begin. 'Thanks for coming over,' Cathal Mac Coille told him, 'before your breakfast.' Mac Coille had seen Cowen and chatted briefly to him before the RTÉ presenter retired for the night at about 1 a.m. Cowen's aides had inspected where the interview was to take place the following morning and stipulated that the Taoiseach should sit with his back to the rest of the room, to prevent distractions. Facing Cowen now, Mac Coille didn't think there was anything amiss.

But the Taoiseach was immediately in trouble. He was hoarse, hesitant and crusty, clearly the result of a late night. Often an indistinct speaker anyway (though he could be clear and articulate when he wanted to), he seemed especially slurred today.

Mac Coille is one of the sharpest interviewers in the country, and he seized on comments made by Brian Lenihan the previous evening after his arrival in Galway. Lenihan had dropped a budget bombshell, suggesting that the end-of-year budget might require more than the €3 billion in cuts and taxes that had been the previously accepted figure. Cowen's aides had been furious about it, regarding it as a typical Lenihan attempt to make himself the centre of attention. Cowen obfuscated and played for time, but Mac Coille toasted him. Cowen stuck to stonewalling. Though there was little or no comment about it afterwards, Cowen's problems in that fateful interview were as much about the budget questions as his ropy voice. It was the substance, as well as the style, that did for him. After the interview, the two men chatted briefly; nobody in the room seemed aware of a problem. Cowen was a bit hoarse, and it was a bad interview, they thought. No big deal. It was only when they went outside and turned on their phones that they began to suspect it was a very big deal indeed.

Ministers, TDs, aides, political opponents: anyone with a functioning political sense who was listening to the radio knew that this sounded pretty bad. But the powder keg was lit when Simon Coveney sent the most influential tweet in the history of tweets about Irish politics. Cowen, Coveney suggested, was 'halfway between drunk and hungover and totally disinterested'. Boom!

Now Cowen was fair game. A lightning charge of excitement ran through the reporters already assembled at the hotel and those rapidly making their way there through the driving rain. When Cowen appeared in the lobby, surrounded by staffers who were beginning to grasp the scale of the disaster, it was – characteristically – TV3's Ursula Halligan who put the question. 'Were you drunk or hungover?' 'Absolutely not,' a flustered Cowen replied. 'That's ridiculous. It's not true at all.' He was immediately ushered away. The cat was out of the bag now.

Micheál Martin hadn't heard the interview but dashed into the press office when he saw the commotion. 'Play me the interview,' he demanded. A five-alarm media mob immediately congregated in the hotel lobby, rushing to interrogate any unfortunate minister who happened to stick his or her head out of the conference hall. The phones of the ministers and TDs inside started to hop with calls and texts about the interview. Mary Hanafin was sitting in the back row and ducked out to find party officials. She had been interviewed on *Newstalk* herself that morning and had switched on to RTÉ to listen to Cowen afterwards. She was horrified by how Cowen had sounded. 'We have to do something about this!' she raged at party staff. The only response was to send out ministers to say there was no problem.

As the media mob rampaged through the lobby, some ministers ducked for cover; others tried the tut-tut/what's-all-the-fuss-about tack. All privately raged at Cowen. Ministers were fighting a rear-guard action, but it was pointless. 'Are you seriously suggesting that any person can't have a drink of an evening time after a full day's conference?' Micheál Martin asked, hardly with genuine incredulity. The issue wasn't of course whether he had a drink; it was whether he had several, with the result that he was unable to function properly the next morning. In a larger sense, the issue was whether he could any longer lead the country. With perceptive bluntness, Michael Noonan summed it up later that day: 'This can't continue,' he said. 'The game is up.'

Sometimes these controversies blow themselves out. This one clearly wouldn't. Cowen had to go out to face the media, and try to beat back the story. A press conference was hastily arranged for the afternoon. It was awful, pitiful, a cringe. TDs and senators jammed the room, intermingling with the press and loudly harrumphing their disapproval at some very obvious questions. All the Fianna Fáil ministers flanked Cowen, as though they could form a phalanx to protect him from the consequences of his own actions. Some thought it unbearable; for others, whom he had lost months before, it was the last straw. The worst of it was that they now had to go out and look like idiots by defending him, pretending that he'd had nasal conges-tion, or wasn't a morning person, or whatever the cock-and-bull story of the hour was. The people of Ireland know what a hangover sounds like; many of them have some experience in the field. Many of them also don't regard ten to nine in the morning as especially early. All over the country, people came to the same conclusion: it was what it sounded like.

At the press conference, Cowen was plastered in make-up, desperately trying to look chipper and sound in control. He tried a few throwaway lines. Pausing mid sentence to cough theatrically, he apologized 'for my voice', saying he wanted to be careful not to 'make a mistake'. The loyalists greeted this as if it were a witticism of Wildean acuity. Cowen had a reputation for drinking; everyone knew that. Asked if he drank too much, he cited the old Chinese proverb 'moderation in all things', adding 'including moderation'. At this, and at Cowen's several attempts at humour, Mary Coughlan guffawed with all her might. It was impossible to tell whether she was just desperately trying to lay down covering fire for her friend, or whether she really thought Cowen was hilarious. But it wasn't funny. If it wasn't so serious, it would have been pathetic.

For Fine Gael and Labour, it was scarcely believable that the Taoiseach had placed himself in such a position. Simon Coveney's tweet was every bit the instant, unscripted response that the medium so powerfully facilitates, but by finally saying plainly in public what had until now only rarely and then reluctantly been referred to, it kicked off an unstoppable media hurricane. Many journalists, caught – as Miriam Lord noted in the *Irish Times* – between censure and complicity, were queasy about discussing the Taoiseach's drinking in public. Now most of them got over it. The media reaction was predictable, instant, damning. Sometimes in politics you have to spin a story to within an inch of its life to get any traction with the media; sometimes you only have to sit back and stay out of the way while the furies do their work. By the time Cowen was fighting his desperate rearguard action in Galway, he was already on the front page of the Fine Gael website. The story almost instantly went global. The British edition of the *Daily Mail* was typical of the international reporting: 'Irish prime minister Brian Cowen is battling to save his leadership of the country and of his party today after claims he was drunk during an early-morning radio interview.' Media analysis later showed 457 articles worldwide had cited his interview in the following twenty-four hours. Most infamously of all, *The Tonight Show with Jay Leno* played the recording on American television, knocking much predictable fun out of it. Irish prime minister denies being drunk: it was irresistible.

It wasn't just the Taoiseach's ill-discipline that the interview demonstrated; it was also his inability, or unwillingness, to say things in simple, clear language. Asked if the budget was going to be more severe for people listening at home than they had previously feared, here's what he answered:

> 'Well, what is going to happen now of course is . . . what people need to know is for the next year we're in discussions at the moment about that, our budget will be for the next year and what we have to do is to align the estimates campaign with the industrial-relations agenda and what that'll involve . . . where every department will be setting out based on the amount it will be able to have next year, it will be – it will be dealing with its own management and its own personnel and its own staff over the coming months, explaining simply that we have to get more for less, we want to avoid, eh, the impact –'

At which point Cathal Mac Coille mercifully intervened to ask, 'But "when" is the question?'

Cowen continued: 'During the course of this estimates campaign that we will be ending up with a situation where the allocations that will be made will require the implementation in many respects of the Good Friday – of the, eh, sorry, the Croke Park – Agreement, which is about re-employment, it is about letting work practices . . .'

And on it went. This is the language of someone who has given up trying to talk to people, who has actually given up on politics. Part of it was cussedness, part of it was shyness, part of it was arrogance, part of it was laziness. He had hired a communications consultant, Cilian Fennell, to advise him, but either he didn't take the advice or the advice was bad. None of the staffers in Government Buildings were able to make Cowen understand the importance of communication in modern politics, the basic need to talk to voters and to tell them what their government was doing.

4

Bailout

Like his father before him, Brian Lenihan was liked and respected by people right across the political and party spectrums. Partly this was because of his astonishing courage; he had been diagnosed with what was probably a fatal cancer in late 2009 but continued to serve as minister while he tried to fight the disease. His bravery inspired many, but it especially bound his officials to him. If he can beat this cancer, one of his senior officials told me in the summer of 2010, then the country will get out of this economic mess. Alas he was clutching at straws on both counts, but it is to Lenihan's credit as a man that those who saw most of him and knew him best were most admiring of him.

Lenihan was also liked across political boundaries, because he was fantastically indiscreet, discussing political and economic problems freely with political opponents whom he happened to bump into in the corridor. Among his regular interlocutors was Labour's Pat Rabbitte. Despite their political differences the two were drawn together in the way that clever people often are. Rabbitte found their conversations at once terrifying and fascinating, though, as he later said to people, 'Being a Lenihan, you suspected that it was 50 per cent bullshit and 50 per cent true. The difficulty was in working out which was which.'

But the time for bullshitting was rapidly coming to an end. On Thursday, 30 September 2010, the Dáil's second day back after a summer holiday, which had lasted since 8 July, Brian Lenihan rose in the chamber to put some final numbers on the cost of a decade of lunacy in Ireland's banks and a decade of somnolence among those charged with their oversight.

It was a long and detailed speech, received mostly in silence, or perhaps in horror. Exactly two years on from the date of the original disastrous bank guarantee, in which the state had agreed to cover all deposits and borrowings for the six main Irish-owned banks, there was a bit of the usual Lenihan guff about putting the past behind us, but only a bit of it. There was no attempt to sugarcoat the numbers that the stress tests on Ireland's banks, including its hopelessly busted state-owned ones, were showing. 'This additional capital requirement,' Lenihan reported, 'brings the projected total gross cost of the restructuring of Anglo Irish Bank to €29.3 billion . . .' There was an audible intake of breath in the House, before Lenihan went on to explain that in the worst-case scenario for the worst of the six banks covered by the guarantee, the bill could potentially be €5 billion higher. Add on what the rest of the banks could cost, and what had already been poured into them, and the bill for the greatest banking bust the world had ever seen was heading for €50 billion. This wasn't far off the total national budget. It was unheard of.

For the first time on a matter of immediate national significance, Lenihan faced Michael Noonan across the floor of the Dáil. The Fine Gael spokesman began quietly and ruefully. But he immediately saw the significance of Lenihan's earlier statement that Ireland was to withdraw from issuing bonds on the international market. 'We can no longer trade in the bond market because our sovereign creditworthiness is gone,' Noonan summarized. Lenihan's anger flashed, protesting that the 'reckless lending' in Ireland's banks had not occurred 'on my watch'. Everyone could see what he was saying, and Noonan obliged him by amplifying it. 'That is true,' he conceded. 'That was the Taoiseach's responsibility.' Cowen sat beside Lenihan, glum and impassive. The tensions between the finance minister and the Taoiseach were by now an open secret.

The government, Noonan said, had chosen to put the sovereign on the line for a bank without having the slightest idea about the extent of its liabilities. He accepted that the minister had been badly served by the Central Bank and the Financial Regulator. But it was his responsibility to safeguard the finances of the state, and he had failed. Noonan was talking as if a bailout were already inevitable. It was.

Labour's Joan Burton realized it too. Lenihan relished political cut and thrust with most of his opponents, but he could only take Burton in very small amounts, perhaps because her criticisms had an infuriating habit of being proved correct. She suspected that, for all Lenihan's articulacy and apparent command of his brief, he was at heart just a very good barrister arguing a case. She thought he had no idea whether what he was saying half the time was correct or not; his job was simply to say it in as convincing a manner as possible. 'We are trying to encourage "Brian the Barrister" to provide some insights into his legal mind. Barristers can tell one anything; that is what they are paid to do,' Burton jibed witheringly. She demanded to hear about the legal advice that Lenihan said precluded the burning of the bondholders. 'Otherwise,' she said, as Lenihan glowered, 'we are entitled to think this is barristers in parliament chancing their arms.'

Burton, who had extensive contacts in the banking and financial worlds, knew where it was all going. 'Today is a day of infamy in Ireland,' she accused. 'It is Black Thursday.'

The following morning, the *Irish Times* experimented with its version of a new trend in newspaper design, one in which graphics – rather than photographs – attempt to convey the data central to a story. Its front page featured representations of Ireland's banks in the style of black holes, with sums of money being sucked into them. In case readers couldn't interpret this design whizzery, the headline inside explained morbidly and simply: 'Taxpayer facing €50bn bill for saving banking system'. The paper went on helpfully to explain what else the country could have bought for this staggering amount of money. Among the items listed was the Real Madrid star and world's most expensive footballer, Cristiano Ronaldo. Ireland could have bought him 373 times, it said. It was best left at footballers. To have focused on the schools and hospitals and childcare and pensions and tax cuts would probably have been too depressing for everyone.

But, for all the serious economic analysis in the broadsheet papers over the following days, the Irish *Daily Star* probably summed up the consequences better than any of them. Its front page featured a large headstone emblazoned with the words IRELAND R.I.P. The paper blamed 'greedy bankers and gormless politicians'.

The *Times* was right that the money was disappearing into a black hole. What it didn't say was where that left the state. In fact, the significance of the Anglo numbers, and the consequences that stemmed from them, dawned only slowly in a political arena that was still transfixed by the circus in Fianna Fáil following the infamous Galway think-in. A couple of not-as-bad-as-expected opinion polls – as well as a sort of paralysing sense of foreboding in the party – had dampened the chances of a revolt against Cowen, though it was difficult to find a TD or minister who had anything good to say about him in private, and many were vicious. What the Anglo numbers did was to demonstrate, to anyone who was minded to see it, that the country's problems went a whole lot further than Brian Cowen.

Amid general fear and uncertainty in the markets, investors had begun to take fright at Ireland's prospects. The yields on Irish government bonds started to nudge steadily upwards, signalling emerging difficulties in obtaining the funding necessary to run the country. Lenihan tried gamely to stem the tide, but it was no use. The *Daily Telegraph* reported that on an investors' conference call with hundreds of traders, a technical malfunction meant that for a brief period the traders could hear each other instead of just Lenihan's presentation. The call descended into farce, the *Telegraph* reported, with one participant making 'chimp sounds', while others shouted 'Dive! Dive!' and 'Short Ireland!' The Department of Finance denied the report, unconvincingly. Among ministers, the sense that they were not in control of the country's destiny began to harden. The Green leader John Gormley startled one cabinet meeting by asking bluntly if they were headed for an IMF bailout. Neither the Taoiseach nor the finance minister wanted to discuss it. In public, ministers kept up the mantra that Ireland was 'fully funded until the middle of next year', seemingly not realizing that, for the markets, saying you were going to run out of money next year was more or less the same thing as saying you were out of money now. The notion of re-entering the bond markets any time soon was always a fantasy.

Perhaps some ministers believed what they were saying. If they did, it just meant they didn't understand it. A week after the Galway débâcle, the cabinet had met for a special session on the budget, due at the beginning of December. It was obvious to everyone there that they had to construct a budget with at least one eye on what the markets wanted. And even then it might not be enough. 'Investors have panicked over Ireland's economic crisis,' noted the *Wall Street Journal*. The government was being assailed by forces it could not control, certainly, but its self-inflicted misfortunes weren't helping either. On the same day that the cabinet held its budget session, the *Guardian*'s website published its regular list of articles most viewed in the past week. Among them was: 'Irish PM Brian Cowen under pressure after "drunk" radio interview'.

During the countless radio and television debates about the effect of threatened cuts to government spending programmes, Colm McCarthy – the economist and author of the 2009 Bord Snip Nua report recommending a raft of public spending cuts – was fond of observing that the government wasn't short of compassion; it was short of cash. The influential Lex column in the *Financial Times* was impressed by the government's determination, but pessimistic about its prospects. Lex framed his thoughts in a similar style to McCarthy. 'Ireland's problem is not a lack of will,' he wrote. 'It's a lack of options.' As September turned into October and the autumn gathered in, those options began to narrow inexorably.

Soon after Black Thursday, a draft of the Flannery group's election blueprint arrived on Enda Kenny's desk. It was a prescient document in a number of ways, especially since it anticipated the extent to which the economic crisis would work to set the agenda in Fine Gael's favour in any forthcoming election. This is the real genius of political strategizing: not just to know the mood of the country, but to understand it, and to anticipate how it is likely to react to the stimuli of events and political messages. Later, in hindsight, senior Labour figures would realize this too. 'The country was moving from anger to fear,' one of the most senior figures in the party told me of those crucial months in late 2010. 'But we stayed with anger.'

The government had announced that it would produce a four-year plan for fiscal correction in November, and throughout October ministers sought to draw in Fine Gael and Labour support for it. Green leader John Gormley went so far as to write to the leaders of the other parties, asking them to contribute to an agreed all-party approach to the budget and the financial crisis. Gormley was genuinely trying to open the door to a national government. But this wasn't a decision he was in any position to make. Cowen thought it was naive and pointless, but, after initially pouring cold water on the proposals – prompting a spate of excruciatingly dismissive headlines for Gormley – he agreed to a series of briefings for the opposition leaders. Nobody really expected anything to come out of it; nothing did. The most cutting summary appeared in, of all places, the Sinn Féin newspaper *An Phoblacht*. Faced with the prospect of having to vote for the harshest budget in Irish history, wrote the paper's columnist Mícheál Mac Donncha, the Greens were 'looking for a group hug'.

Janey, they thought over in the Fine Gael backroom, if they're asking us to join them, they must really believe it's all over. We had better be ready.

Actually, the Greens' proposal, if done properly, wouldn't have been a completely silly political strategy. Any budget plan, whether implemented at the behest of the markets or anyone else, was going to have to decrease the deficit, and that meant huge spending cuts and tax hikes. Labour and Fine Gael couldn't avoid spelling out their approach forever. They could, however, avoid doing it on Fianna Fáil's or the Greens' terms. But this was all just politics, and the situation was quickly moving beyond politics.

Work on the four-year budget plan was in any case already proceeding among a group of senior officials in the Department of Finance. Discussions with the European Commission had settled on a figure of €15 billion as the total adjustment the government – however constituted – would have to achieve to bring the budget deficit down to the permitted European level of below 3 per cent by 2014. For an economy deep in recession, it was a gigantic ask, inevitably necessitating deep cuts to public spending and steep tax hikes every year. Nonetheless, a group of officials in finance knew that a bailout, or some form of external assistance, was by now inevitable sooner or later, and that it would come with terms and conditions in the shape of a rigid budget plan. They wanted to influence that plan as much as possible, rather than having it dictated to them by outsiders.

In Brussels, the officials in the European Commission could read the political signs as well as anyone, and they knew that a Fine Gael–Labour government would probably be in place before too long. They sought to make contact with figures from both parties. The senior officials in both Kenny's and Gilmore's offices were now being briefed by finance officials, usually the secretary general, Kevin Cardiff, and assistant secretary, Ann Nolan, on a weekly basis. The Central Bank sent them updates on Ireland's creaking banking system. The banks had long since realized that a change of government was coming and sought to keep lines of communication with the opposition parties, particularly with Fine Gael, constantly open. The messages were not cheerful. There was 'massive capital flight', recalled one recipient of the briefings. 'The money was leaking out of the banking system.' The fears for the Irish banking system and for the sovereign were intensified hugely when French president Nicolas Sarkozy and German chancellor Angela Merkel, meeting in Deauville in Normandy, announced that, from 2013, investors and bondholders would have to share the burden of any state bailouts. Whatever slim chance Ireland had of regaining market confidence was now gone. As one finance official told the *Irish Times*'s Simon Carswell, it was 'the final kick in the bollocks'. As funds fled from the Irish banks, they had to be replaced by funds from the ECB and from the Irish Central Bank. By the end of October, Irish banks owed the ECB €130 billion. Ireland was now centre stage in the Eurozone crisis.

That Halloween, Colm O'Reardon, Gilmore's most senior finance and economics adviser, went to Luxembourg to meet with senior European Commission officials and members of the staff of Jean-Claude Juncker, head of the Eurozone finance ministers group and prime minister of Luxembourg. O'Reardon reported back that, as far as most of Europe was concerned, Ireland was being lumped in with Greece, and would be treated in a similar fashion. They respected Brian Lenihan; but Brian Cowen, he found, had 'zero impact' at European level. The European officials wanted to send one very important message: any new government in Ireland, as far as they were concerned, would be bound by the promises made by its predecessors. The Commission was very hardline on the fiscal adjustments that would have to be made in Ireland. It understood the underlying strength of the Irish economy, and approved of the adjustment measures taken so far. But it was clear there was an awful lot more pain to come in Ireland. One official from Juncker's team told O'Reardon, 'If you guys go into a programme, I hope you're interested in gay marriage. Because that's what's going to happen to you.' It was not the most comforting of thoughts to bring home.

There was a sense of nervousness and foreboding everywhere. 'The days of bluffing and false promises are over and the harsh reality of truth has dawned,' Kenny told the Dáil at the end of October. The entire country had the jitters. The government, seemingly oblivious to the mood, announced a scheme on 5 November to give away free cheese to those in need. The agriculture minister Brendan Smith went on *Morning Ireland* to explain the benefits of the scheme. It would also promote the use, value and importance of nutritional dairy products, he said. It was a small measure, he acknowledged, 'but it is helpful to those in need.' Comedians hardly knew what to do with it. It was beyond satire.

A few days later Olli Rehn, the European Commissioner with responsibility for economic and monetary affairs, arrived in Dublin. Reuters reported that his visit was intended to 'bolster Irish efforts to lance the worst budget deficit in the EU'. It was, sort of. And also to 'convince' the markets that the country didn't need 'a Greek-style bailout'. This was codswallop. The markets had already made up their minds. The yields on Irish ten-year bonds when Rehn was in Dublin were over 8 per cent, way beyond what was remotely sustainable; they weren't going to be convinced otherwise by a few photo ops at Government Buildings. Rehn was in town to clarify what the European Commission expected to happen, and to reinforce the message that O'Reardon had brought home from Luxembourg. In public, he called for 'political consensus' – a blunt message to the apparent successors to the beleaguered government. At private meetings, he asked both Fine Gael and Labour what would happen after the election. Fine Gael's leaders told him that they didn't know what the Commission was going to agree with the existing Irish government, but that they understood a significant budgetary consolidation was necessary. Banking, and specifically the question of 'burden-sharing' – the polite term for burning the bondholders, or at least toasting them a little – was another matter. It would keep cropping up.

Rehn's visit didn't calm any nerves, but that was hardly its purpose. He had been sent to gauge the extent of the political chaos that Brussels feared Cowen's government was sliding towards. Rehn had hardly departed from Dublin Airport when the punch-drunk administration received another haymaker in the shape of an op-ed piece in the *Irish Times* from Professor Morgan Kelly of UCD.

It would be difficult to overstate the impact of Kelly's pieces on national debate. He had predicted as far back as 2007 that the Irish property bubble was about to crash – a prediction for which he was widely excoriated, including by the then Taoiseach, Bertie Ahern, who memorably wondered why the likes of Kelly didn't commit suicide. By November 2010 Kelly's predictions had all come horrifyingly true, and he was looked to as a sort of national seer, a Cassandra whom bitter experience had taught everyone to believe. Now his latest augury landed in the government's in-tray with a sickening thud. Ireland, he wrote on 8 November, had 'ceased to exist as an autonomous fiscal entity'. It had become instead 'a ward of the European Central Bank'. 'Ireland faced a painful choice between imposing a resolution on banks that were too big to save or becoming insolvent, and, for whatever reason, chose the latter,' Kelly concluded. 'Sovereign nations get to make policy choices, and we are no longer a sovereign nation in any meaningful sense of that term. From here on, for better or worse, we can only rely on the kindness of strangers.' It was devastating. And it was true. The national mood began to darken further.

Events accelerated now. Four days after Kelly's article, Reuters reported that Ireland was in talks to access a bailout. These reports were backed up by ECB sources in Frankfurt, who briefed that Ireland should seek outside help. The genie was out of the bottle, but Fianna Fáil ministers tried to force it back in. Dermot Ahern told RTÉ's *The Week in Politics* that such reports were 'a fiction'. The BBC and Bloomberg also reported that Ireland was in talks. It didn't matter to Dublin: ministers kept denying it. Cowen insisted no application for funding had been made. Noel Dempsey and Ahern went on television to deny there had been any contacts between the Irish government and the European authorities about a bailout. 'I'm not aware of any contact, are you, Noel?' Ahern asked. Dempsey shook his head gravely. The two ministers had been briefed by Lenihan personally. But he was lying to them. Irish officials were already in exploratory talks with Europe and the IMF. When the bailout emerged, the two ministers looked ridiculous. Two lifetimes spent in politics, with substantial achievements to their names, all now reduced to an idiotic lie. Both were incandescent with Lenihan, and the way he had casually regarded their credibility as dispensable. But he had bigger things to worry about.

At a meeting of the Eurozone finance ministers in Brussels, Lenihan was put under massive pressure to announce that Ireland was seeking a bailout, but he refused. Two days later, his Central Bank governor, Patrick Honohan, took the decision out of his hands. In Frankfurt for a meeting of the ECB governing council, Honohan contacted RTÉ's *Morning Ireland*. Ireland, he said, was in talks, and he expected a very large loan – 'tens of billions' – to be extended to the government and accepted by it. Lenihan was apoplectic when he heard the broadcast. He wanted to sack Honohan immediately and discussed the possibility with his staff. He thought his governor had 'stabbed him in the back'.

But now Frankfurt was on the phone. 'We are exceeding our mandate,' the ECB president Jean-Claude Trichet warned Ireland's finance minister in a phone call, which Lenihan immediately related to his officials; 'we cannot continue.' Lenihan's most senior aides discussed Trichet's threat to downgrade Irish banks' collateral and so disqualify them from the massive loans Frankfurt was extending to them. The funding would cease, and the banks would collapse. Would he really do it? 'Fuck them!' one of his officials urged Lenihan. 'Call their bluff!' But you should only call a bluff if you have some sort of a hand yourself. And Lenihan had no cards left to play. On the Sunday, 21 November, journalists were summoned to Government Buildings in the bitter, biting cold. The Irish government, Cowen announced, was applying for a programme of assistance. It was over.

5

The government implodes

Once the government said it was applying for a bailout, the political dam burst. The following day, 22 November, with the deluge rushing around their ears, the Greens scrambled for the lifeboats. As the cabinet was taking the formal decision to ask for external financial assistance that weekend, the Greens were deciding to leave government. Their view was that the government could not possibly continue once the IMF arrived, though they believed that the budget and finance bill would have to be passed before an election could be called. The announcement bore the hallmarks of the Greens' participation in government: long-agonized over, well-meaning, politically inept and badly communicated. Gormley couldn't get Cowen on the phone to tell him until minutes before the press conference began. Green TD Paul Gogarty brought his eighteen-month-old daughter to the press conference. She sat at the top table with her daddy and her teddy. Neither said much. Confusingly, the statement issued was ambiguous in its conclusion: it wasn't clear whether the Greens wanted an election in late January or wanted the finance bill done by late January and an election called then.

In the Dáil the next day, Noonan was withering. 'What they have done to the coalition government was outrageous at a time when credibility and certainty were required and members on this side of the House were walking on eggshells in case we got the cabinet and the country into further difficulty.' 'Outrageous,' agreed Pat Rabbitte.

Noonan compared the behaviour of the Greens unfavourably with the 'responsible' way Labour had left when the 1982–7 coalition broke up. 'Arrangements were made for a withdrawal with the minimum of damage. Everybody was in the loop. Furthermore, when the Labour Party deputies decided to go, they went. This crowd decided to go, but stayed. One would send for security if it was a Christmas party.' Joan Burton was in the chamber too, and registered her approval. Noonan wasn't just flirting with Labour, though: he was reflecting the joint understanding between senior figures in Fine Gael and Labour that would be one of the foundations of the next government: the belief that you needed grown-up politicians making hard decisions to fix the mess they had inherited.

Noonan never wavered in his belief that Fine Gael would need Labour to form the next government; it was a view that was strengthened over the following weeks as he watched Lenihan desperately horse-trade constituency favours in return for Michael Lowry's and Jackie Healy-Rae's budget votes.

Fianna Fáil went through the roof when they heard about the Greens' departure, with many deputies and ministers howling about betrayal to anyone who would listen. Meanwhile, privately, Lenihan was talking about resignation to his senior officials; after all, he was the finance minister on whose watch the ignominious bailout had finally come to pass. Other ministers urged Cowen to call an immediate election. But where would that leave the country? A Christmas election with banks tottering and any new government destined for an immediate bailout. Cowen's administration had been a disaster, but he had a highly developed sense of his responsibility and would try to do the right thing, however difficult. Sometimes this meant that he charged ahead, with catastrophic decisions. Now, despite his fury at Gormley and the Greens, it meant that he resolved to stay in government with them, pass the budget and the finance bill, and take the electoral consequences. For the country, it was probably, on this occasion, the right thing to do. It probably cost Fianna Fáil – who knows? – a dozen seats.

On 24 November, two days after the Greens announced their departure, the long-awaited 'four-year plan' was published. It would form the basis of the bailout agreements and act as a template for not just the budget due within weeks, but for the budgetary policy of at least the early stages of the government that would follow Cowen's administration. The plan was predictably brutal, containing a raft of tax increases and spending cuts amounting to some €15 billion over four years. Garret FitzGerald said it would take 4 per cent off GDP.

On the last Sunday in November, the terms of the agreement were published. The day before, a huge demonstration of bewildered and angry citizens organized by the Irish Congress of Trade Unions, numbering in the tens of thousands, braved the icy wind and rain. The *Sunday Independent* was in no doubt about their message. 'Default! Say the people' roared its front page. As to what might happen then, its normally voluble columnists were not of a single mind. Nor was anyone else. The Greens fretted about civic disorder, and there were indeed a few half-serious attempts to break through the gates of Government Buildings and the Dáil, though they were mostly driven by competition between the radical Republican group Éirígí and Sinn Féin, the latter determined not to be out-gunned in the agitation stakes by its rivals on the streets. But there were others who had revolutionary agendas too. Fintan O'Toole, probably the country's leading newspaper commentator, called for the government to be replaced by a 'short-term technical administration (led by non-political people of integrity and competence)' – an idea that appeared to require the suspension of the constitution, by an authority O'Toole did not make clear.

Both Labour and Fine Gael were watching all this with a sort of horrified fascination. Their political opponents were falling apart before their eyes. Throughout October and November, as fiscal control and political authority gradually ebbed away from Cowen's administration, both parties were conscious of the need not to do or say anything that could make the situation worse. After all, it was a situation they would soon have to contend with themselves. Gilmore, especially, eased up on the Dáil rhetoric that had served him so well earlier in the year. There was no repeat of the April accusation of 'economic treason' he had aimed at Cowen – not because he didn't believe the accusation was warranted, but because he was concerned that if the opposition piled on the pressure in the Dáil and the media, the government could simply collapse in disarray. Gilmore wanted Fianna Fáil routed, and he wanted to be in power certainly, but he needed to inherit a functioning government. There were times, during those febrile November weekends, when that seemed an uncertain prospect.

Behind the scenes, the realities of impending government were looming. Delegations from both parties met the Troika both before and after the memorandum of agreement was finalized with the Irish authorities. Already a few things were becoming clear: while the two parties could live with the broad terms of the fiscal adjustment package, there were likely to be problems on the banking side, especially with the ECB's insistence on ruling out burden-sharing with the bondholders of Ireland's busted banks. For a start, both parties knew they would be going into a general election campaign in which the issue would certainly surface. One thing Fine Gael quickly learned was that the Troika itself was split on the question of burden-sharing. 'Look, the MoU [Memorandum of Understanding] is silent on this but it is something we have to discuss,' Ajai Chopra of the IMF told a meeting with Fine Gael figures. But the ECB said 'absolutely no way', according to one person present. Moreover, the ECB insisted on speaking for the Troika on the matter. 'It would be a fundamental breach between Ireland and the Troika if the new government attempts to shift policy on this,' Fine Gael was told, months before it was part of that new government.

Somehow, Cowen's coalition staggered through until Christmas, having suffered a crushing by-election defeat in Donegal, but clung on to pass the budget in early December. His party was in bits; each week brought news of another senior Fianna Fáiler announcing his or her retirement. Dermot Ahern. Seán Ardagh. M. J. Nolan. Beverley Flynn. Then Bertie Ahern. In all, twenty Fianna Fáil TDs, including some of its highest-profile ministers and ex-ministers, chose not to contest the general election. The party would lose every one of those seats.

Over the previous three elections, Fianna Fáil had brought campaigning to a new level of sophistication. Now the party was in utter disarray. Headquarters struggled to establish any level of preparedness for the general election to come; officials all but begged Cowen to focus on the election. It seemed to junior minister Conor Lenihan that the party was 'sleepwalking towards the precipice and outright disaster'. To all intents and purposes, as a political force, it was leaderless. Lenihan joked with people that it was like the last days of the late Soviet leader Leonid Brezhnev. 'He might be dead but the different factions can't agree on a successor, so we have to pretend he's alive,' he said, half seriously. Several senior figures expected Cowen to resign over Christmas, but when he came back in January after the break, there was no sign of it; just the same dogged, myopic, destructive determination. Micheál Martin resolved to act.

By contrast, Fine Gael had been polling and preparing, organizing and war-gaming, as they had for no other election before. For the first time in its history, the party was facing a general election campaign with more money, more candidates and more favourable opinion-poll ratings than its historic enemy. Its 'five-point plan', the summary of its entire appeal to the public, was focus-group tested, refined and tested again; an online campaign would be mounted seriously for the first time in Irish politics; and, while the election steering committee, led by Frank Flannery, would continue to tweak local strategies and the division of constituencies right up until polling day, the organization was ready and raring to go. In fact, some of them had already started. Campaign-finance laws restricted the amount of money each candidate and the party nationally could spend during the period of the election campaign proper, so many just started spending money in the months before the campaign. No sense in having a pile of money left over after the thing had finished. The party's election base would be the same building at Leeson Street Bridge that it had used in 2007. Back at its Upper Mount Street headquarters, the IT infrastructure was in place that would enable a team of volunteers, under the direction of Ciaran Conlon and US consultant Ravi Singh, to run an intensive social media campaign. The election grid, a detailed day-by-day map of the campaign plan, colour coded for key messages, had been agreed. Blue for jobs. Green for reform. Orange for health (from the Dutch model). 'We need to stop worrying about the answers,' Conlon told meetings. 'We need to define the question.' He thought the five-point plan could do that. For a time, he was correct. All the questions were about it.

Enda Kenny was now the unbackable favourite to become Taoiseach – a remarkable turnaround for a man who only months before had had to face a challenge from within his own parliamentary party.

Fine Gael insiders were dismissive of the notion that the electorate would never settle for Kenny as Taoiseach. They reckoned there was no mysterious alchemy to becoming Taoiseach – all they had to do was ensure that Fine Gael got enough votes. Actually, whatever misgivings the electorate may have had about Kenny as Taoiseach, events had overtaken them. By the beginning of the year he seemed ready to confound those who had said he would never succeed to the highest office. Yet it could hardly be said that he had risen in the midst of the crisis to take up the role of national leader. Rather, he had simply stayed standing for long enough to see the prize come his way. Perhaps the most underestimated man in Irish politics, certainly the most resilient – however you chose to describe him, as the political world waited for the election to be called, it was going to take an earthquake to stop him from winning it.

If Fianna Fáil was in a state varying between panic and terror, the Green Party was just resigned to its fate. Its ministers were exhausted and largely demoralized after two and a half years of more or less continuous crises in government. Every one of its six TDs knew that there was a strong chance they would lose their seats; every one of the party's staff knew that they would then lose their jobs. Media coverage of the Greens tended to concentrate as much on their impending wipe-out as on anything the party was actually saying about policy. In the *Irish Times*, Deaglán de Bréadún likened them to the 'early Christians' who, though massacred, would pass on beliefs that endured. As Green candidates contemplated the hungry lions in the arena, the promise of the political hereafter wasn't much of a consolation.

Despite having called time on the government in the aftermath of the IMF's arrival, and thus set the election countdown clock in motion, the Greens appeared to have done little to prepare. In fact, the Greens had fallen into two of the classic traps for a small party in Irish politics: in government, they had concentrated all their resources – physical and intellectual – on governing, and none on preparing for the next election; and in government with Fianna Fáil, they had found themselves being contaminated by the larger party's unpopularity.

The Green Party leadership felt that a 'narrative' that was highly unfavourable to the party had already settled among both the public and the media. 'It didn't matter what we did. We were going to be faced with an immovable object: the narrative of propping up Fianna Fáil and everything that went with that,' John Gormley told me subsequently. 'It didn't matter what we said,' he said. 'They had made up their minds.'

Sinn Féin was buoyed by two things: one was the stunning victory of Pearse Doherty in the Donegal South West by-election at the end of November; the second was the long-predicted arrival of party leader Gerry Adams into southern politics. Adams had announced in November that he would resign his seat in Westminster and stand in the Louth constituency. Having a northern leadership had damaged the southern party, and the Adams question had been agonized over within Sinn Féin for years, without ever really being settled. Now it was. His arrival shifted the party's centre of gravity and gave it what it had always lacked in southern elections: an immediately recognizable leader.

An unprecedented number of non-party, small-party and newly independent candidates were also preparing to enter the electoral fray in response. They were, and remain, an eclectic bunch. Left-wing and far-left groups came together to form the United Left Alliance, an umbrella organization rather than a party, which included the Socialist Party of the Dublin MEP Joe Higgins, several councillors of the People before Profit Alliance and some independent left-wing figures like the former Tipperary South TD Séamus Healy. There were also existing independents such as Finian McGrath, who likewise sought to capitalize on their 'outsider' status, despite in his case having previously been a government supporter. A number of 'non-traditional' independents would also stand, principally on a platform of opposition to the government's banking policy and the EU/IMF deal. These included candidates with a high media profile – including the Trinity senator Shane Ross and financial commentator Paul Sommerville – and some without any, including Stephen Donnelly, who would stand successfully in Wicklow. There were the traditional 'constituency-based' independents such as Michael Lowry and Michael Healy-Rae, son of the retiring Jackie; these also included candidates who had recently left Fianna Fáil, such as Mattie McGrath of Tipperary South. Perhaps most intriguingly – certainly for the media – was a group of high-profile figures that included journalists Fintan O'Toole and Eamon Dunphy, who toyed in private and then publicly with running as a group, with candidates in every constituency, but who ultimately withdrew. The guys who were going to save the country couldn't do it because they couldn't order their posters on time, sneered activists in the established parties. The reasons for the no-show were more complex than that, but there was a grain of truth in it. Even without them, it was a huge and disparate field of independent candidates preparing for the election as 2011 dawned. Despite their many differences, there was one thing that united them: they all claimed to offer a new departure in Irish politics. Before they would get their chance, however, the old order represented by Fianna Fáil would enter the final stage of its collapse.

The Dáil returned earlier than usual in January, and when it did, Fianna Fáil was in turmoil. The atmosphere was rife with rumour and counter-rumour; when a supposed challenge to Cowen failed to materialize at the Fianna Fáil parliamentary party's first meeting, Miriam Lord summarized, 'More night of wrong vibes than night of long knives, as Cowen lives to fight another day.' But the question was not yet settled, because it could be settled in only one way. Following revelations in the book *The FitzPatrick Tapes* that Cowen had played golf with the disgraced former chairman of Anglo Irish Bank, Sean FitzPatrick, back in July 2008, just weeks before the bank's near-collapse prompted the government's bank guarantee, the Taoiseach told the party he would 'consult' with them about his future. When he did consult, several of his most senior colleagues, including Mary Hanafin and Micheál Martin, told him he should resign for the good of the party. Martin told him he should stay as Taoiseach until the election, but resign as party leader. Others swore loyalty no matter what. That Saturday morning Cowen held a breakfast meeting at his home in Offaly, attended by John Moloney, one of his closest friends in politics. It was the rasher-and-sausage summit.

Cowen told Moloney that he had received tremendous support, especially from the party's younger TDs. 'I've a duty to work for these guys,' Cowen said. 'They have to work for you too,' Moloney encouraged. Fortified by the rashers and sausages and the support of his doomed party, Cowen decided he was staying.

On that Sunday, 16 January, he called a press conference in a Dublin hotel to announce that he intended to continue as leader of Fianna Fáil and, furthermore, that he was putting down a motion of confidence in his own leadership for the following Tuesday. Flanked by the Tánaiste, Mary Coughlan, in a strikingly colourful dress, and by his chief whip, John Curran, Cowen was relaxed, determined and confident. Less than three hours later, his foreign affairs minister, Micheál Martin, announced he would be voting against the motion. The long-awaited heave against Cowen was finally on.

It was a relatively mild-mannered affair. Cowen and his lieutenants canvassed hard, but discovered that many TDs just did not have the stomach for knifing a leader they personally liked, even if they could see the disaster that awaited them at the polls. The outcome was fixed when none of Martin's frontbench colleagues saw fit to join him publicly in rebellion. Of the two other potential leaders, Brian Lenihan confounded the expectation of many backbenchers when he announced his support for Cowen. Lenihan had spent months encouraging backbenchers to challenge Cowen, many of whom saw the finance minister as their only hope of salvaging their seats. It was a commentary on the state of the party and of Cowen's leadership that a man with terminal cancer was considered a better alternative for the leadership. When Lenihan told Sean O'Rourke on RTÉ's *News at One* that he would be supporting Cowen, backbencher John McGuinness was on hand to relate how the finance minister had encouraged him and others to mount a campaign against Cowen. The economic disaster had ruined Lenihan's credibility among many of his colleagues anyway, but his U-turn was the final straw for them. His relations with Cowen were broken too. One person with regular contact with both men described their relationship at the end as 'utterly, utterly poisonous'. Mary Hanafin simply refused to say what she would do. Isolated, Martin lost the vote, and resigned from cabinet. The mood among most Fianna Fáil TDs was utter despair, and resignation to their fate. It seemed there was no hope for the party. They were right, but there was one further twist yet to come. Whatever their real view of his leadership, Cowen's colleagues had proven unwilling to guillotine his premiership. Now, he was about to do it himself.

Perhaps not surprisingly, this most ill-starred of leaders brought his final tragedy upon himself. Having defeated Micheál Martin's leadership challenge on Tuesday, 18 January, Cowen, claiming 'vindication', sought on the following day to reshuffle his cabinet, bringing forward the resignations of four members that evening – Dermot Ahern, Noel Dempsey, Tony Killeen and Mary Harney – some of whom complied with the request to resign more cheerfully than others. Another minister, Batt O'Keeffe, would follow early the next morning. Disaster awaited. Even those Fianna Fáil TDs whom he had intended to appoint to cabinet could see that such a blatant political stroke would backfire. Barry Andrews was called late at night and offered the job of minister for health. He played for time, and consulted with his father, party elder statesman David Andrews, who asked, 'Are you out of your mind?' Earlier that evening Martin had asked Andrews to go over to Cowen's office and implore him not to go ahead with the reshuffle. Andrews did, but nobody would listen to him. Government Buildings was chaotic, with people coming and going, some begging Cowen not to proceed with the reshuffle of the cabinet, others telling him that he was the Taoiseach and it was his prerogative. 'You can't do this!' Mary Hanafin pleaded. Billy Kelleher, TD for Cork North Central, rang his wife. 'I'm not going to take it if I'm offered it,' he told her. 'Of course you're not!' she said. It seemed everyone outside Cowen's immediate circle of loyalists could see impending disaster if the reshuffle went ahead.

More dangerously, he had failed to secure the agreement of the Green Party, which simply refused to back any new appointments. As accusations and threats flew, the Greens threatened to leave government immediately and vote against the new appointments in the House. Faced with the prospect of being defeated on a vote in the Dáil, Cowen had no choice but to back down. After a morning charged with high political drama, he was left with a cabinet of just nine ministers, and his authority in tatters. After repeated adjournments of a Dáil chamber which was, justifiably, entirely in uproar, a humiliated Cowen, shoulders hunched and eyes downcast, returned to the chamber and announced that the general election would be held on 11 March.

Fianna Fáil TDs wandered around Leinster House in a state of stupor. Many simply could not believe what had just happened. Others were spitting absolute fury. 'If he comes to my fucking constituency,' hissed one, 'I will not meet him.' Others were even less polite. That night on Vincent Browne's television show, Conor Lenihan demonstrated the extent to which the entire party was losing its temper by losing his. The host, in fairness, just shouted back at him. At Fianna Fáil headquarters, officials tried to assess the damage and to plot a way forward. They reckoned there were now two, maybe three safe seats in the country. Cowen himself, Martin and maybe Éamon Ó Cuív. No other seat could be relied upon.

The Fianna Fáil parliamentary party was in open revolt, and on the following Saturday the seventh leader of Fianna Fáil at last faced political reality. At a packed, hastily arranged press conference in the Merrion Hotel, Brian Cowen announced his resignation as party leader. Fianna Fáil, he said, would fight the election with 'good heart and determination'. It was about the opposite of the truth.

But the implosion of Fianna Fáil had also collapsed the government. On the following day, the Green Party ministers filed in sombre fashion into the same room and announced that they were leaving government. 'Our patience has reached an end,' said party leader John Gormley. The party would, however, vote in favour of the finance bill in the Dáil in the following days. After frantic talks with Fine Gael and Labour, agreement was reached that the finance bill would be rushed through the Dáil that week, clearing the way for a dissolution. After a brief leadership contest, Micheál Martin was chosen to lead Fianna Fáil. Five days later, his face was on the lampposts, and the election campaign was on at last.

6

'Tomorrow the people are in charge'

The dying days of the Fianna Fáil–Green coalition had seen some raucous sessions in the Dáil, as the country's parliamentary system struggled to accommodate a government that was clearly falling apart. But when Brian Cowen rose on Saint Brigid's Day, 1 February, the chamber was subdued, rueful, fearful even. As he brought down the curtain on both the thirtieth Dáil and his career in public life, the outgoing Taoiseach quoted Raftery the Poet's optimism on the coming of spring: *Anois teacht an earraigh/beidh an lá ag dul chun síneadh/Is tar éis na féil Bríde/ardóigh mé mo sheol.* As they contemplated what awaited them on the doorsteps, Fianna Fáil deputies were anything but optimistic. And though Fine Gael and Labour expected to return as a government, the immensity of the task that would await them was clear by the way it had destroyed their predecessors.

Most politicians are a mixture of altruism and egotism. It is deep in their nature to think of their own seat, their own future, first. How else can they achieve great things for their fellow citizens if they don't first attain elected office? But those departing Leinster House that chilly afternoon also wondered what would become of the place and of the old post-civil war political dispensation, with its clubby two-and-a-half-party certainties. The feeling that change was on the way was everywhere. But change to what?

Cowen's lyrical farewell to the TDs was his swansong as a player in national politics. Though still Taoiseach, he would play no part in the Fianna Fáil campaign and fulfil his duties as head of government only as a caretaker. For someone in whom such hopes had once been invested, by his own people and by the country, his end was brutal, even by the essentially unsentimental standards of politics. By the end, he cut a figure that was almost tragic. There was always a strange sort of nobility to his basic honesty, his bluntness, his cussed refusal to engage with the norms of modern politics. But his administration had ended in an utter shambles.

Kenny and Gilmore followed Cowen's valedictory words, wishing him and his family well. But the niceties were brief; both delivered strongly political speeches. Thereafter the Dáil exchanges descended into the rancour that had characterized the final months of the doomed coalition government. Poor John Gormley, whose dreams had been of a government remembered for its green policies and political reforms, was hollered down as he attempted to list the over-looked achievements of his coalition. Gormley, a decent, able and sincere man, had been overwhelmed by circumstance, and he railed against the unfairness of it. But it was useless. 'I am very proud to have served in a government that produced civil partnership,' he pleaded. 'Yesterday, a gay couple came up to me in Ranelagh and thanked me for it. I am proud we delivered the legislation.' But all the gays in Ranelagh would not save Gormley; and the opposition benches fairly hooted their derision. Half to himself, Gormley gloomily predicted little change in the future. 'Tweedledum and Tweedledumber. That is what we will get, unfortunately.' Someone shouted at him: 'You had your chance!'

Enda Kenny lingered in the Dáil chamber after the Ceann Com-hairle, Seamus Kirk, adjourned the House for the last time. As other TDs held back respectfully, Kenny had a few quiet words with the departing Taoiseach. Although Cowen and Kenny were different animals, they had a lot in common. Both were elected in by-elections following the deaths of their TD fathers. Each was twenty-four when elected, becoming the youngest deputy in the House at that time. The two men had grown up in Leinster House, and after a shared half-lifetime in politics they appreciated the significance of this moment.

There had been little rapport between them any day ever, as they faced each other across the floor of the House. Cowen had little respect for Kenny, whom he considered a lightweight, a poseur try-ing to play the role of tough political leader, without ever really convincing even himself. Cowen rarely bothered to disguise his dis-dain. Kenny bridled at it, but never quite managed to overcome the impression he gave of being slightly afraid of Cowen. Now both men could plainly see who history would judge to be the winner in their confrontation. Kenny was polite enough not to rub his opponent's nose in it during his formal contributions. He was always warmer and more human in his personal contacts with political rivals; he once confessed privately to having hated the necessity of attacking Bertie Ahern over his personal finances. Now he had words of honest goodwill for his departing rival. Cowen's innermost thoughts remain his own, but he accepted Kenny's good wishes with apparently genuine gratitude.

In Áras an Uachtaráin later that afternoon, Brian Cowen's political life would come to a close, and with it an era of dominance for Fianna Fáil that had spanned nigh on eighty years. As a pale sun shone wearily over Dublin City, Cowen's black Mercedes-Benz, habitually splattered with mud from the by-roads of Offaly, sped through the Phoenix Park towards the Áras with his security detail following. Shortly before 4 p.m., President McAleese signed the formal dissolution. The thirtieth Dáil was no more. Perhaps half an hour later, Cowen emerged, now with his family. They passed a gaggle of reporters without stopping. The cars were waiting. The doors clunked, the engines purred into life. They moved off slowly down the driveway at first, then more quickly, disappearing into the gathering gloom.

For those who were still in the game, the starting gun had been effectively fired months earlier. By the time Cowen announced that polling day would be the revised date of 25 February, the parties – with the exception of his own – had been in election mode for months. Yet, however intense the pre-election period has been, and however well advertised the coming contest, there is always a discernible intensification of activity and mood when the Dáil is dissolved and the campaign proper starts. TDs scatter to their constituencies in the four corners of Ireland, to be dragged out of them only under extreme duress; many of the party headquarters' staff relocate to a specially designated election facility that brings all the campaign workers under one roof, designed for the daily press conferences; the media tools up for blanket coverage. Hectic the pre-campaign may be, but everyone feels the difference when the Dáil actually rises. Morning meetings, long days, late nights. When it's on, it's really on. Campaigns matter.

As Kenny lingered in the chamber having a few words with Brian Cowen, his TDs were already scattering to their constituencies. In Dublin South East, the constituency that hosted Leinster House, Lucinda Creighton already had her posters up. All over the country, the best-planned, best-prepared and best-financed Fine Gael general election campaign in the history of the party swung into action.

Everything that Fine Gael had done since the post-heave reorganization had been done with this moment in mind. Detailed planning had been in place since the previous summer. Even before the Green Party's announcement that it was pulling out of government, Fine Gael was expecting to mount a campaign in the first half of 2011. It was a judgement driven by simple arithmetic: the Fianna Fáil–Green government had been losing TDs steadily, and was now dependent on the support of independents. Indeed, Fine Gael had tried to use the budget and IMF bailout as a sort of dry-run for the election campaign, rehearsing messaging and strategies, and developing its idea of a 'five-point plan', which would become the centrepiece of the election pitch. The party's aim was to be 'ready to go' from the start of the year.

In planning its campaign, the core group of Fine Gael strategists – Phil Hogan, Mark Mortell, Frank Flannery, Mark Kennelly, Andrew McDowell, Ciaran Conlon, Tom Curran – had come to one very important conclusion: that its principal opponents would be Labour, not Fianna Fáil. They had had doubts about the accuracy of the *Irish Times* polls that showed Labour leading Fine Gael and rubbished them to nervous Fine Gaelers – but there was no doubt that there was a surge in support for Labour that posed a significant threat, if not to Fine Gael's chances of leading the next government, then to its hopes of dominating it. They figured voters had made up their minds on Fianna Fáil, but many had yet to decide between Fine Gael and Labour. Mortell looked at the research and figured that a great body of swing voters was choosing between Fine Gael and Labour. He told the others that this should underpin not just what they wanted to do, but how they did it. They then set about trying to persuade them to choose in favour of Fine Gael. In other words, they put Labour, not Fianna Fáil, in their gun-sights.

This was to have profound consequences for the way that the party designed and approached its campaign. Fine Gael strategists were heavily influenced by the advice of its American political consultants, Greenberg Quinlan Rosner, in reading the mood of the electorate and crafting a message that would fly with voters. The Americans' involvement arose from Kenny's and Frank Flannery's determination after 2002 that Fine Gael would match Fianna Fáil in every department. Fianna Fáil had been secretly employing the hotshot Washington consultants Shrum Devine & Donilon since 1997. Bob Shrum was such an important figure in Democratic politics in the US that the competition for his services among aspirant Democratic candidates for the presidency had become known as 'the Shrum primary', though it was Tad Devine who would have most involvement with Fianna Fáil. The Americans were masters at interpreting the research and crafting messages that would fly with specific target groups. Fianna Fáil learned a lot from them and paid them a small fortune. The Americans stayed in the Merrion Hotel, across the road from Government Buildings, worked all the hours, ate in the best restaurants. Everyone benefited from the arrangement. When the relationship became public after the 2002 general election (much to Bertie Ahern's annoyance), Fine Gael resolved to tool up to meet the challenge.

Fine Gael went to another leading firm of Democratic consultants, Greenberg Quinlan Rosner. Led by Stan Greenberg, they were an old ally of, and competitor for business with, Fianna Fáil's American pals. The involvement of Greenberg's firm began before the 2004 local and European elections and increased steadily in volume, influence and expense. By the time of the 2011 election, there were several members of Greenberg's staff advising Fine Gael on various aspects of its campaign. When I discovered their names – Jeremy Rosner, Kristi Lowe, Sean Dryden, Catherine Silvey and Ben Goldfarb – and published them, it turned out nobody in Dublin had heard of them. But they were hugely influential. According to post-election filings with the Standards in Public Office Commission, the campaign-finance watchdog, they were paid some €109,000 for work during the few weeks of the campaign, but this was just the tip of the iceberg. Most of their important work had been done before the formal campaign, and their total bill was several times greater. This is just one of the areas where money buys a political advantage, and it's a big one.

The 'five-point plan' which would form the centrepiece of the party's political marketing arose not just from the Americans' input, but also from exchanges among the backroom staff – particularly Ciaran Conlon, Andrew McDowell and Sean Faughnan – in the autumn of 2010. Constant referral to the five-point plan by the candidates and the leadership was to become a point of parody, even for Fine Gael itself: Kenny jokingly made reference to it in his homecoming speech in Mayo after he was elected Taoiseach. But the party understood one of the tenets of modern political campaigning, as Leo Varadkar observed on a television documentary broadcast soon after the election: at the moment when politicians are almost physically sick of mentioning something, the public might just be starting to hear it.

Along with the five-point plan, the other central plank of the Fine Gael strategy – and the one principally directed at winning votes from Labour – was the Fine Gael pledge not to increase income taxes. The complementary promise was that the greater part of any future budgetary adjustments would be met by spending cuts, rather than new taxes. It was a tactic that enabled Fine Gael to target Labour as a high-tax party. When the campaign started, it was to prove highly effective.

But for all the careful preparation and meticulous, poll-tested planning, events also moved in Fine Gael's favour. Party strategists felt something decisive shift in the political landscape once the IMF arrived in November: it was the point when many voters finally and irrevocably gave up on Fianna Fáil. Ciaran Conlon sensed that the whole country had finally tuned in to hear what Fine Gael was saying. Tellingly, a similar thought occurred to Seán Dorgan, the Fianna Fáil general secretary, when he was in Donegal assisting with the doomed by-election campaign. After the IMF, he thought, it was like a different country.

Bertie Ahern always wanted to fight general elections during the summer. He reckoned the long evenings and fine weather worked to Fianna Fáil's advantage, allowing the party's bigger election machine more scope to canvass. He won three elections, all held during the summer. The campaign of February 2011 was as far from the sunny summertime contests of the Celtic Tiger period as it is possible to imagine. It wasn't just the weather. Fianna Fáil was in disarray, and Fine Gael had the momentum of a juggernaut.

The election called, Kenny hit the ground running, taking off on a high-octane tour of border counties, the media trailing behind. In Cavan a crowd cheered him, with one man repeatedly calling after him, 'Hello, Taoiseach! Hello, Taoiseach!' He turned out to be a Fine Gael councillor. But the point was made, and the pattern set. Kenny smiled and waved and winked, and gave the thumbs-up. But he also had a deadly serious message. Fine Gael had a plan, a five-point plan, to fix the country. And it would not raise income taxes.

In those crucial early press conferences, Kenny performed well, taking some questions himself and passing others on to his front-bench colleagues. Despite confident predictions by its opponents, Fine Gael strategists didn't hide Kenny; or, if they did, they hid him in full view. He was front and centre at many of the press conferences, though he was always surrounded by colleagues. This was not just a way of providing practical support; it reinforced the idea of Kenny as leader of a strong team.

Kenny was still regarded as weak on detail by the press corps, but, discerning that the chances of catching him out with a killer question were diminishing, journalists began to lose interest in pursuing him. On Day Four, when one reporter mischievously asked him to explain cloud computing, he batted the question out of the park with a sufficient explanation and a large dollop of self-deprecation. I may not know how it works, was the message, but I know it's important and I'll listen to people who know what they're talking about on it. It marked an important moment. The Fine Gael handlers sighed with relief.

An important early question for the Fine Gael backroom team was whether Kenny should take part in the televised leaders' debate. In general, there is little to be gained from such contests for a front-runner – if a party is leading in the polls, why risk a television debate that could derail the campaign? All Irish political strategists follow British politics closely, and the Fine Gael handlers knew that Tony Blair had won three elections without ever doing a televised debate. They also knew that in his first campaign in 1997, as an uncatchable front-runner in the polls and opposition leader, Blair had strung along television stations and increasingly desperate Conservatives, never quite ruling out a debate, but never agreeing to it either.

Fine Gael now sought to employ the same tactics, as TV3 pressed for the first debate of the campaign. Kenny reheated an old beef with TV3's Vincent Browne – wilfully misinterpreting a metaphorical suggestion that Kenny be left alone in a dark room with the 'whiskey and the revolver' as a literal invitation to kill himself – and used it as an excuse for not taking part in TV3's debate. Then Browne offered to step aside as moderator in favour of Ursula Halligan, TV3's political editor. Kenny answered this by saying that he wanted to leave an empty chair as the symbol of all those who'd been forced to emigrate. Kenny's preposterous gesture and Michael Noonan's vain but earnest attempt to remain impassive were captured on camera and became one of the YouTube hits of the campaign. But the focus groups assured Fine Gael that Kenny would get away with it.

On the weekend before the debate, TV3 chief executive David McRedmond was flying to Rome to watch the Ireland v. Italy rugby match. Sitting on the tarmac in Dublin Airport awaiting takeoff, he told the producers, 'Get on to Mark Mortell! Get Mortell!' – but Mortell was thinking about tax, not TV3. He had already concluded that there was little to be gained by an early debate. The Fine Gael backroom team held their breath. The debate happened. Kenny looked a bit silly for not turning up, but suffered no lasting damage. Fine Gael was on its way. Kenny would later take part in a five-man debate on RTÉ, where, predictably, nobody was heard in the clamour, and also in an Irish-language debate, which had negligible impact. There would be a final television three-man debate on RTÉ that would not work out so well, but by then Kenny was almost home and dry. Ironically, Labour's overseas advisers, in the shape of its friends in the British and Australian Labour parties, also advised Gilmore not to take part. He overruled them.

Tax became a mantra for Fine Gael, as Michael Noonan and Leo Varadkar especially hammered Labour as a party of high tax. The more seats Labour wins, Varadkar warned, the higher your income taxes will be. Fine Gael's plan for controlling the public finances centred on a programme of great swingeing cuts to every area of public spending – a budgetary adjustment that it said would be in a ratio of 73 per cent cuts to 27 per cent tax increases.

Fine Gael headquarters had a bag of tricks. During the 2007 general election campaign Fianna Fáil strategists contrived two set-piece events in order to bolster Bertie Ahern's flagging appeal to voters. He entertained Ian Paisley at the site of the Battle of the Boyne, and he addressed British MPs and peers at Westminster. Fine Gael had watched their enemies, and learned. This time it was Kenny who was doing the statesmanlike encounters: one with European Commission president José Manuel Barroso and the other, bang in the middle of the campaign, with German chancellor Angela Merkel. The photos from Berlin seemed to show Merkel looking a bit uncertain about the whole thing. Enda, naturally, looked delighted. So he should have been. It was a brilliant PR coup. Kenny mentioned the visit at every opportunity over the following few days; Merkel less frequently.

Labour's campaign had been planned around Gilmore's appeal as leader. 'It was a central part of our campaign strategy – to make it about leadership,' the party's national organizer David Leach said later. 'Every focus group, every poll, showed Gilmore beating Kenny hands down. So obviously we wanted to play to our strengths.'

Perhaps the party had spent too much time wondering how best to capitalize on their new-found support, and not enough consolidating it; too much time telling people that Eamon Gilmore could and should be Taoiseach, and not enough time telling them why, or what he would do once he got there. Certainly, by the time Kenny was hobnobbing with Merkel in Berlin, it was obvious to Labour that the Fine Gael leader was going to be Taoiseach after the election. As Fine Gael's campaign steamrollered ahead, Labour's stumbled, and the Gilmore for Taoiseach logos – ubiquitous on posters, banners, mugs, t-shirts, everything – stood as a silent reproof to paying too much attention to mid-term opinion polls. A party official would later try to collect all the Gilmore for Taoiseach mugs.

At the start of its campaign, Labour unveiled a new campaign headquarters on Dublin's Golden Lane. It looked like a golden opportunity for Labour. It had never been so high in the polls; no previous Labour leader could ever have credibly offered to lead a coalition government. On Day One, Gilmore stood on a box in headquarters to rally the troops, surrounded by Gilmore for Taoiseach banners. On Day Two he launched the party's campaign in the Gravity Bar at the Guinness Storehouse, high above the heads of the people of Dublin. On Day Three, he laid out an aggressive approach, promising a renegotiation of the terms of the EU/IMF bailout deal. Coining what would become one of the quoted soundbites of Irish political history – but not in the way he anticipated – Gilmore thundered, 'It's Frankfurt's way or Labour's way!'

The phrase immediately generated a buzz among the assembled journalists. Joan Burton was less impressed. She was standing beside Gilmore on the podium and immediately thought: Holy God, that's stupid! How the hell did that get in the script? She looked down at the audience of journalists and party workers and saw old hands Brendan Halligan and Willie Scally. Judging by their faces, she thought they had come to the same conclusion. She tried to look impassive when she heard Gilmore brush away concerns about the attitude of ECB president Jean-Claude Trichet, describing him as a mere 'civil servant'. *Jesus Christ! You don't do insults in diplomacy!* she almost shouted.

Burton had been out on the road campaigning for much of the time in the run-up to the election and felt she was being isolated from the decision-making back at headquarters. She was. She had become completely alienated from Gilmore and thought the strategy of focusing on him as leader was ridiculous. When she got her consignment of Gilmore for Taoiseach posters for Dublin West, she put them in her dad's garden shed. That's where they stayed.

On the choice that always faces Labour leaders, Eamon Gilmore had reversed the stance of his predecessor, Pat Rabbitte, and taken the key strategic decision not to join an alliance with Fine Gael, but rather to fight the contest as an independent party on an independent platform. In fact, Labour had drifted apart from Fine Gael after their shared failure to wrest power from Fianna Fáil in 2007. Then, the two parties had agreed a common platform and held joint events as part of the 'alliance for change'. Now, despite the likelihood of a coalition government comprised of the two parties, they were further away from each other on policy than they had been at any point since the 1980s. For example, while Fine Gael had backed the bank guarantee of September 2008, Labour had opposed it (though with nothing like the vigour it now claimed). On other issues too Labour's stance – or rhetoric, at least – had moved to the left, Fine Gael's to the right. Privately, Gilmore thought that many of Fine Gael's 2007 intake were 'Tories'.

Conscious that the last great Labour surge, the 'Spring Tide' of 1992, had produced fewer Dáil seats than it might have, party handlers had set about recalibrating their candidate and constituency strategies, adding new candidates and attempting to divide constituencies on a scale the party had not seen before. Labour would field candidates everywhere, and sitting TDs were required to accept a running mate, something that few relished.

There was one further way in which Labour was determined to learn from past campaigns and past mistakes. In both 2002 and 2007, Labour had been praised for its thoroughly planned, expertly executed, 'professional' campaigns. The only problem was neither produced any new seats. Some in the Labour leadership felt that perhaps these campaigns had been almost too well planned – and consequently less flexible or reactive to events. So, on this occasion, the campaign directors decided to hold much of their advertising budget in reserve. Whatever might develop in the course of the campaign, they reasoned, they would be in a better position to react to it if they had plenty of money at their disposal. They wanted a 'speedboat, not a supertanker'; they wanted to be able to change course quickly if they needed to. In this, they were prescient.

It was, Kenny noted at the launch of the party's manifesto in the grand echoing hall of the Royal College of Physicians, the anniversary of the birth of Galileo, 15 February. 'Measure what can be measured,' the great astronomer had said. By now, more than halfway through the campaign, the opinion polls measuring political support were clear about one thing: Fianna Fáil was stuck in the mid teens, and Labour's votes were ebbing away. But Fine Gael was growing all the time.

This now became the central question of the final phase of the campaign: would Fine Gael win enough support to form a government without the Labour Party? Leading Fine Gaelers pooh-poohed the notion, and a battery of heavyweights was sent out to proclaim their preference for a stable and solid coalition with Labour. Kenny himself was asked the question by a journalist at a press conference: was he now looking for an overall majority? 'I'm not, actually . . .' he began, before giving the five-point plan another turn. Taken at face value, it was an astonishing admission – that the putative Taoiseach wasn't actually trying to win the election. But when you're on the up, you can get away with these things.

Even as they publicly dismissed the notion of a single-party government, the Fine Gael campaign went into overdrive behind the scenes, carefully recalibrating its operation on the ground to give weaker candidates a boost. Leaflets appeared in key areas of key constituencies: 'To maximize Fine Gael's representation in this area, vote number one for . . .' Day after day, Fine Gael repeated its simple message: *We have a five-point plan; we won't raise income tax; Labour is a high-tax party.* They hammered it home with relentless efficiency. It wasn't subtle, but the polls said it was working like a dream. 'George Bush said, "Read my lips, no new taxes,"' Kenny told a *Morning Ireland* interview in the middle of the campaign. 'The Fine

Gael view is you should not increase taxes. Our view is retain your capital programme and cut current spending ... Sort out your budgetary problems by way of dealing with current spending.' However, Kenny added a bit of small print: you should not take money from the disabled or the blind or pensions or children ... That was cutting down his options a bit.

The party was also starting to give hostages to fortune, making promises and commitments – many small and local, some big and national – that it would not be able to keep. In what would become almost as celebrated as 'Frankfurt's way or Labour's way', Leo Varadkar promised that 'not another red cent' of taxpayers' money would go into Ireland's banks unless bondholders were burned. What Varadkar meant, and what he said most of the time, was not another cent of taxpayers' money *beyond what the Fianna Fáil–Green government had already committed to*. Of course, when you examined the small print, it turned out that Brian Lenihan had already committed to a colossal recapitalization of the banks, which would be revealed within a few weeks, at a cost to the new government of an eye-watering €24 billion. That's a lot of red cents. What Varadkar managed to do was give the impression that Fine Gael would impose burden-sharing on the banks in the future, but without categorically promising to do so. The suggestion that they would burn bondholders would come to naught; but at a crucial stage in the election it neutralized the banking question, which could have knocked the entire Fine Gael campaign off course.

Labour had known that, like all left-wing parties, it would be vulnerable on tax questions. The introduction of the universal social charge at the beginning of the campaign – the opposite of the old pre-election wheezes that Fianna Fáil used to employ – meant that many tens of thousands of people who were previously outside the tax net were suddenly within it; of those already inside, their tax wedge had grown enormously over the previous three budgets. It wasn't surprising that tax became a central issue in the election. It always is, of course. But it was just more so this time. Labour hoped that it could minimize the damage by its pledge that individuals earning under €100,000 a year would be unaffected by any of its tax changes. But Fine Gael's message was simpler and sharper, and it put Labour on the hook.

As Labour, wounded by Fine Gael's attacks, tried to get beyond the charge of being the high-tax party of the public sector interests, SIPTU president Jack O'Connor waded into the debate to ensure that the spotlight was kept firmly on it. A single-party Fine Gael government, he warned, would be 'a recipe for disaster'. Fine Gael's Lucinda Creighton shot back that O'Connor was right to be worried: Fine Gael would put taxpayers ahead of the 'vested interests' that Mr O'Connor represented. Is Jack O'Connor a Fine Gael sleeper? wondered one Fianna Fáiler.

Labour was bleeding now. When Gilmore, his campaign managers and key strategists reviewed their latest private polling halfway through the campaign, it showed Fine Gael on 40 per cent, Fianna Fáil on 18 and Labour on 16. The election was slipping away from Labour, and Gilmore was slipping towards disaster. They could yet be beaten by Fianna Fáil! It was a moment of profound crisis for the Labour campaign.

At emergency meetings, the political leadership and the key campaign figures, David Leach, Mark Garrett and Colm O'Reardon, surveyed their progress and their prospects, with the gloomy polls hanging over them like the sword of Damocles. 'We are getting hammered on tax,' Garrett told them. They had to change tack. People weren't listening to positive plans from Labour; they had to focus on the negative aspects of the Fine Gael plans. 'We can't change now,' protested O'Reardon. 'We have to,' Garrett repeated, 'we're getting hammered.' Rabbitte and others were wary about attacking Fine Gael and poisoning relations in a future coalition. He had previously suggested the two parties should agree not to outbid each other's promises in the course of the campaign. He had a horror of what an old-style auction election could do to the subsequent government. But it was beginning to look as if Labour would be lucky to get into the next government, let alone lead it. Gilmore understood Rabbitte's concerns, but the campaign and Labour's fortunes – and his own leadership – were hanging by a thread. The politicians and the handlers made a vital decision. Labour changed its campaign completely, and went negative.

The party launched its manifesto at the new stadium on Lansdowne Road, two days before the Ireland–France rugby international. As Ronan O'Gara and Jonny Sexton banged over penalties, and the Irish pack practised its lineout calls on the pitch below, Gilmore stuck out his elbows and hit Fine Gael a few digs. Fine Gael, Gilmore asserted, would 'attack families by cutting child benefit'. A Fine Gael government would 'attack pensioners' and 'attack frontline services'. The mood was aggressive and determined. Labour candidates posed for pictures in the stands overlooking the pitch and clustered around their leader for the group shot. 'Everybody wave!' called the photographer. But Gilmore wasn't waving. He was drowning. The only question was: Would anything rescue him now?

It would. 'We hit them as hard as we could for two days,' David Leach said later. Labour targeted Fine Gael with a series of statements, savaging their plans to cut child benefit particularly. Colm O'Reardon is nobody's idea of an advertising man, but he came up with the idea of aping a Tesco ad campaign, using the company's famous slogan 'Every Little Helps'. The party's creative types produced a series of newspaper and online advertisements with the slogan 'Fine Gael – Every Little Hurts'. The ads claimed that Fine Gael policies would result in significant cost increases for ordinary people, while at the same time introducing water charges and cutting child benefit. Labour headquarters received several angry phone calls from Tesco's representatives. Garrett and company waited in the hope that Tesco would seek an injunction against them, which would have hugely increased the ads' impact, though sadly for Labour no writ arrived. At the end of the two days, they reviewed the new strategy. The signals – as best they could interpret them – were that the attacks on Fine Gael were getting some traction, both with the media and with the public. They resolved to continue and escalate.

Just as important, Labour ceased talking about Gilmore for Taoiseach and concentrated instead on the dangers of a Fine Gael single-party government. Now the wisdom of holding back on its campaign spending became clear. Labour printed 350,000 leaflets, which were distributed to candidates all over the country. Posters were heralding its warnings about Fine Gael, and a flurry of further newspaper ads hammered home the message. On the doorsteps, Labour candidates pushed the message about Fine Gael cuts hard. Voting Labour, candidates said, was the only way to achieve a 'fair and balanced' government. At the homes of public servants, candidates and canvassers translated this into blunt terms: a Fine Gael government will dump the Croke Park Agreement and cut your pay. We need Labour votes to protect the public service.

Backs against the wall, Labour came out fighting. One morning, following another gruesome opinion poll, party staffers prepared gloomily for that morning's press conference. David Leach grabbed a chair and stood up on it. 'If ever there was a day to stand up, this is the day!' he roared. 'The press are coming in here in an hour – what are you going to look like? Like you're a beaten docket? Or like you think you can win? This is the day to stand up!' Even if we're fucked, that's great stuff! a few of them thought.

As the campaign entered its final week, the battle lines were clear: Fine Gael was powering ahead, and Labour was desperately begging voters to give the party a slice of the government. Fine Gael began the week with a rally of its Dublin candidates, presided over by *Newstalk* broadcaster George Hook, whose station was advertising itself with the slogan 'News without the state-run spin'. The day's polls were showing that not only was Fine Gael within touching distance of an overall majority but that Kenny – derided by so many for so long – was the most popular choice for Taoiseach.

Kenny seemed to be bulletproof, unstoppable now. He brushed off a *Sunday Business Post* story about his teacher's pension, amassed after just four years in the classroom, promising not to take it up. The *Sunday Independent* – some of whose most influential columnists had been calling for Fine Gael to govern alone without the troublesome impediment of a left-wing coalition partner – had a poll which it insisted showed that (yet again) the public was in tune with the *Sunday Indo*. 'Poll: Give Us Enda without Gilmore' klaxoned the front page. There was another banner headline across the top on the front page: 'If you really want a single-party government, vote for it'. The second story on the front page accused the trade unions of trying to 'interfere' in the election by calling for a Fine Gael–Labour coalition. Actually, the 'Give Us Enda' headline was based on a pretty tendentious reading of the poll data. But it, and other polls that day, really showed that, while an overall majority wasn't the most likely result, it was firmly within the range of possibilities. Certainly, if the movement towards Fine Gael seen in the previous week continued, it was on the cards. But it didn't. That last weekend was the high-water mark for Fine Gael.

With four days of campaigning still to go, the Fine Gael vote now went into reverse. Perhaps it was Labour's attacks; perhaps, as Mark Mortell privately believed, there was now an 'inherent distrust' of single-party government in Irish politics. Certainly, the question of a Fine Gael overall majority was the only one discussed in the final days. The *Sunday Independent*'s influence has long been hotly debated in political circles. Its huge circulation suggests that it enjoys some sort of connection with middle Ireland. But the paper has a 'love it or love to hate it' appeal, and key Labour figures thought that attacks by the *Sindo* were likely to galvanize their core voters and send nervous public servants flocking to them. They weren't alone in the belief. 'If the *Sunday Indo* had shut their fucking mouths, we might have won it,' one Fine Gael minister later privately reflected. Whatever the reasons, the tide had now turned.

Kenny may have been within sight of the finish line, but he began to stumble. First, he did a poor interview with TV3's Ursula Halligan, floundering on questions of renegotiating the EU/IMF programme and weakly reaching for the insipid generalities of the five-point plan when asked specific questions about something else entirely. Watching Kenny retreat behind platitudes ('Politics is about finding solutions and making decisions'), the handlers found themselves gripped by old fears. Then he faltered noticeably in the second half of the final television debate on RTÉ. Having avoided danger by ducking the first debate, Kenny achieved messy draws in the Irish-language and five-way debates that followed. Behind the scenes, Kenny's staff strained to keep upbeat and to reassure him; but in the final debate, between just him, Gilmore and Martin, he did not perform well. It was watched by an audience of 964,000 people. Two days later he did another poor interview, this time with Bryan Dobson on RTÉ; watched by half a million people, he flailed about as Dobson pressed him on detail. It has largely been forgotten because of his success, but Kenny did not finish the campaign well. Labour, seizing the moment, turned up the volume again, constantly warning of the dangers of an overall majority, that a Fine Gael government unmitigated by Labour's presence would clobber social welfare, the public sector and child benefit. The final battle in an election campaign that had promised to eschew the bidding wars of old closed with a very old-style scrap on pocketbook issues.

On the twenty-fourth and final day of the campaign, Kenny travelled as far away as possible from Dublin, swinging through Sligo and Donegal before taking the road home to Castlebar. Addressing the party workers in Donegal North East and gesturing to the two candidates, he urged them, 'Don't have any breakfast, don't have any dinner, don't have any tea. Starve yourself in the interest of getting votes out for these people.' He was nearly there, and he knew it. Liberated by the certainty of victory, and a world away from the dreaded television studios, Kenny set aside the five-point plan for once and let his own words pour out.

When Kenny spoke in debates and interviews, he often seemed to be trying to remember what he had been briefed to say, and often didn't seem to be remembering very well. Like most politicians he had a spoof setting, and when it was turned on he could talk around an issue without really committing to anything. Sometimes the spoofing was painfully obvious, and he often got himself in dreadful muddles. But when speaking in generalities, about needs and emotions and about loss and hope, he was fluent and clear. He could talk about individual cases, and of their wider symbolic importance. Sometimes, when he wasn't being self-disciplined, this could descend into near-gibberish. But when he really knew what he was talking about, and he really wanted to say it, he could rouse an audience. This was one of those moments.

'Today, yes, we have to tell the truth. We are living in many cases with a national heartbreak, reeling from the national confidence trick pulled on us by the government and those to whom they ceded power, the developers and the banks,' he said.

'Every week, as we know, and from this historic county of Donegal included, a thousand mothers and fathers watched their children pack up their lives, put their degrees in beside their dollars and their bitter disappointment as they head for Sydney or Brisbane or Vancouver or the United States. Today, another generation of Irish is building the future of another country.

'Tomorrow, as they pick up their pencils and mark their ballot paper, I want to ask the people of Ireland to turn their anger into action and vote with their power, vote with their pride.

'Because if this election is to take the political pulse of our nation, I want every beat and every vote to show a nation that looks with hope and generosity and courage to the future – not with regret or hurt and bitterness of the past. Just as grudges paralyse us in our own lives, root us in the pain of the past, they will do the same to us as a nation.

'That's not to say we can forget the past and that we should forget the past – we don't, we can't, nor should we. In fact, with our plan to get our country working, we're saying "never again"; never again can such a travesty be allowed to happen.

'We have to close that gap between government and the people, between politics and the people. Because it was in that gap that the rot started and the rot flourished. Tomorrow, then, the people are in charge. Governments may govern, but it is the people who rule.'

Even the jaded staffers and reporters, sick of the sight of one another after three weeks of endless miles, late nights, early mornings, food on the run, and of hearing the same speech over and over again, paused to take note. Lise Hand captured the scene vividly in the *Irish Independent*, writing, 'There's not a bruised and heartsick Irish voter left who believes in a Brave New Dawn any more. Not after all this country's been through and what still lies ahead. But just for a moment on a chilly hillside, the glow of those words warmed us.'

Then the would-be Taoiseach could do no more. He turned for

home, leaving Donegal behind, passing Ben Bulben and Drumcliffe, hills to the left, wild Atlantic to the right, past Sligo, making for the heart of Mayo, and sleep, at last. He would wake up to a political landscape that had been turned upside down.

7

Deal or no deal

The two political systems with which Ireland has the most in common have dramatically different procedures for the transfer of power following a general election. In the United States, the presidential election takes place on the first Tuesday in November, but the new president has until late January's inauguration to organize the transition to a new administration. In Britain, the leader of the largest party travels to Buckingham Palace as soon as he is sure he can form a government – usually, though not always, in the hours after the result of the election is known. While he or she is kissing hands at the Palace, the removal vans are outside 10 Downing Street, hurrying the loser out the door. The winner returns to his new home.

Ireland lies somewhere about equidistant between these two opposites. Because the new Dáil will not usually meet for a few weeks after the date of the election, the outgoing Taoiseach and his ministers remain as a caretaker government until the new Dáil elects a new Taoiseach and approves his government. This hiatus has the advantage, in a system where coalition governments are the norm, of allowing some space and time for both physical and mental recuperation after a gruelling campaign, and for the necessary horse-trading over a coalition deal.

In early 2011, with Ireland's government barely functioning, the window available to form a government was narrow. Unlike previous occasions, there would be no time for recuperation from the campaign, striking political poses or prolonged horse-trading. The Dáil was scheduled to meet again on 9 March, just two weeks after polling day. The rush was principally because an important European summit was scheduled for the following day, though Fine Gael and Labour spinners suggested they were just anxious to get on with the job. Whatever the reason, it meant that the two parties that were virtually certain to form the new government, but which had spent an election campaign battling against one another, had barely a week to agree a deal on how the country would be governed for the next five years. Even before Ireland's crisis coalition was formed, the pressure was on.

Votes were still being carefully counted when senior staff around Kenny and Gilmore began to reach out to set the wheels in motion. As the soon-to-be-Taoiseach and the head of the larger party, Kenny made the first contact, leaving a message for the Labour leader on his mobile phone on the Saturday. Kenny and his aides thought it odd when it wasn't replied to promptly.

But Gilmore had received no message. Fine Gael called an old mobile number, which was diverted to Gilmore's office phone, unattended over the weekend. As Saturday gave way to Sunday, Gilmore's aides wondered, What's with the 'radio silence'? Why the hell haven't they called? Are they playing it cool? They weren't worried about it; but they did wonder if Fine Gael were sending a message that it might not need Labour if the smaller party didn't play ball in the negotiations. 'The ball is in Fine Gael's court,' one staffer told the *Irish Times* a bit nervously. Mark Kennelly and Mark Garrett had an urgent conversation on the Sunday.

'Why hasn't he called?' Garrett asked.

'He did!'

'He didn't!'

'He did!'

The confusion was eventually sorted out, and a meeting between the two principals was arranged for the Monday, though not until a few reporters found it difficult to get a straight answer about who called whom and when. Fine Gael was a little taken aback at Labour's nervousness; 'They were a little perturbed,' remembers a senior Fine Gael figure. It didn't exactly augur brilliantly for the negotiations to come, never mind five years of government.

On the Monday morning, Andrew McDowell rang Colm O'Reardon and suggested they meet for coffee in Bewley's on Grafton Street. The two men threw their eyes up to heaven about the mix-up over the phone messages and then agreed they had bigger things to worry about – most pressingly, the logistics of the forthcoming negotiations.

The O'Reardon–McDowell axis would become one of the foundation stones of the coalition. On the face of it, they had little in common. O'Reardon, a Northsider, deeply embedded in the traditions of the Labour Party, is distinctly a man of the left, but one who insisted that stable public finances could not be the preserve of right-wing parties. McDowell is as Southside as his Labour counterpart is Northside, and his growing influence – and eventual overlordship – of economic policy had chimed with the more conservative instincts of the younger intake of Fine Gael TDs. He was not, as some reports had it, a nephew of the former Progressive Democrats leader Michael McDowell, but his cousin. That was close enough to arouse considerable suspicion about him in Labour. 'Immensely powerful, courteous, self-effacing, dogmatic and ideological' is one Labour minister's description of him.

On closer inspection, though, there were considerable similarities between the two men. Both were prodigiously bright and had had glittering academic careers. After a Master's degree in finance at UCD, McDowell studied in the rarefied halls of Johns Hopkins University in Baltimore, Maryland, before returning to the UCD Smurfit Business School for an MBA; O'Reardon completed post-graduate degrees in the universities of Oxford and Cambridge. It wasn't quite the government of the eggheads, though; while both were policy wonks, they knew that policy was often the slave of politics. And both knew that if this government didn't work, the future for the country was highly uncertain. Each was the father of a young family, and the prospect of a failing country was real to them in a particular way. They had different ideas about how best to get there for sure, but they were committed to the same destination. As the most important economic voices in their respective parties, they knew how important it was that they get on with each other – and they did.

When O'Reardon returned to Leinster House, he went to see Gilmore about the talks. The Labour leader had a surprise for him.

'You're on the team,' he told him. 'You're not supporting them – you are one of the team.' In the Fine Gael offices, McDowell was being given a similar message.

In previous negotiations, advisers like McDowell and O'Reardon would have been supporting and assisting the elected politicians who were the principals in the negotiations. By including the two economic advisers as full members of the teams, the two party leaders not only emphasized the primacy of economic and budgetary policy in the formulation of a new programme, they also ensured that a watchful eye was kept over proceedings. Crucially, the two advisers couldn't be asked to leave the room while the politicians thrashed out a deal. It was a subtle but important shift.

The two sides met in the Sycamore Room in Government Buildings, a large room on the first floor dominated by a huge oblong board-room table, hewn from sycamore. Foreign heads of state had been received here; social partnership deals struck in the small hours of the morning, the better to emphasize how hard each side had pushed the other, even as shivering reporters outside told their editors it was all for show; and a few programmes for government thrashed out across the polished hardwood. But the room had never seen such desperate times as these.

The delegations mostly kept to the same places at the table for the week. Michael Noonan sat at the centre of the Fine Gael side with Phil Hogan to his immediate right and Andrew McDowell beside Hogan. To his left were Alan Shatter and – often but not always – another Fine Gael adviser, usually Angela Flannery. Brendan Howlin was the anchor at the centre of the Labour side, with Pat Rabbitte and Joan Burton to his left, and Colm O'Reardon on his right. To O'Reardon's right was the rotating adviser slot, usually occupied by Jean O'Mahony but occasionally by Richard Humphreys, Finbarr O'Malley or Maev-Ann Wren.

They first met on Tuesday, 1 March, and most of that day and the following one were taken up with a series of briefings from senior officials, largely focusing on the economic and fiscal situation. Two things struck the politicians and their advisers pretty quickly: the economic situation was vastly worse than they had feared, and the quality of some of the briefings from the officials was dire.

One of the first briefings was from a team led by Kevin Cardiff, the secretary general of the Department of Finance. The negotiators thought it was dreadful, unhelpful, shocking. Several of them couldn't believe how bad it was. Cardiff spoke almost in a murmur – some of the participants down along the table could barely hear him. Noonan was caustic even while they were there; he was scathing about them after they left.

'How many senior bonds are out there in the banks?' O'Reardon asked at one point. The officials gave three different answers.

Noonan asked exactly how many public servants the state was employing. Ciaran Connolly, the second secretary at the Department of Finance in charge of the public service, hesitated and shuffled 'a couple of bits of paper' around, looking for a definitive number. He had no copies of his notes, but produced another piece of paper 'with biro marks on it'. There was no clear answer.

The politicians looked at one another in horror. Jesus Christ, one of the participants thought to himself, I didn't realize things were this bad. When the finance team left after this first briefing, the room was genuinely shocked.

Later, some of the talks teams discussed the chaos of the presentations. They thought that the senior civil servants had looked beaten down, demoralized by the situation in which they found themselves. 'Physically they looked destroyed,' said one. The talks teams thought the officials had seemed content enough with the safety-net of the bailout programme, but had put forward no ideas about how the country was ultimately going to get out of it.

The Department of Finance officials were only too aware that things were going badly. Later Cardiff paid a visit to another senior official. 'How did it go?' the official asked. 'It didn't go well,' Cardiff replied. 'They're not happy.'

The finance officials tried to regroup. Robert Watt, assistant secretary in the Department of Finance, was called into the negotiation room: he gathered himself and his papers and went into the lions' den. Unlike his colleagues, he gave a top-drawer performance, with clear information and clear explanations.

'You guys are the politicians, you have to decide. I'm just a civil servant,' he told the two teams. 'But here's what we think is possible and what's not.'

Watt impressed Howlin especially; when he came to create his new Department of Public Expenditure and Reform, Howlin chose Watt to head it. For Cardiff, the briefings had a different sort of outcome: within six months, the government asked him to become its representative on the EU Court of Auditors.

That episode would bring its own political troubles, but there was a curious interlude on the second day of the talks when the Department of Finance released a report into its performance in advising the government during the reckless years of the boom. To the amusement of the negotiators in Government Buildings, the report – which was splashed all over the front page of the *Irish Times* – found that the department had prudently warned the Ahern governments about the dangers of their spending and tax policies, but that these warnings had been ignored. The mandarins were absolved of blame. Yeah, right, thought some of the negotiators. Others thought, These guys still have a few tricks: we'd better watch ourselves.

Some of the briefings were scary for a different reason: they were all too clear. The representatives from the National Treasury Management Agency, headed by John Corrigan, gave a cogent and professional presentation. During the questions, they were asked if the current debt profile of the country was sustainable. They didn't sugar-coat the answer. No, they said. It isn't. A number of the would-be ministers and political rainmakers around the table had half expected this – after all, it had been declared often enough by many of the new breed of economists who had shot to fame since the crisis began – but it was still shocking to hear it from the people whose job it was to manage the debt. It meant that the fate of the incoming government was partly out of its own hands – dependent, rather, on other governments and the EU institutions agreeing something that would reduce Ireland's crippling debt and interest burden. The political teams started to ask the briefing delegations about what level of debt might be sustainable. Everyone had different ideas. Jesus, thought one of the Fine Gael negotiators, no wonder the country is in the state it is.

When the team from the NTMA left, the issue of default was aired briefly. Though nobody really thought it was a serious option for the new government, there were those who wondered whether it could be avoided.

As the briefings dragged on throughout Tuesday and Wednesday, the mood inside the room got darker. Economist Colm McCarthy, author of the Bord Snip report that had recommended wholesale slashing of public spending, addressed the group. Everyone there knew McCarthy, a popular and gregarious – if professionally lugubrious – figure who had been an independent, and vital, adviser on public sector cuts to Brian Lenihan. No one expected his briefing to be uplifting. It wasn't. Central Bank governor Patrick Honohan outlined the state of the country's banks and advised that recapitalization on a massive scale should be one of the new government's first priorities. Despite the teams' familiarity with the spectacular implosion of Ireland's financial sector, the numbers still made some of them queasy.

A delegation from the Department of Foreign Affairs arrived and gave a polished performance. But they admitted to not knowing exactly where Ireland stood with several important European allies with regard to the progress and future of the bailout. Irish attendance rates at European meetings had plummeted in 2010 and stopped altogether in the early months of 2011. These guys have no idea exactly what's going on, thought one of the talks participants.

Every incoming government everywhere says that the state's finances are worse than they thought; at no time was it as true as it was now. Pat Rabbitte reminded the Fine Gael delegates that they had no choice: they had to lead the next government. Labour, however, could contrive some reason to 'fuck off' out of Government Buildings and lead the opposition. So, after a barrage of briefings on Tuesday and Wednesday, the teams knuckled down and began to hammer out drafts of agreements in the various policy areas. Meanwhile, there was a separate engagement between the two party leaders. The first meeting, for over an hour on Monday, did not go well. Uh-oh, thought some of the aides, there could be a problem here. It didn't help that Kenny was two hours late for the meeting. Gilmore's aides wondered to one another: What the fuck? Is this some sort of power play? What are we dealing with here? Later they would discover that was just the way Kenny was. It wasn't the way Gilmore was. A Labour source later told the *Irish Times* that the two men's rapport 'was immediate and successful'. Precisely the opposite was the case.

Kenny and Gilmore are utterly different. Kenny is gregarious and perennially good-humoured; Gilmore serious and intense. 'Kenny is an open book,' says an aide. Gilmore is not. For years John Drennan, the *Sunday Independent*'s political commentator, had half taunted the Fine Gael leader with the sobriquet 'Kenny lite'; no one had ever accused Gilmore of being 'lite'. Yet it was Kenny's ability to combine his own natural optimism with a seriousness of purpose, reflected across his party, that had spoken more powerfully to voters in the just-concluded campaign.

More important than their divergent personalities were the very different expectations each had of what would come out of the talks. For Kenny, Fine Gael had nearly achieved an overall majority; it was the indispensable party and, if Labour didn't play ball, he had options. The options weren't brilliant, but they were better than Labour's. Kenny would do a deal with Labour – and he never, says one person involved throughout, seriously contemplated otherwise – but he wanted to do that deal on his own terms. He believed Gilmore simply couldn't turn down government, having run the final weeks of its campaign as an explicit appeal to voters to put Labour in coalition with Fine Gael.

Gilmore knew that Kenny could cobble together a majority in the House to get himself elected Taoiseach, but he believed that a minority Fine Gael government wouldn't last until Christmas. Especially not if what was coming out of the briefings in the Sycamore Room was half true. Gilmore never seriously considered staying out of government as a strategic political choice, but he needed Fine Gael to know he wouldn't take a bad deal either. He went out on to the Leinster House plinth on Tuesday evening with his hugely expanded parliamentary party and told reporters that if the negotiations didn't succeed, Labour would go into opposition.

It wasn't subtle. It was also evidence that the earlier meeting between the two party leaders had not gone well: they were still communicating through the media. As the two negotiating teams were getting closer through the shared experience of the Sycamore Room briefings, the leaders seemed to be getting further apart. Word reached the negotiators that there were problems with the bosses. Surely not, they thought. Then, late in the week, as the process neared an end, the two leaders were scheduled to join the talks teams for a session. The appointed time passed. The hours ticked by. Then word filtered through to the Labour team: Gilmore had been seen leaving Government Buildings. Fuck! thought one of them. It's gone!

Despite the various bumps in the road, Mark Garrett and Mark Kennelly kept the lines between the two leaders open. Garrett also had a back channel to Mark Mortell. All three Marks knew there was no realistic alternative to a deal between the two parties. They also knew they had to coax the leaders into a working relationship. Early meetings between the two men were held in a small meeting room on the ministerial corridor in the Leinster House complex (though structurally it is part of Government Buildings). Later in the week, the encounters moved to a meeting room beside the Taoiseach's office. The advisers took this as a good sign.

The differences on economic policy – and the overarching issue of the reduction in the enormous annual budget deficit – were ones of degree, rather than profound differences of substance. Fine Gael wanted to reduce the deficit to 3 per cent of national income by 2014; Labour wanted it put off until 2016. Fine Gael wanted spending reduced by €9 billion in that time; Labour's target was €7 billion. And Fine Gael argued for an adjustment comprised of spending cuts to tax increases in the ratio of about three to one; Labour wanted a fifty-fifty split. With regard to the general, macroeconomic approach, the two parties were pantingly ready to compromise.

As the negotiators thrashed out agreement across the table, the advisers swapped drafts on the various sections of the programme –

Maev-Ann Wren and Sean Faughnan on the health programme, Jennifer Carroll and Finbarr O'Malley on the justice content. O'Reardon and McDowell were the 'clearing house'. As the teams neared a compromise on the shape and parameters of the fiscal correction, the list of issues to be 'kicked upstairs' to the two leaders got longer – water charges, a property tax, overseas aid and abortion among them.

Whatever the problems on the range of measures the new government would adopt, the knottiest problem of all was cabinet numbers, and in particular the question of which party would occupy the Department of Finance. It almost brought the talks between the leaders to breaking point.

For much of the history of the state, the Department of Finance has run government. It has dwarfed the Department of the Taoiseach in size and in reach; and, in terms of imposing his will – and the minister has always been male – on the mechanics of government, the minister for finance was in some ways more powerful even than the Taoiseach. This power was greatly eroded during the Ahern era, when the centre of gravity moved across the Merrion Street quadrangle to the Department of the Taoiseach. The vector for this, as it always is in government, was money. The political imperative to spend the rivers of cash flowing into the exchequer from the economic boom had loosened the finance department's control over the purse strings. And the growth of the social partnership system – the tripartite agreements between government, unions and employer bodies from the late 1980s, anchored in the Department of the Taoiseach and utilized as a tool for political and social construction by Ahern and his top civil servant Dermot McCarthy – also undercut the control of the once all-powerful finance department.

However, the collapse of social partnership as a result of the brutal fiscal corrections of the post-boom years had reversed that process. Under Brian Lenihan, the finance department began to retrench and to regain its power. In private, many of its senior officials thought the catastrophe of the economic collapse was the inevitable result of the department's caution and conservatism –

the hallmark of its culture since its foundation, and which it had imposed on an unwilling political system for decades – having been abandoned. For them, the bust was evidence that they were the ones who should be back in charge.

The Fine Gael and Labour politicians who had been watching all this in opposition had a different view. They saw the department and its senior officials as part of the problem – and a significant part at that. The banking-supervision function of the department had been a calamitous failure, and the cosy migration of senior mandarins from Merrion Street to Central Bank headquarters in Dame Street was a symptom of what was wrong. And when it really counted, on the night of the bank guarantee, this much vaunted engine of government and its celebrated mandarins had been little more than poodles of the banks. The abject performance of some of the briefing teams topped it off: the new government wasn't just out to change the personnel (though that would come); it wanted to break the power of the Department of Finance for ever. The end of finance as the dominating monolith of government was in sight.

But, whatever the revised architecture of the heart of government, the two party leaders still had to agree on a cabinet split. After that they had the even more troublesome task of deciding on who their ministers should be. In Gilmore's case this would be a bruising task.

There are fifteen cabinet ministries and Gilmore's opening bid to Kenny was for an eight-seven split, in a 'partnership' government. The Labour leader knew it was a long shot, but he reminded Kenny that the last time the two parties had been in government the left/right split had been along these lines; on that occasion, however, the Rainbow administration of 1995–7, the deal had been between a weakened Fine Gael leader and two other parties, Gilmore being a member of the smaller one, Democratic Left. This time Kenny was in a more commanding post-election position than any Fine Gael leader before him, a handful of Dáil seats away from an overall majority. Phil Hogan laughed when he heard the eight-seven suggestion. 'Tell them there are seven independents we could talk to,' he said.

Gilmore's real goal was a nine-six deal, but it simply wasn't on.

The general two-to-one rule that had manifested itself in many areas of the talks was asserted again: Fine Gael had twice as many Dáil seats, so got twice as many appointments as Labour. It was crude, but there was a political logic to it – to politicians, elections are the grounding law of everything.

The two leaders and their surrogates, the three Marks, batted it back and forth all week. The idea to split the Department of Finance between a public expenditure ministry and a department responsible for banking, taxation and overall economic management gained ground. Not only was it a good idea in itself, they thought, but it helped with the political problem of Labour's unrealizable ambition to get the finance portfolio.

Gilmore and Kenny had both travelled to meetings of their respective European political parties on Thursday and Friday, but by Friday night the deal on the Programme for Government was as good as done. By 10.30 p.m., when proceedings were finally halted, the negotiators were exhausted. Joan Burton set about ordering a Chinese take-away for everyone, heading down the corridor to visit the Fine Gael room to take their orders. She was amazed – and a little taken aback – to discover so many people there. The Labour room was a lot emptier. There were about twenty-five people on the order. Burton paid with Brendan Howlin's credit card.

Burton had had several reservations throughout the process, ranging from the trivial to the substantive. For one thing, she thought Michael Noonan shouldn't be eating so many biscuits – she had an idea he might be diabetic and half seriously wondered, What if he keels over? More seriously, when the negotiating teams met the two party leaders, she thought Kenny was in buoyant form and Gilmore was annoyed. The alienation between the Labour leader and his deputy, Burton, was now entrenched, and she wondered privately about Gilmore's ability to deliver the best deal for the party. She worried that Kenny was 'gaming' Gilmore. When the ministerial split became public, she thought he had failed to get finance because Gilmore was fixated on getting foreign affairs for himself.

By Saturday evening, Kenny and Gilmore had reached agreement on the outstanding issues that had been 'kicked upstairs', on the cabinet split and on the crucial finance restructuring. It was to be ten-five in the cabinet, but Labour would take both the attorney general's job and could appoint a 'super-junior' minister, a confection which dated back to the last time the two parties were in government and which had been created to give Pat Rabbitte a seat in cabinet. The rigid Irish system of restricting cabinet to fifteen ministers allowed for flexible Irish solutions when an extra job was needed.

The teams had had the run of Government Buildings for the week. On Saturday evening, at eight o'clock, the two leaders met in the room outside the Taoiseach's office and signed off on their agreement. Weary but satisfied, the two teams went back to the Sycamore Room one final time to put words on Kenny and Gilmore's deal and incorporate them into the final Programme for Government. They were working together now, rather than swapping drafts, and the backup staff brought in a printer that whirred and clacked its way into the early hours. By 4 a.m. on the Sunday morning, they had a final draft. Exhausted, the teams filed out of Government Buildings. The two party meetings to approve the deal would begin in a few hours.

The Labour delegates' mood in UCD's O'Reilly Hall on Sunday, 6 March, was earnest and determined – but also celebratory. Having fought an election in the cold and wet for the past month, the party had triumphed in greater numbers than ever before. Sure, the election hadn't delivered what Labour had once hoped. But it now had the biggest haul of TDs in its history. Political parties exist to wield power, and Labour was on its way back to doing so after too long in the wilderness. And, while there were some misgivings about what it would be facing in government, there wasn't a hope in hell that the coalition deal would be rejected. As the thirty-six TDs were introduced on the podium, they were cheered to the rafters.

A small number of speakers opposed the motion. North Dublin delegate Cian O'Callaghan waved round the copy of the Programme for Government that had been distributed to the delegates. 'It might have a red cover,' he thundered. 'But the cover should be blue!' Serial dissident Tommy Broughan was the standard bearer for the left. If delegates approved the deal, he warned, it would ruin the party and 'the dream of a left-wing government will remain just a dream.' Gilmore replied that he could see the argument for waiting 'to sweep to power in 2016 – but the families that are in trouble with their mortgages can't wait until 2016!' The hall erupted into applause. Few paused to wonder exactly what the new government could do for families in trouble with their mortgages. After three and a half hours, a vote was finally called. A show of hands demonstrated what everyone already knew: support for going into government was overwhelming. Gilmore and Joan Burton took the applause at the centre of the stage. The leader attempted a hug; Burton stood upright, not exactly rejecting it, but not warmly accepting it either. Her body language said: We'll see, pal, we'll see. The snappers snapped. The following day's newspapers carried the shot. Gilmore looked like a grinning koala bear clinging to his tall, statuesque deputy leader. It would be a long time before he attempted to hug her again.

If the Labour Party leadership wanted the party membership to acclaim the deal, Fine Gael felt no such need to bulletproof itself against future criticism. Its TDs met in the Shelbourne Hotel that Sunday afternoon to be briefed on and to approve the coalition deal. There is something about the Shelbourne that appeals to Fine Gael. Perhaps it's the Old World grandeur about the place, Celtic Tiger era brutalizations notwithstanding. Perhaps it's that Michael Collins was associated with it. Maybe it's that the Free State constitution was drafted upstairs. Fine Gael likes to be reminded of that, of the decent people of Cumann na nGaedheal standing upright and building the state while the hooligans on the other side had taken to the hills. Wasn't this exactly what was happening again? With these ancestral echoes in the background, the seventy-six beaming Fine Gael TDs, its senators and its MEPs streamed past the top-hatted doorman and into the hotel lobby as photographers and television crews clamoured outside. The same thought struck several of them: God almighty, there's just so many of us!

Kenny's ally, Senator Maurice Cummins, chaired the meeting. Kenny spoke briefly at the outset, sounding a sober and determined note about facing up to the challenges ahead. Michael Noonan did most of the talking. He went through the Programme for Government with special emphasis on the economic and budgetary elements. Noonan often adopted a folksy sort of tone in such meetings that some – particularly those who still felt a betrayal from the heave – thought was condescending. One of their number seethed in the audience as he looked up at Noonan 'grinning like a Cheshire cat'. Negotiators Phil Hogan and Alan Shatter answered questions.

There were those in the audience who felt that Fine Gael could and should form a government on its own, but they were smart enough to keep such thoughts to themselves. It was part-rally, part-coronation, and over the course of three hours not a single voice was raised in dissent. This was not only because the TDs had been assured that the Programme for Government reflected Fine Gael's numerical superiority, but also because the thoughts of the politicians had moved, inevitably, to the subject dearest to many of their hearts: who would get the jobs? As the meeting broke up and TDs gathered in knots around the hotel, this was the subject which dominated most discussions.

Noonan himself and a group of twenty or so TDs eventually left the hotel and went for a meal in Saba, a city-centre Thai restaurant. Several of the group had been in the anti-Kenny wing, and they were fatalistic about their prospects for preferment. But Noonan was in 'flying form'. He was constantly interrupted by fellow diners asking him to pose for photographs with them. Look at him, he's loving it, thought one of the former plotters.

After the conclusion of both parties' meetings, Kenny and Gilmore met in Herbert Park in Ballsbridge for a photocall to mark the formal consummation of the partnership. Kenny was waiting by the bandstand when Gilmore arrived, and the two men went through the usual handshaking and playful punching and laughing and smiling. They walked together. Purposefully, they hoped. A child was produced. More handshakes. Then the handlers called time. Kenny left, while Gilmore lingered, chatting to his aides. When the Labour leader and now Tánaiste-in-waiting went to leave, he found the gates had been locked. A few moments of panic for the spin-doctors ensued, until an open gate was found. The park-keeper waited impatiently by the gate, jangling his keys; park-keepers do not like to be kept waiting by anyone. A passer-by looked on in amusement. 'That's your first clash with the public sector,' he told Gilmore. The sketch-writers resisted the temptation, but it was a pretty appropriate metaphor. The two leaders and their parties were stuck in this together now.

8

Hang out our brightest colours

For the two days before the Dáil met, the mobile phones of TDs and advisers were hopping, as the political world pulsated with gossip, hints, advice, discreet lobbying and naked pleading. Politicians differ in their approaches to these things. Simon Coveney went to Kenny and made his case for a place at the cabinet table. Michael Ring spent days telling everyone he only wanted a cabinet job and he wouldn't settle for a junior ministry. Ruairi Quinn travelled to Athens with his leader while the Programme for Government was being negotiated and never once mentioned the issue; Gilmore thought his reserve remarkable. Others leaked to the newspapers that they were sure bets.

There would be just one certainty in all of this. When the appointments were made, the anointed would be sure they deserved their elevation to high office; the disappointed furious at the injustice of their omission.

When the Dáil met on 9 March, Fine Gael's Simon Harris – aged twenty-five and the freshest of all the fresh faces that assembled that day – nominated his leader for the post of Taoiseach. As the political correspondents scrambled through the hastily issued thumbnail pictures of the members of the thirty-first Dáil to find out about this self-possessed schoolboy, Harris nodded to George Bernard Shaw's words to Michael Collins's sisters. 'Today, the period of mourning for Ireland is over. Today, we hang out our brightest colours and together, under Deputy Kenny's leadership, we move forward yet again as a nation.'

Labour chose its youngest deputy, Dungarvan single mother Ciara Conway, to second Kenny's nomination. 'The two largest parties in the state have joined together in the nation's interest to form a strong and stable government,' said Conway. The newly elected leader of the newly relegated third largest party rose next and did not oppose Kenny's nomination. Pondering his twenty-strong cohort of TDs, utterly dwarfed by the massed ranks of Fine Gael and Labour deputies, and a minority even on the opposition benches, Micheál Martin, like everyone else present, knew there had never been a Dáil like it.

Other things didn't change. Independent TDs had been returned in greater numbers than ever before, and one by one they rose to speak on Kenny's nomination. The proceedings quickly became farcical. Séamus Healy spoke about the campaign to save hospital services in Clonmel. Tom Fleming told the Taoiseach-elect that he wanted to speak to him before the evening was out about the proposed closure of a factory in his constituency. That meant his South Kerry rival Michael Healy-Rae had to get one up by telling the Dáil he had *already* raised the matter with the man who couldn't actually become Taoiseach until the independents shut up. Luke 'Ming' Flanagan demanded respect for the people of Longford–Roscommon who had elected him. Ming had taken his name from Ming the Merciless, the intergalactic tyrant of the *Flash Gordon* comic books and television series. He was a campaigner for the legalization – and, by his own admission, an enthusiastic former user – of cannabis and had once mailed a joint to every TD. He had entered local politics and become mayor of Roscommon. He wasn't exactly Dick Whittington, but it was still a remarkable achievement for a man who called himself Ming the Merciless. To the massed ranks of Fine Gael TDs in their new suits he couldn't have seemed more eccentric if he actually *had* come from the planet Mongo. He would turn out to be a pretty conventional independent TD, concerning himself principally with constituency matters and making his greatest national impact on the issue of the rights of turf-cutters. Wexford independent Mick Wallace wanted to know why the taxpayers of Ireland should 'carry the burden of mistakes made by the banking system'. A year later, the thirty-first Dáil would learn that Deputy Wallace was not one of the taxpayers of Ireland, or at least not one of the compliant ones. One of the mistakes made by the banks that the new deputy was decrying, it turned out, was to lend money to the pink-shirted and exotically tonsured Mick. As ever, the election of so many independents would be heralded, mostly by themselves, as a new dawn in Irish politics. As ever, the truth would turn out to be more prosaic.

Enda Kenny was elected Taoiseach by the thumping margin of 117 to 27, with Fianna Fáil deputies abstaining on the vote. The long-windedness of the independents meant that the schedule for the Taoiseach's visit to Áras an Uachtaráin, and therefore for the subsequent cabinet appointments, was pushed back. The affable new Taoiseach then spent forty-five minutes longer than expected having a cup of tea with the president. The two party leaders had agreed that no cabinet appointees were to be called over to Government Buildings to be told of their appointment until Kenny got back from the Phoenix Park, so by the time he returned, Leinster House was in a frenzy of rumour and speculation.

Many of the cabinet appointments were expected by everyone. Noonan had sewn up finance a long time back. James Reilly, Shatter and Hogan – Kenny's praetorians from the days of the heave in 2010 – got the departments they wanted. Simon Coveney's lobbying was successful, and Leo Varadkar was deemed too useful to leave out. Likewise Richard Bruton. Jimmy Deenihan and Frances Fitzgerald were helped by their geography and gender respectively. Those omitted were, of course, furious. Michael Ring was 'fit to assassinate Kenny', colleagues joked; somehow he found it in himself to accept a junior ministry. Fergus O'Dowd was 'inconsolable'. He, too, got a junior ministry. Andrew Doyle had told colleagues he was confident of getting the agriculture job. He got nothing, and was 'bitter and angry'.

But if the Fine Gael appointments were largely predictable, Eamon Gilmore's appointments ignited a political storm for Labour before the administration was even a day old.

In the days before the new government was appointed, newspaper speculation pointed almost unanimously towards Joan Burton's appointment to the second finance job, with responsibility for public expenditure. She was 'widely tipped to lead public sector reform in a new-style Department of Finance', the Press Association told the world, taking its cue from the domestic experts. The fact of the new Department of Public Expenditure and Reform – and of Labour's imminent tenure there – was accurately briefed; the identity of its first minister was not. Gilmore and his aides, naturally, suspected Burton of doing the briefing as part of a strategy to make the appointment a *fait accompli*. Whatever the reason and whoever was doing it, it was everywhere. Not only that, but the political world also expected Burton's coronation.

Those inside Gilmore's circle knew that Burton hadn't a hope of getting a finance job. Neither of his two top aides, Garrett and O'Reardon, entertained the slightest expectation that she would get next or near finance. Even – or actually, especially – if Labour had managed to secure the old, unitary finance portfolio, Burton was never going to get the gig, they believed. Gilmore simply no longer trusted her, or at least not enough to entrust her with a finance portfolio and membership of the new Economic Management Council. The EMC was a radical innovation – a four-member team comprising Taoiseach, Tánaiste and the two finance ministers, supported by officials and advisers – that would recast the architecture of political leadership in Ireland. It would turn out to be the engine of government, the forum in which almost all the most important decisions of the new administration would be made, deciding all economic and budgetary policy. Gilmore did not see a role for Burton in that set-up.

The relationship between Burton and Gilmore – and between Burton and O'Reardon especially – had been deteriorating for a long time. Gilmore and his aides believed that Burton was 'not a team player' and that she was more interested in pursuing her own profile and ambitions than in helping the leader achieve his. 'Team Joan', they called it. They fingered her for months as briefing against Gilmore's leadership. They also thought that she had performed poorly in the election campaign.

Burton, in turn, felt a disdain for Garrett and O'Reardon that went far beyond the usual elected politician's dislike of unelected advisers. She thought Garrett was very controlling, and O'Reardon hugely powerful, but with little ability to work with other people. The whole leadership operation, she thought, was too centralized, too intolerant of other views and too redolent of the democratic centralism that old

Labour always suspects stems from the Workers' Party background of its last two leaders.

While both Burton and Gilmore maintained civility personally – save for one bad-tempered exchange in the lift at Leinster House – Gilmore's office was constantly exasperated by Burton. Inevitably, it got personal. They hooted with laughter at the satirist Mario Rosenstock's impressions of 'Moan' Burton wailing at Vincent Browne. More seriously, they pointed out that the new job covered the areas of public expenditure and reform – neither areas in which Burton had previously expressed much interest, they felt. Instead, taxation and the economy were supposed to be her forte – and it was in both of these areas, senior aides told one another, that Labour had been especially vulnerable during the general election campaign.

On her part, Burton did not have enormous respect for Gilmore. For a start, she believed that he had little or no grasp of economics. During the fevered discussions on the bank guarantee and whether Labour should support it, she had formed the view that Gilmore had no idea what was going on. She also believed that Labour's credibility on economic issues was built on her criticisms of the tax incentives and shelters that had allowed many very wealthy people to pay smaller proportions of their income in tax than ordinary taxpayers, and also on her resistance to the bank guarantee. In fact, whatever about Burton's own view, the Labour Party's opposition to the guarantee was a good deal less strident at the time than the party liked to pretend subsequently. Burton liked pointing out that Ruairi Quinn hadn't actually voted against it.

With time running out and the Dáil on tenterhooks that Wednesday evening, nervous cabinet aspirants began to receive calls from Gilmore's office. *The leader would like you to come over to Government Buildings.* Eventually, Burton's phone rang. She made her way across the 'Bridge of Sighs' that links the Leinster House complex to Government Buildings. There is a small waiting area in advance of the corridor that houses ministers' Dáil offices and the security-controlled door into the Merrion Street buildings. There she met Richard Bruton. 'Well,' they joked, 'we're in!' But to what? Neither knew which job they would be offered.

An aide came to collect them and they clattered through the chequered corridors, until they arrived at the far side of the courtyard to the suite of offices on the second floor that houses the Taoiseach and his office staff. Gilmore was occupying one of the rooms before the Taoiseach's office at the end of the corridor. The meeting between the leader and the deputy leader was brief and cold. Burton thought Gilmore was feeling sorry for himself, because he had just been dealing with an unhappy Ruairi Quinn. She was being sidelined into the Department of Social Welfare, she felt, to keep her busy with cuts to the most sensitive areas of government spending. Gilmore protested that the department had by far the largest budget of any government department. Burton wasn't buying that line, but Gilmore wasn't budging. It was a take-it-or-leave-it offer. Burton told people afterwards that she had been given sixty seconds to make up her mind. She took it. Then she was told that she had to wait in another office to see the Taoiseach. She was surprised to find Leo Varadkar, Jimmy Deenihan and Frances Fitzgerald there. They too were in, but still didn't know what their jobs would be. Burton's emotions whirred, her mind raced. It was an odd place to be.

For Burton, this failure to get the public expenditure job was the culmination of a series of moves to belittle and exclude her. As government had neared and the power of the advisers around Gilmore had grown, she had felt that she had been pushed out from the centre of decision-making in the party. 'We've been a very good team,' she said to Gilmore once. 'There's a complementarity there. Don't risk it.' Now she knew her fears had been well founded.

Most of the insider speculation centred on Rabbitte for the public expenditure job. He certainly wanted it, but Gilmore was wary of having Labour's presence in government headed by two former Workers' Party/Democratic Left figures as the DL/old Labour divisions had never entirely disappeared. Given the degree of centralization of decision-making that he, Kenny and their aides were planning under the new Economic Management Council system, the Labour leader could anticipate the potential pitfalls of appointing Rabbitte. Rather ruefully, Rabbitte himself could see the logic.

Ruairi Quinn, who had been a solidly parsimonious finance minister the last time Labour was in government, was fancied by some as an outside bet. In fact, Quinn only made the cabinet after having to fight for it with Gilmore. Stories of the angry confrontation between the two men swept Leinster House, and Quinn was the subject of much resentment from those who were left out, who suspected he had 'bulldozed' his way in. He had threatened to resign his seat, staff told people. Some thought: What chutzpah! Others thought: Why did Gilmore give in?

It was Brendan Howlin, now one of Gilmore's closest allies, who was handed the role.

Like his ministerial twin, Michael Noonan, Howlin was something of a resurrection man. He had twice been a candidate for the leadership of the party, but had semi-retired from active parliamentary politics when he became Leas-Cheann Comhairle after the 2007 election. His career – respectable and substantial but hardly stellar – seemed to be a long down-slope to retirement.

But politics sometimes throws up the most unanticipated opportunities, and Howlin possessed three things vital in any political leader: judgement, a sense of strategy and impeccable timing. The three came together to propel him into a pivotal role in Gilmore's operations during 2010. As Brian Cowen's government began to buckle with the slow recognition of a fast-moving economic implosion, Howlin knew Labour would be catapulted into office, and perhaps sooner rather than later. As Leas-Cheann Comhairle, his office was on the same corridor as many of the junior ministers in the Fianna Fáil–Green government. Junior ministers are often among the most frustrated politicians in any administration: a little responsibility, but not much power; some visibility, but little independence. Often, they chafe under ministers they regard as their political or intellectual inferiors. Howlin is a good listener and discreet with the press. When they talked, he listened. He knew Cowen's embattled administration was descending into rancid fissiparousness before many of its members did, and he used the knowledge to help Gilmore prepare and position. His appointment as lead negotiator on the Programme for Government talks recognized his importance to Gilmore and the absolute level of trust that his leader had in him. His appointment as the new minister for public expenditure and reform surprised people, but it shouldn't have shocked them.

When the Taoiseach led the new cabinet into the Dáil chamber, as tradition requires, Howlin fairly bounced along in the procession. Joan Burton's face was like thunder.

When the news of the cabinet appointments became public, there was a general ho-hum about the line-up – most were, after all, along expected lines. There were rumours – accurate ones, unusually – about a tantrum by Willie Penrose, who had been offered the 'super-junior' job in charge of housing. 'I'm not fucking having that. I'm only interested in a cabinet job,' was his reaction. Pat Rabbitte was dispatched to soothe his bruised ego. No less distinguished a figure than Rabbitte himself had been a super-junior in the Rainbow government: it was a real job. No, he hadn't had a vote, but cabinet votes were extremely rare, almost unheard of. No one in cabinet would look down on him because he was in the high chair. This was not entirely true, but Penrose relented. He was never happy, though. Still, in a Leinster House hothouse made hotter by the presence of hundreds of excited Mayomen and Fine Gael supporters, the Penrose story fizzed for the evening.

In an age of instant reaction and social media, where established 'old' media is terrified of lagging behind in the 'real' story breaking on its newer counterparts, stories can suddenly veer off in an unanticipated direction. So it was with Joan Burton's non-appointment. On the Wednesday evening and into the Thursday morning, the story began to erupt. The charge was that Burton had been omitted as part of an old boys' operation. Sexism and misogyny were alive and well in the Labour Party.

At first they didn't take it too seriously in Gilmore's office. But it gathered momentum. As the traditional media began to wake up to the reaction, the airwaves and social media were humming with the outrage of high-profile women who perceived a slight to a woman in public life who was clearly able to cut it with the boys. The National Women's Council proclaimed Burton's non-appointment a 'disgrace'.

Several prominent women journalists took up their cudgels on Burton's behalf. Olivia O'Leary, who had marked International

Women's Day earlier in the week with a radio column hailing Burton's expected appointment to one of the finance jobs, was typically effective in her indignation, decrying the fact that the cabinet's two women ministers were given the welfare and children's portfolios – 'nanny and housekeeper', as she put it.

Justine McCarthy in the *Sunday Times* put the non-appointment of Burton squarely down to her gender. Moreover, she detected a campaign of sexist briefing against Burton by the lads in Labour who were threatened by a bright and capable woman. Online commentary flayed Gilmore as a sexist and a misogynist who had denied Burton her rightful position because he believed women were inferior and couldn't do sums. Medb Ruane wrote that Gilmore and Kenny were making decisions 'emotionally rather than rationally'.

The truth was that Burton had never been in the running for the job. Perhaps a part of her knew that. She still felt utterly shafted. Publicly, she said she was 'surprised and taken aback and bemused'. Privately, she was furious. Like all women in public life, she had experienced sexism on many occasions. When he was finance minister, Brian Cowen used to delight in doing impressions of her in the Dáil bar while half seriously pleading with the Labour leadership to reshuffle her away from the finance brief because he found her voice so annoying. She knew all this, and for Burton it was all of a piece: the boys' club was keeping her out again.

Gilmore rolled helplessly with the blows. Among the public, Burton's stock soared; among her colleagues, it plummeted. Rabbitte thought it was hilarious. He had known Gilmore all his political life and believed that he hadn't a sexist bone in his body. Whatever you could say about the rest of the party, he thought, the notion that Gilmore was sexist was utterly mad. Nonetheless, Gilmore's staff believed he was 'genuinely hurt and taken aback'. Moreoover, the new Tánaiste and his aides saw the controversy as evidence that he had made the right decision in passing her over. *Joan was in it for Joan*, they thought. She simply didn't care that the launch of the new government had been blown out of the water. The staff were now grinding their teeth in fury to one another. 'She has been handed a €20 billion budget to manage and all she can do is complain to journalists,' raged one. And they all – including Gilmore – knew that the affair was damaging to him and to Labour. It wasn't quite the worst possible beginning for Labour in government, advisers thought. But it must be close.

That weekend, Burton gave an interview to the *Marian Finucane* show. The redoubtable Charlie Bird was presenting on the day. Burton knew that things had got out of hand, and that the smart thing to do now was to row back a bit. She was 'honoured' with such a great responsibility. 'It's about the people, Charlie,' she told him. She mentioned that she had travelled in to Leinster House that morning on the Number 39 bus. 'I felt warm and comfortable with my people on the bus,' she said. Gilmore's aides – who up until that point had been listening in a state of terrified fascination – hooted. Burton was half trying to pull back from the controversy, but half egging it on too. What about the suggestion, Bird said, that women in Labour get more support from an underwire bra than they do from the party? 'I got a lot of sympathy,' she said. 'I want to move on.'

Bird played an interview with Gilmore from a few months previously. Marian Finucane had asked him who would be minister for finance, should Labour be in government with Fine Gael. Gilmore replied with clipped certainty: 'Oh, Joan Burton of course.'

Well?

Burton – just about – didn't take the bait.

Relations between Gilmore and Burton had deteriorated long before the cabinet appointments. Now the hostility was openly acknowledged. It would become a feature of everyday life in the coalition.

The fuss over Burton distracted from the new government's two most significant initiatives: the creation of a new finance department and the establishment of the Economic Management Council. Together, these arrangements represented the biggest reform in the operation of the government since the foundation of the state.

The idea of splitting the finance responsibilities in government had been knocking about for some time. Early versions of the idea proposed by Richard Bruton suggested that public spending should be made the preserve of a minister subordinate to the finance minister

– reflecting the position in the UK, where the chief secretary to the treasury runs public expenditure, while the chancellor of the exchequer sets the overall numbers and is responsible for economic and budgetary decisions. In Ireland, however, it is established constitutional doctrine that one minister cannot be legally subordinate to another; the unwritten British constitution allows for much more flexibility. Later versions of the idea suggested that two co-equal ministers might serve in the same department. The negotiations on the Programme for Government gave a final shape to the model: there was to be an entirely new department, responsible for public expenditure and reform. This had the additional benefit for Labour of providing political cover when it was denied the finance job.

The new department was effectively hewn out of the hulk of the Department of Finance – or, as Howlin told people, 'I designed my own department and I picked the people in it.' This was certainly true for his senior staff. Finance mandarins who had expected to slot in were sometimes disappointed. Ciaran Connolly had been second secretary general in the Department of Finance in charge of the public service. On the day after the government was appointed, he went into Howlin's office to tell him, 'I'm your new secretary general.' The new minister replied sharply: 'No, you're not!'

Instead, Howlin chose Robert Watt, the young rising star of the Department of Finance whose briefings during the coalition talks had so impressed him. His new secretary general (or 'sec-gen' in civil service argot) was very different from the grey eminences who had held the top role in the finance department. Though Watt joined the Department of Finance after university, he later left the civil service to join Indecon Economic Consultants. He rejoined his old department in January 2008, just as the tsunami was about to hit. Watt realized quicker than anyone the implications for the public service budgets, and he knew that if the public service as it was understood was to be saved, it had to be changed radically. Highly intelligent, with a keen political sense, he became one of Brian Lenihan's most trusted aides.

Since his college days, Watt had been friendly with Ronan O'Brien, whom Howlin appointed to be his special adviser. O'Brien had joined the Labour staff in Leinster House from UCD and been recruited by Ruairi Quinn when Quinn became leader of the party after the election disaster of 1997. He left when Quinn resigned after the 2002 election defeat, but remained a party activist. While Bertie Ahern was using the fruits of Ireland's extraordinary economic boom to dominate its politics for most of the 2000s, and Pat Rabbitte was heading up a new regime in Labour, O'Brien and a group of party activists, politicians and sympathetic journalists would often meet in Toner's Pub on Baggot Street on Friday nights to grumble, reminisce, bemoan past mistakes and occasionally plan for the future. They wondered if Labour's time would ever come again. Most figured it would; the world turns. But they never thought it would be in such grim circumstances.

O'Brien got himself a reputation for being a tough negotiator. 'I had your Rottweiler in to me this morning,' one minister complained to Howlin. The other advisers – and some of their ministers – regarded him as rather impatient and grumpy. But he was also a shrewd reader of politics in both the long and the short terms.

Physically, the new department remained in the finance buildings. After some initial toing and froing, Kevin Cardiff offered to vacate his office for Howlin. The secretary general's offer was polite and also symbolic. Howlin immediately accepted. It meant that his office and the adjoining rooms for his key officials were on the second floor of the department, looking out on to Merrion Street. Those housing Noonan and his team were on the floor directly below. Pretty soon the two suites became known as the 'JC Corridor' (after James Connolly), and the 'MC Corridor' (after Michael Collins). Nobody dwelt too much on the fact that both historical figures ended up being shot.

As Joan Burton fumed in the modernist brutalism of Busáras, where the Department of Social Welfare (now renamed Social Protection) had its offices, Howlin fairly skipped around the polished corridors of Government Buildings. When people asked about the responsibilities of the new job, he quoted a senior official's assessment. 'Michael Noonan is the minister for banking,' he said. 'I'm the minister for everything else.'

The first meeting of the cabinet took place, as is traditional, at Áras an Uachtaráin, after ministers had received their seals of office from President McAleese, on 9 March. The first meeting of the Economic Management Council was the following day in the Sycamore Room in Government Buildings. Noonan and Kenny sat together at the centre of the table, flanked by their secretaries general, Cardiff from finance and Dermot McCarthy of the Department of the Taoiseach (within months both senior officials would have departed, to be replaced by Martin Fraser and John Moran). To the right of Cardiff sat Andrew McDowell. (Later, Geraldine Byrne Nason, appointed as second secretary general in the Taoiseach's department in charge of European Affairs, would join the group and sit on the Fine Gael side. Finance second secretaries general Ann Nolan and Jim O'Brien also usually attend now, as does Noonan's special adviser Eoin Dorgan. The Department of the Taoiseach sends John Callinan, an assistant secretary, while Sharon Finnegan, a principal officer in that department, keeps the minutes.)

Across the table, Howlin and Gilmore sat together, confirmation of the partnership at the heart of Labour's role in government. Beside Howlin sat Watt (and later Ronan O'Brien would attend). Beside Gilmore, to his right, was Colm O'Reardon and to his right David Cooney, secretary general of the Department of Foreign Affairs. (Later, as European negotiations in Ireland's debt levels became more and more important to the government, O'Reardon would walk across St Stephen's Green once a week to join a conference call between Cooney and the Irish ambassadors in the Eurozone countries. Progress reports were supplied to the EMC at its meeting a day later.)

At the first EMC meeting, Kenny welcomed everyone and gave a brief outline of how he and Gilmore envisaged the new arrangement working. Discussion moved quickly to the European Council meeting in Brussels, for which Kenny was due to depart in a few hours. The Department of Finance had circulated talking points for the Taoiseach to take with him, but the new ministers and their advisers thought they were 'not robust enough'. They rewrote them to 'toughen them up'. The new Irish government would meet its partners in Europe with messages of friendship and cooperation and commitment to the programme – but it would also display a harder negotiating stance. It was an important moment: the civil servants were nervous, but the politicians held firm. Afterwards, the advisers beamed. 'Politicians, 2: Civil Servants, nil,' one of them told his colleagues.

The EMC was created in an attempt to deal with a number of recognized needs and inadequacies. First, there was the imperative of keeping a functioning and open relationship between the two party leaders and their staffs. Second, there was the widespread realization that cabinet government had simply failed to operate properly in the final months of the Fianna Fáil–Green administration. Third, both Mark Garrett and Mark Kennelly had been intrigued by suggestions from the management consultants McKinsey (where Garrett had worked in New York, and which had provided managerial advice before the government took office) that some sort of joint structure was needed to direct and oversee the work of a necessarily disparate governing system. They called it a 'watchtower'. Finally, the Troika liked the idea.

For Labour, the EMC had one vital extra advantage: it guaranteed the party an equal say in economic policy-making. The composition of the cabinet might be two-to-one in Fine Gael's favour. But at the EMC, it was fifty-fifty all the way. It's the solution, thought one senior party figure, to the problem of 'Does Labour get finance?'

The EMC continues to meet weekly in the Sycamore Room. Originally, it was envisaged that it would meet before cabinet, so it started at 8 a.m. on Tuesdays (cabinet begins at 10.15 a.m.). It was quickly seen that this was impossible. The Labour and Fine Gael ministers have separate meetings at 9. The Taoiseach and Tánaiste like to meet around 10 for a brief chat – usually Kenny drops into Gilmore's office, which is nearer the cabinet room, being on the same wing of the Government Buildings quadrangle. ('It's Charlie Haughey's old office,' he tells visitors.) EMC meetings can go on for a few hours, and 'the last thing you want to be doing is having a row at 8 about something that's going to cabinet at a quarter past ten.' So now the EMC meets on Wednesdays at 2.30 p.m. It is the start of the weekly political schedule, rather than the end.

The cabinet agenda is circulated on Friday afternoons. Andrew

McDowell and Colm O'Reardon take turns chairing a meeting of all government advisers at 1 p.m. on Mondays, clearing items for cabinet and troubleshooting any potential problems. The advisers' meeting rarely deals with matters of sensitivity or substance. But it does offer a contrast in style between the two parties. 'The Fine Gael guys think it's *The West Wing*,' observed one attendee, 'and the Labour guys think it's *The Sopranos*.' If necessary, McDowell and O'Riordan meet with Mark Garrett and Mark Kennelly later in the afternoon. So the EMC is usually considering issues and proposals a week ahead of the government meeting. It is an accurate reflection of the role of this 'inner cabinet'.

While formally the EMC is a committee of the cabinet that reports to the full cabinet and is not empowered to reach decisions on its own, in reality it is the decisive organ of leadership in Ireland. It is the very apex of power. Over time, more and more government matters have come to be considered and decided by the EMC before going to the cabinet for a formal decision – in reality, approval of what has already been decided by the leaders of the government. Partly, this is because all coalition governments need a sort of clearing house to avoid division at cabinet (the British coalition government operates a similar system, 'The Quad'); partly it's because most of the big decisions are financial and economic; and partly it's because – in the words of one of the most senior people in the administration – 'the cabinet leaks like a sieve'. The marginalization of cabinet government is a source of constant unhappiness among excluded members of the cabinet who feel – correctly – that they are being kept from the forum where the real decisions are made. Some ministers suspect the whole thing is actually unconstitutional.

However those on the outside felt about it, those involved were soon congratulating themselves on the workings of the new arrangement. And the relationships between the principals and their advisers were as important – and perhaps more important – as its architecture in making it work. Here, Howlin and Noonan were the central figures. On the face of it, the two men were very different. Noonan is a big, brooding, deliberate presence, his physicality seemingly an outward manifestation of his heavyweight political presence; Howlin is small, a staccato livewire, a bundle of energy who frequently stands on his toes when talking. Noonan slouches; Howlin bounces. The men had been friendly previously, and their relationship had again flourished at just the opportune time. Indeed, when Noonan was made finance spokesman for Fine Gael, Howlin confided over a pint that he was certain he would be in any new Labour cabinet. It was a prospect Noonan was entirely comfortable with; even then, he knew he would need all the help he could get. 'You know, Brendan,' he would later tell Howlin, 'maybe we should have three finance ministers.'

9

'Burden-sharing, my arse'

The senior civil servants gathered around the new Taoiseach in the Justus Lipsius building in the heart of Brussels' EU quarter were not optimistic. It was the new government's third day in office, and Ireland was in a corner. The Taoiseach was more isolated than any Irish prime minister had ever been at a European summit. The country was in a bailout. France and Germany were offering an interest rate cut on the Irish bailout loans, but they wanted Kenny to agree to a move on Ireland's corporation tax arrangements. The German chancellor Angela Merkel, whom Kenny had previously delighted in portraying as one of his best friends, had turned nasty, explicitly linking the corporation tax issue to the Irish interest rate. A lot of the Irish delegation agreed with the assessment of one official: it was 'fucking blackmail', pure and simple.

Ireland's low rate of corporation tax had long been an irritant to many European governments, and Irish politicians and diplomats had been unyielding in defending it for years in Brussels. Many regarded it as 'unfair competition'. French president Nicolas Sarkozy had taken to calling it 'shameful'. Now, relying on financial assistance from its European neighbours, the country had never been in such a weak position to resist moves towards greater European harmonization of tax arrangements. The Irish delegation, including both Brussels-based diplomats and officials from Dublin, figured a push might come. They just didn't know what form it would take. In the event, it came in the shape of an attempted mugging.

The Irish delegation was cloistered in its rooms during a lull in the proceedings when the Taoiseach received a message asking him upstairs to a meeting with the European Council president Herman Van Rompuy. When he went up, Van Rompuy hummed and hawed for a few minutes without really saying anything. Kenny thought it was a bit odd. What was this about? Then the door to the conference room opened. The Taoiseach looked up to see Merkel and Sarkozy walk into the room. Sarkozy was without his jacket. Neither sat down. Kenny immediately realized, It's an ambush: they're here to browbeat me into it.

According to an account he gave to his aides shortly afterwards, the two leaders subjected him to 'fierce pressure'. You must do this, he was told. You have no choice. You will not get your interest rate cut without it.

No way. I cannot move on this. It's sacrosanct, Kenny said.

The meeting ended on a pretty hostile note. You can forget about your interest rate reduction unless you do this, his erstwhile friend Merkel said.

When he went back downstairs to the Irish delegation, officials found him taken aback at the exchange. Was this how it was going to work for Ireland in Europe now? The officials were divided. Then the message came from Van Rompuy that France and Germany would settle for 'soft language' on tax from the Irish, promising future cooperation and commitment but without immediate concessions. 'There's a formula here that doesn't commit you to anything,' Van Rompuy urged. So that was the plan, officials thought – rough him up a bit and then offer an easy way out. Nonetheless, it would be going further than any Irish government had ever gone on maybe the most sensitive issue for Ireland in Europe.

Some of the officials thought that he was in a corner and had no choice but to agree; the moves towards greater tax harmonization could be fought when Ireland was in a stronger position. In any event, there was lots of opposition elsewhere in Europe to such a move. Others thought it would be a political catastrophe for Kenny to attend his first EU summit and immediately concede on corporation tax. Kenny's political instincts agreed. 'If that's what's on the table,' he said, 'we won't be having any agreement tonight.' But it would also be a blow to return empty-handed, especially with Greece having been granted an interest rate reduction – albeit just 1 per cent – on its loans. The government press secretary Eoghan Ó Neachtain reckoned they could spin the story another way: as Kenny standing up for Ireland against the bullying of the Europeans. Mark Kennelly was sceptical. He had clashed with the press secretary already, and their disputes would escalate over the coming weeks. But Kenny pulled Ó Neachtain aside and said, 'Do it!'

Publicly, Kenny acknowledged a 'good vigorous and vibrant debate' with Sarkozy. 'I'm not sure whether you would call it a Gallic spat or not but obviously the French president has had very clear views about the corporation tax rate for some time – and then, so have I,' Kenny told reporters afterwards. But the French and German leaders did not mince their words, making it perfectly clear that this was the condition attached to an interest rate cut for Ireland. 'It's difficult to ask other countries to bail out Ireland when Ireland is determined to keep the lowest tax on profit in Europe,' Sarkozy told reporters. 'Ireland is going to have to come to terms with that, but there's a very clear request from the members of the Eurozone that there must be at least some gesture.' Merkel was if anything even blunter. 'We weren't satisfied with what Ireland agreed to today, so the question of lowering interest rates has only been addressed for Greece.' Though France and Germany were leading the push against the Irish on corporation tax, the big two weren't by any means alone. 'It's difficult to make any change to the contract, but of course we will look at the comprehensive package. Finland is ready to negotiate some details, but Ireland will also have to make new commitments,' the Finnish prime minister Mari Kiviniemi told RTÉ. Like a lot of EU governments in the donor nations, she was feeling the domestic political fallout from the bailouts.

Brussels briefed heavily against Kenny; the Channel 4 economics correspondent Faisal Islam tweeted that he had received a report of proceedings at the council in which Kenny was described as 'very cocky', in stark contrast with the humble Greek prime minister George Papandreou. Kenny was to blame for Ireland's failure to get a rate cut, it implied. Sarkozy and Merkel were 'very upset'. The 'Charlemagne' European politics blog on the *Economist*'s website also wondered if Kenny had missed a 'golden opportunity'.

In the Irish media, it was a different story. Ó Neachtain worked the phones hard and his energetic spinning succeeded; the papers lapped it up. Kenny had played 'hardball', the *Evening Herald* complimented. The *Sunday Independent* was typically forthright in its support and admiration: '"Suicide" if we give in to EU on Taxes' blared its front page. '"No surrender" insists Enda Kenny'. If Kenny was an unlikely heir to the spirit of the siege of Derry, former Progressive Democrat leader Michael McDowell was an unlikely admirer of the new Taoiseach's mettle. But even he was on board. 'Sarkozy deserves a gesture,' he harrumphed in the pages of the *Sindo*, 'but a gesture involving two digits and no other numbers.' On the day after the summit, with the papers throwing garlands at him, Kenny rang Ó Neachtain at home. 'You've made me into a national hero,' he said.

Ireland's corporation tax regime would remain a source of irritation for several EU countries, and a vital national interest to be defended for Kenny and his ministers. The next time it blew up, the fingers were being pointed in London and Washington as well as Brussels. Though coming under increasing pressure, the government has continued to hold firm. Future years are likely to see further attacks on Ireland's tax laws, and the massive avoidance of tax that they facilitate.

If Kenny was delighted with Ó Neachtain's success in putting the right spin on his performance in Brussels, the rest of his staff were in no doubt that the press secretary's continued presence was only temporary. Ó Neachtain had been an enemy for too long for them to suddenly accept him as a colleague. He didn't expect to hang around himself either. He had been getting ready to leave the previous Sunday with the departing Brian Cowen when Phil Hogan rang him. Hogan wanted to see him to talk about something important. Okay, said Ó Neachtain, come to the House. Hogan didn't go in much for small talk. 'Will you stay on?' he asked him. Ó Neachtain refused, though he could guess what he was likely to hear next. 'Look,' Hogan said, 'talk to Kenny.' Ó Neachtain was a former army officer. Hogan knew that if the Taoiseach asked him to do something, he would do it.

The next day, Kenny called. 'Look, I'm going to be elected Taoiseach on Wednesday. I have to go to Brussels immediately and then I have to go to Washington. You know how it works. We need your help.' So Ó Neachtain stayed for a few months. The tension between him and Mark Kennelly, however, was never far beneath the surface. They often clashed on whether the Taoiseach should do 'doorsteps' – brief interviews with reporters, usually as he entered or exited from appointments. Ó Neachtain thought Kennelly was over-protective. 'Look,' he snapped at Kennelly on one occasion, 'leave this to the people who actually know what they're doing.'

For all the bluster about Kenny going toe to toe with Sarko to defend Ireland's corporation tax – so much of a national shibboleth at this stage that Sarkozy might as well have asked for the keys to Áras an Uachtaráin – the episode showed the new administration another side of the task it faced. Officials found that Ireland had little credibility in Brussels. There was 'zero sympathy for Ireland'. The 'stigma' of the bank guarantee was still evident. And there was, according to one official, 'no appreciation that the banking debts were anyone's responsibility but our own'.

Over the coming months Kenny and Gilmore would often seek to exaggerate the extent to which the Fianna Fáil–Green government had disengaged from contacts in Europe. In fact, Ireland's attendance rate at ministerial meetings had been fine right up until the final months of the coalition, when it dwindled to zero. What was more damaging was the perception that Ireland had 'partied' – as Brian Lenihan put it – while paying no heed to warnings from Europe. And now it was depending on Europe to bail it out. Some humility – and some pain – would not be out of order, Brussels thought. And, said one official, 'Every conversation you had – Charlie McCreevy came up.' And not in a good way.

The outcome of that first summit was certainly positive politically for Kenny, and demonstrated that the good luck he had enjoyed in the past was holding. Or so thought some of the Labour leadership, as they surveyed the media wreckage of their first few days in office. Because, as the new Taoiseach basked in media plaudits on his first weekend in office, the new Tánaiste was experiencing just the opposite, as the fallout from his decision not to appoint Joan Burton to one of the finance ministries continued to rumble on. As the newspapers hailed Kenny for standing up bravely to the bullying Sarkozy on their front pages, they examined Burton's 'shafting' and Labour's turmoil on the inside pages. Gilmore hardly suspected that this was going to become a running theme for his party, but it wouldn't be the last time that Labour ministers and party figures, comparing Kenny's sunny fortunes with their own gloomy lot, wondered, in the words of one minister, 'How the fuck does he do it?'

Most of the coverage ignored the fact that the much hyped renegotiation of Ireland's bailout terms – repeatedly promised by both parties since it was signed, and a cornerstone of their election campaigns – had pretty spectacularly failed to get past its first hurdle. Over the coming weeks and months, senior figures in the administration would come to believe that a renegotiation of the terms, and most especially of its cost, was essential if the government were to have any chance of success. Yet the 'Gallic spat' did postpone the day of reckoning on the bailout costs for a few months, by which time events in Greece had changed the landscape in such a way as to help the coalition's case.

But the new government was about to be confronted with a much more immediate issue, one that could not be postponed or spun. Ireland's politics may have been renewed by the general election, but its busted banks were once more in need of attention. And money.

When Brian Lenihan first came up with the idea, his Fianna Fáil aides were barely able to contain their amusement. It was mid February; the general election campaign was well under way, and the reaction on the doorsteps to Fianna Fáil candidates was every bit as hostile as the party had feared. Ministers, TDs, aides, party staff – they were all on course to lose their jobs. The party itself was beginning to understand that it was facing a defeat that might not just reduce its parliamentary representation but might actually obliterate it altogether. Yet it is a human characteristic, and one especially evident in Ireland, to find some amusement in the midst of the bleakest situation. And now the Fianna Fáil campaign team had found something that greatly tickled them.

Lenihan announced that he was postponing the €7 billion recapitalization of some of the Irish banks – agreed with the Troika under the bailout arrangements and due to take place by the end of February – until after the general election. Such a decision, he indicated, was more properly the preserve of a new government. He told *RTÉ News* piously, 'I think you have to respect the mandate you have.' The high moral tone especially tickled the Fianna Fáilers. It was, admittedly, late in the day for Lenihan to have concerns about the parameters of his government's mandate when it came to shovelling taxpayers' cash into the banks, but he didn't let that bother him. Lenihan managed to avoid a campaign explosion by throwing the ticking time bomb under the next government. And he did it while managing to sound plausibly statesmanlike and non-partisan. The aides loved it. 'We thought it was brilliant, hilarious. It completely wrong-footed them,' one told me. Lenihan was pretty pleased with himself too.

'It's a typical Fianna Fáil stroke designed to avoid announcing bad news during the campaign,' Michael Noonan fumed. 'The government is the government until a new government replaces it – there's no mandate required.' He knew then that one of his first acts as finance minister would have to be the ploughing of more taxpayers' money into the banking sector. But he also knew he would have to address the vexed question of the bondholders.

The Troika was concerned above all with continuity and with ensuring that the next government should continue the programme agreed with the outgoing administration. Troika officials had had a number of meetings with Fine Gael and Labour while they were in opposition, and had even sought to sit down with Fine Gael during the election campaign. Fine Gael declined, fearing it would look presumptuous if it leaked. The questions would be: What were you talking about? What commitments have you made? In any event, senior Fine Gael figures didn't want to engage on the contentious banking questions until they were ready.

As soon as the election was over, Andrew McDowell received a call from Kevin Cardiff in the Department of Finance. 'Chopra wants to meet,' Cardiff told him. The talks on a programme for government hadn't even begun. The Irish side stalled for a few days. Later, Cardiff arranged a conference call between Andrew McDowell, Colm O'Reardon and the top Troika officials: Ajai Chopra of the

IMF, Klaus Masuch of the ECB and Istvan Szekely from the European Commission. The Programme for Government had not yet been finalized, but the Troika was already elbowing its way into the negotiations. In a way, it would be the third partner in the coalition.

The bondholder question had become a sort of shorthand for the unfairness that many ordinary people felt about the situation. Here were international finance houses, banks, hedge funds and so on being repaid their investments in busted banks – failed businesses, essentially – with money that had been raised, in one way or another, from ordinary taxpayers. It was an each-way bet in the amount of billions of euros for the masters of the universe, financed by the little guys. If people had known that in recent years many of the bonds had been traded at far below par value – in effect at prices that reflected the unlikelihood of their being repaid – they would have been even more outraged. It meant that the investors who had bought these bonds since the economic collapse, for as little as 25 per cent of their value in some cases, were going to make an enormous killing when they were repaid in full. The buying and selling of various types of debt with different levels of risk attached is just the way financial markets work, but at a political level nobody could possibly stand over it. The election campaign and the period before it contained many promises and half-promises to burn, or to try to burn, or to at least renegotiate stern-facedly with the bondholders. Leo Varadkar's 'not another red cent' was the most notorious, but it was hardly the only one. However, only Sinn Féin and the far-left said plainly that they would not pay and would tell the Troika to leave, comfortable in the knowledge they wouldn't have to make good on their promises.

Privately, officials and ministers pointed out that there could be extraordinarily destructive immediate and long-term consequences from a default on bonds by Irish banks guaranteed by the state, though to many, even in the financial world – some of whom thought the Irish government's approach was lunacy – those fears were overblown. They also pointed out that the alternative – bailout and long-term, perhaps endless, austerity – wasn't very attractive either. But commentators just talk; politicians have to take real decisions that affect people's lives, and then they have to face those people.

In a sense, here was the essence of Ireland's approach to the financial crisis by both the Fianna Fáil and Fine Gael-led governments: cautious, a bit deferential to Europe, conscious of the dreadful state of the national finances and of the consequent weakness of any hand they might choose to play and, perhaps above all, concerned to maintain the existing social, political and economic order. That wasn't by any means an illegitimate strategy; but it was a conservative one. Then Ireland is in many ways a conservative country, with a conservative political establishment. A unilateral default was a shot in the dark whose consequences began with banks crashing and might end anywhere, and they just weren't willing to risk that. Now, caught between the political imperative to burn bondholders and the probable consequences of unilateral action, the only thing politicians of both the old and the new governments could find to say was that they were being forced into it by Europe. Pretty soon, Europe would confirm it intended to do just that.

By the time Michael Noonan took office in March, he had been thinking and preparing quietly for the showdown on the bondholders. His daughter worked in Paris for the investment bankers Lazard, which had implemented, Noonan knew, the burning of senior bondholders in Russia. He spoke to the Lazard bankers while in opposition and they produced for him a 200-page report on the steps necessary to implement burden-sharing with senior bondholders in Ireland. If he could get the ECB to agree, he had a definite process.

The Central Bank had also engaged Blackrock, a specialist consultancy, to perform 'stress tests' on the Irish banks to gauge their exposure to bad debts in a variety of future scenarios. The tests would then determine the extent of the recapitalizations that AIB and Bank of Ireland required to insulate them against future eventualities and thus, it was hoped, enable them to attract the investment and funding they needed to function normally and support economic activity. Barclays Capital was also hired to provide advice.

The stress tests gave Noonan his number: €24 billion. With the Lazard plan, he had a roadmap. At a briefing for ministers in the Sycamore Room on Monday, 28 March, along with officials from

Barclays and the Central Bank, including its whizz-kid new boy John Moran, Noonan laid out his plan for the recapitalizations but also his plan to enforce burden-sharing on the remaining senior bondholders in Anglo Irish Bank and Irish Nationwide, though not those in AIB and the Bank of Ireland.

For a government only weeks in office, these were huge, risky decisions, and there was, recalled one person present, 'a great deal of fear in the room'. The numbers were colossal and the financial engineering completely alien to many of the ministers. Some also found themselves getting lost in the terminology – the officials had code names for each of the banks – Alpha was AIB, Bravo was Bank of Ireland, and so on. They saw the political imperative for burning the bondholders but were nervous about taking the step, given all the previous government's warnings about it. But Noonan put on a 'bravura' performance. Neither Kenny nor Gilmore was present, so Noonan was in command of the meeting. 'We are the sovereign government of the Irish republic,' he reminded them. The time had come for such decisions. The following day, at the regular Tuesday cabinet meeting, the subject was formally on the agenda. Noonan proposed the recapitalization and the burden-sharing plan. Joan Burton, Pat Rabbitte, Leo Varadkar and Willie Penrose all spoke strongly in support of Noonan's plan. The cabinet decided to proceed with the recapitalizations – and the burning of the Anglo bondholders. Or so several cabinet ministers and senior officials understood.

'The understanding was that Noonan would burn them. That's the understanding we had,' one minister told me. 'The government decision was to burden-share,' said another. 'The decision was taken not to repay €6 billion in Anglo senior bonds,' says another. 'It was taken half for political reasons and half because we wanted to save the money.' Another minister present also confirmed that this was his recollection. The ministers' account is endorsed by several senior officials with knowledge of the talks.

By Thursday morning, 31 March, the ECB had woken up to the Irish intention of imposing losses on the senior bondholders in Anglo. ECB officials were vehemently opposed to a unilateral announcement by the Irish. Throughout the day, there was a series of increasingly hostile telephone conversations between Frankfurt and Dublin. Noonan was on the phone to Jean-Claude Trichet, the ECB president, and the discussions were becoming more and more fraught. Trichet was implacable. No matter how Noonan argued, Trichet would not consider agreeing to the burden-sharing. After the first conversation, finance officials arranged for a phone conversation between the Taoiseach and Trichet, which took place after 4 p.m. The ECB president told Kenny: 'I have just had a conference call with Jens [Weidmann, president of the Bundesbank and member of the ECB Governing Council] and the members of the executive board. I am here to tell you the outcome of that discussion.' If the Irish proceeded to burn bondholders, he said, it would mean that the Irish banks were insolvent, and the ECB could not support insolvent banks. Bullshit, thought the Irish aides. The reason for burning bondholders was to keep them solvent and then recapitalize them. But Trichet was not for turning.

The clock was now ticking down to Noonan's scheduled 4.30 p.m. announcement in the Dáil. A 'flustered' and very rapid meeting of the EMC took place, in which Noonan briefed his colleagues on Frankfurt's resistance. The finance minister said he would push again.

With minutes to go before he was due to make his announcement, Noonan was again on the phone. 'No, no, no,' Trichet insisted. 'If you do it the bomb will go off. It will not go off in Frankfurt, it will go off in Dublin,' he warned, according to accounts of the call Noonan and his officials later delivered to colleagues. Trichet urged Noonan to think about Ireland's financial-services industry and whether it would be able to raise finance on the markets, if the ECB withdrew support. He also pointed to Ireland's dependence on foreign investment, and the damage unilateral action would cause to it. The call ended inconclusively. Noonan didn't tell Trichet that he would row back, but he knew when he was beaten. 'He pushed and pushed but they just refused,' said one person closely involved.

Noonan's and the Taoiseach's conversations with Trichet had revealed that the benefits of unilateral action could be outweighed by the risks. The ECB was providing Irish banks with emergency funding and was also a part of the Troika – which was overseeing the bailout and supplying the money the state couldn't raise on the markets. The Troika possessed, Noonan understood, a pretty big stick. Officials again ran calculations on the money. Was it worth it? Someone came up with a figure: hundreds of millions of real savings would be made. Such calculations are usually made as a justification, and they were now looking for a way out. The real calculation was this: the risk was too great, while the benefits remained uncertain.

Now Noonan had to dash from his office in the Department of Finance to the chamber with an amended speech, which the officials had been furiously writing and rewriting in accordance with the ebb and flow of the Frankfurt negotiations. The finance minister is not the quickest of movers either. In the Dáil an uneasy silence settled as the press and the assembly waited for Noonan to fill his seat between an impassive Tánaiste and a smiling Taoiseach. In the row behind, chief whip Paul Kehoe spoke urgently into his mobile phone. Where the hell is he? Finally Noonan arrived, ten minutes late and out of breath; in the confusion, the pages of his script were mixed up, page four appearing before page three. Noonan just read it out anyway. It meant that parts of his speech didn't make sense, but nobody noticed.

No one noticed that a drama of huge proportions had just taken place – no one, that is, except for the members of the cabinet, who knew that a different course of action had been decided upon a few days earlier. Varadkar, though he was in Brussels, was especially angry when he heard the news. Some wondered about the legality of Noonan's announcement, given what the cabinet itself had agreed. However, others defined the decision that had been made differently: the burning of the bondholders would be pursued *if it could be done*. 'Officials interpreted the government decision as a decision to try to do it,' says one person involved at every stage in the events. That wasn't the understanding several ministers had, even if they saw the logic of Noonan's late call. At an earlier debate on the universal social charge, Sinn Féin's Seán Crowe had unwittingly summed up the feelings of more than one cabinet minister on the subject. 'Burden-sharing?' he asked rhetorically. 'Burden-sharing, my arse!'

Behind the scenes, officials and advisers scrambled to brief journalists and prepare for a press conference in Government Buildings later.

Mark Kennelly was nervous about putting Kenny out front and centre at an event where the questions were likely to be hostile and detailed. The potential for disaster, to which Kennelly was always hyper-sensitive, was evident to everyone. He clashed repeatedly with press secretary Ó Neachtain, who advised that the Taoiseach had to be seen to lead on such a pivotal issue. The press conference could be managed. Noonan and Howlin would be beside him. Gilmore too. Technical questions would naturally be the preserve of the finance minister.

'But they'll say he's weak on the economy!' Kennelly protested.

'Ye're the ones who promised to burn bondholders!' Ó Neachtain retorted. 'And ye haven't lit a fucking match!'

That's what the Taoiseach has to go out and explain, he thought. Eventually, Kenny intervened. He did the press conference, though Noonan answered most of the questions. It was fine. The press coverage was okay, concentrating as much on the tag of the 'pillar banks' as on the absence of burden-sharing. 'Noonan's pillars had better be good,' concluded Miriam Lord in the *Irish Times*, 'or we'll all end up going the way of Admiral Nelson by the time the next stress test rolls around.' They were riding their luck, and they knew it.

The cabinet was not yet a month in office and the weekly meeting was working its way through another lengthy agenda. Some of the experienced politicians around the table thought fleetingly (and some not so fleetingly) that officials were piling up the agendas, lest ministers should begin to show troublesome inclinations towards independence or reform. There was, to be sure, a lot for the new government to do, even as new ministers were familiarizing themselves with their departments, their new staff and the set of problems they would be living with for the next half a decade, if things went according to plan.

The meeting had begun as usual at 10.15 a.m. Soon after midday, whispers began circulating around the table. Ministers having finally learned what silent mode was, phones illuminated silently, flashing with incoming text messages. They looked at the devices and showed them to their colleagues. Everyone was getting the same message: 'Moriarty is out!'

For months – for years, in fact – the report of the Moriarty Tribunal's investigations into the award of the second mobile-phone licence to Denis O'Brien's Esat Digifone, and of the role the then Fine Gael minister Michael Lowry had played in the process, had been imminent. Newsrooms around Dublin had lost count of the number of times publication had failed to materialize as rumoured. Now, with the party in office for the first time since a Fine Gael administration had awarded that licence, Moriarty exploded like a landmine under its feet. The Mahon (Planning) Tribunal – still, incredibly, at this time continuing its Homeric deliberations – had been mostly (though not exclusively) a Fianna Fáil affair. The Baroque corruptions of Charles Haughey, the swaggering greed of Ray Burke and industrial graft of Liam Lawlor had firmly associated Fianna Fáil in the public mind with the idea of politicians for sale. The Moriarty Tribunal was Fine Gael's chance to catch up.

The cabinet finished up after 1 p.m. Pat Rabbitte kept an arranged lunch appointment in Leinster House, but his mind was racing. Rabbitte was minister for communications, energy and natural resources – the successor, albeit through several name changes and much portfolio shuffling in the department, to Michael Lowry. It was Rabbitte's department that had recommended the mobile-phone licence be awarded to Denis O'Brien. It was now at the epicentre of a massive political storm. In other words, Moriarty was first and foremost Rabbitte's problem.

When the mobile-phone licence had been awarded to Esat Digifone in 1996, Rabbitte was a 'super-junior' minister in the Rainbow government, a minister of state at the Department of Enterprise but with a seat at the cabinet table as the second Democratic Left representative, along with party leader Proinsias De Rossa. He knew then, as he knew now, that Denis O'Brien was seen as 'close' to Fine Gael – which meant he wasn't obviously a Fianna Fáil supporter and therefore had been tapped for political donations by a series of Fine Gael politicians. As the tribunal evidence showed, O'Brien was happy to oblige. The question was: Would the tribunal make the call that this 'closeness' – and in particular the relationship between Lowry and O'Brien – had undermined the licence-issuing process? If it did, the report was political dynamite.

After lunch, Rabbitte hurried to his department on Adelaide Road, arriving there about 2.30 p.m. All hell was already breaking loose. In his bright modern office, where two-storey floor-to-ceiling windows overlooked the Georgian rooftops as far as the grey-green dome of Government Buildings, the senior officials of the department had gathered in emergency conference. It was chaos. Several conversations were going on at cross-purposes; others were buried in the report, marking furiously. People who were usually so calm and prepared and structured in everything they did were in a complete flap. There was a good reason: their department, their colleagues and in some cases the officials themselves were in the line of fire, and they knew it.

A senior Department of Finance official was also there; some of the rolling cast of officials from the communications department wondered why. One official kept rising from his seat and going into the adjacent boardroom. Several of the former senior civil servants of the department, who had been serving when Lowry was the minister and the licence was awarded, were in there, all furiously reading the report or scanning it for mentions of themselves.

Rabbitte thought the priority of the meeting should be to get him a line he could use in the Dáil when he had to get up and answer questions in a couple of hours. 'Hold on, lads, I have a special-notice question in the House,' he told them. The response was of the 'Ah, sure minister ...' variety. 'Hold on a fucking minute,' Rabbitte barked. 'I need a response to a special-notice question.'

Rabbitte explained what he wanted: 'What's required here is a parliamentary reply that explains the history and context and pays tribute to his lordship and makes some commentary on the report.' The last would clearly be the tricky part of the operation. 'I'll write the last bit myself and you do the other bits.'

The great fear in the department was that they would be found to have participated in a corrupt process. But the officials were utterly and completely – some of them to a degree that surprised observers – convinced that this had not been the case. A draft report of some of the tribunal's findings had been circulated in 2008: this had contained extremely serious findings against named or otherwise identified civil servants. Though the report was only a draft and had been circulated to allow parties to comment on its proposed conclusions, it left the department and the officials aghast. They had strenuously opposed the draft findings and made detailed submissions in response; the tribunal then went on to recall some official witnesses. In fact, the damning findings in the draft report would largely be omitted from the final version.

A finding of corruption would have shocked the civil service to the core. It was one thing to discover politicians were corrupt, the mandarins thought. But to have the civil service implicated as well? It was too horrible for words. If the civil service was shown to be corrupt, some of them thought, it was more or less the same as admitting the country was ungovernable.

This worried the Department of Finance. But it also had more practical concerns. Adverse findings by the Moriarty Tribunal could open up the possibility of legal actions for damages and lost earnings by unsuccessful bidders. Such litigation could result in enormous contingent liabilities for the state. The legal adviser at the meeting in Rabbitte's office continually warned, 'I just wouldn't say anything at all, minister.' The finance officials knew things looked bad. They didn't want Rabbitte making them any worse. But to say nothing, or meeting the questions with formulaic responses, was politically untenable. All this swirled round the minister's office as they frantically tried to put together a response for the Dáil questions.

Before long, Rabbitte's private secretary was at the door. It was time to go. He was due in the House in a few minutes. Officials were working feverishly on his script, but it wasn't finished. They would finish it when he was in the car, email it to his Dáil office and get it to him in the chamber. He dashed downstairs and into the waiting car for the short journey to Leinster House. In the car, he rang Finbarr O'Malley, his adviser, who had digested those parts of the report on which he thought Rabbitte was likely to be questioned. He briefed his minister as completely as he could in the five minutes the journey took. Not for the first time, Rabbitte had cause to be grateful for O'Malley's coolness and thoroughness.

Rushing to the chamber, Rabbitte was pleased to find a procedural wrangle going on between the Ceann Comhairle and Micheál Martin. Brian Lenihan too was trying to get in, as were several others. They wanted a full debate and they wanted the Taoiseach in the chamber to answer questions. They only had Rabbitte. And, though the Fianna Fáilers didn't know it, he didn't have a script yet. Barrett made to move proceedings on and call Rabbitte to answer the questions. The minister hastily sent a note to the chair: 'Let them at it, I've no script.' Barrett didn't seem pleased. Soon he called Rabbitte to speak. As Rabbitte rose, an usher glided in the door nearest to him and handed him an envelope. He took out his speech. 'The tribunal of inquiry,' he began, 'was established on 26 September 1997 . . .'

Moriarty found that Lowry had indeed 'delivered' the mobile-phone licence for Esat Digifone. Later, he had received a number of payments from Esat owner Denis O'Brien, though the report did not make a finding of corruption against O'Brien. Fine Gael basically brazened it out. Labour swallowed hard and said nothing, secretly conscious of what it would have said if in opposition, but believing that it just didn't make sense to kick up about it now; the government had too much work to do. The Taoiseach performed a series of half-endorsements and half-evasions; it would be a number of months before he actually came out straight and said that he accepted the tribunal's findings. Like Rabbitte, he was being implored by some of his officials not to say anything that could support litigation taken against the state on foot of the report. But Kenny was also a bit conflicted by the Denis O'Brien question: no prime minister wants to make an enemy of a press baron. And O'Brien's irresistible advance on the Independent group meant he was on his way to becoming a press baron. The 'Denis question' would remain a source of friction between the two government parties, and would come back to haunt them a year later.

As ministers began to understand just how straitened their circumstances were likely to be in their departments – 'Jesus, what I couldn't do with even a couple of hundred million!' one minister bemoaned to me in the early months – those at the very centre of government were coming to an uncomfortable conclusion: that the bailout as constituted would not and could not work. It was too expensive. It would crush the economy. Unless there were substantial changes to its costs, the new government and the country would be slowly strangled.

'The programme couldn't work. The numbers were just too much,' one person who attended the early meetings of the EMC told me. 'We believed that we had inherited a bailout that couldn't work,' said another source. One thing gave the ministers encouragement, though: the IMF agreed with this assessment. 'The IMF believed it. But the ECB and the Commission didn't.' The Irish assessment was backed up by the informal advice that governments seek and receive from experts in all fields – in this case investment banking and finance. 'This isn't going to work,' one senior government figure was told by one of his interlocutors from the finance world. 'You're better off making a break for it.' He meant that Ireland should default, at least on the banking debts. But it's difficult to make a break for it when you're carrying the country on your back.

According to people at EMC and cabinet level, on both sides of government, on the political and the official side, defaulting on Ireland's debts was never really seriously discussed or considered as an option. There were some cabinet members and some advisers who secretly thought that they would get there sooner or later, but the stance taken by the two parties in opposition meant that the decision to rule out default had been taken almost unconsciously even before the votes were cast, and before they sat down to negotiate a Programme for Government. Ireland's political elite was not going to surrender the country's membership of the advanced nations of the world unless it was forced to.

Officials also knew that if Ireland was going to default, it had to be ready for some pretty hairy consequences. And nothing was ready for that kind of event. But, as tension grew in the Eurozone over Greece's troubles, and analysts and commentators talked reasonably about the breakup of the euro, senior officials realized that they would have to be ready at some point. And so in the early months of the new government, a top-secret committee of senior officials from the departments of the Taoiseach, Finance, Public Expenditure and Justice, with others seconded in at various stages, was formed. Martin Fraser, an assistant secretary at the Department of the Taoiseach – but soon promoted to the top job on the retirement of Dermot McCarthy – chaired its meetings and coordinated its work. There were no politicians or political advisers on the committee, though both groups were briefed on its work on several occasions. Few people in government were aware of its existence. Of those that were, some of them called it 'the most secret committee in government'.

The committee began to work on a plan for what to do to ensure the functioning of the state and society in the event of a sudden Eurozone breakup, though some of its plans could equally have been utilized in the event of a default. Banks would immediately be closed and exchange controls implemented. People would not be able to access their cash except in controlled, limited amounts. A new currency would have to be created as quickly as possible, though in the interim existing notes and coins would be used, their value based on a floating exchange rate in relation to outside currencies.

A Special Powers Act would have to be passed through an all-night emergency session of the Oireachtas; this would effectively give the government wartime powers to control commerce, banking and public order. The draft legislation was duly drawn up.

Because money would be so tightly controlled in the early stages of such an event, plans were made to ensure that pharmacies would continue to supply vital drugs and that the food supply was not switched off. Considerable extra security would be needed, especially around shops and banks. All Garda leave would be cancelled; the army would be on standby to assist. Normality would not resume until economic and market conditions had stabilized, and it was anyone's guess how long that would take. Nothing like it would have been seen in Modern Ireland since the Second World War.

It was this sort of planning that underpinned the decision – or, more accurately, the widely shared disposition in government – not to seriously consider telling the ECB or any of Ireland's other international creditors 'to go fuck themselves', as some were advising. In those fraught, sober, grim early meetings of the EMC, and in the absence of a default option, those present knew there were two alternatives: demand an immediate renegotiation with the Troika, citing their mandate following the election; or stick with the agreement. It was described this way to me: 'This can't work, and they [the Troika] will realize that so they will offer us concessions.' This point of view was strongly held by, among others, Central Bank governor Patrick Honohan, whose views were accorded significant weight by the political principals.

Still, they weren't terribly appealing choices. Said one EMC member: 'We wondered – Jesus! Are we doing the right thing here? Is this going to work?' The truth was, none of them knew. The whole thing was running on hope.

'We might get through this'

The report of the 25-pounder guns of the Second Field Artillery Regiment boomed across the city of Dublin twenty-one times. If residents of the nation's capital had managed to avoid the wall-to-wall media coverage, the traffic disruption and the native water-cooler smartarsery, then the thunder of the guns – which had last seen martial action in the service of her father during the Second World War, before their purchase by the army of the Irish Republic – announced it unmistakably: Her Majesty Queen Elizabeth II of the United Kingdom of Great Britain and Northern Ireland, and of Her other Realms and Territories, had arrived.

The visit, which started on 17 May, was the result of months of detailed and extraordinarily security-conscious logistical planning, years of patient diplomacy and decades of the steady normalization of the relationship between two countries with a tangled and often bitter and bloody past. It was the product of the labours of Brian Cowen and Bertie Ahern, and most especially of Mary McAleese, now entering the final months of her long and productive presidency. The visit was announced a week before Enda Kenny became Taoiseach; if his predecessor had left him a whole lot of troubles, he had left him this gift too. It was rather ungracious of Kenny not to acknowledge the role of Cowen and his administration when repeatedly offered the opportunity to do so by Micheál Martin in the Dáil in the weeks after the visit. For a most amiable man, Kenny often displayed a tribal side in his first years as Taoiseach.

Nonetheless, both Fine Gael and Labour felt a quiet satisfaction that it fell to them, and not Fianna Fáil, to accommodate the historic visit. Both parties have always defined themselves in part by opposition to Fianna Fáil's traditionally more hard-edged Republicanism, and its shadow, a reflexive anti-Britishness that ran like a seam of iron-ore through Irish life. Fine Gael did so for a mixture of class, cultural and historical reasons; Labour because such atavistic impulses were anathema to its sense of itself as a modernizing force. In the post-Good Friday Agreement era these distinctions had largely become redundant, but their echoes remained.

The gushing was intense, widespread and largely justified by the surprising rapport that the ageing monarch appeared to strike up with anyone she met, including the few carefully selected civilians at a few carefully selected events. According to the *Irish Times*'s report of the Queen's stop-off in Trinity College, people who met her 'remarked upon how friendly, deeply engaged and good humoured she was'. That was about as tough as the coverage got. That it should be so was hardly unforeseeable; what was more remarkable was that she appeared to be enjoying herself. There are enough pictures of the Queen looking glum at official events to suspect that her ever-present beaming smile was quite genuine. 'Irish republicans who see her as the personification of the British state were confounded, even charmed,' noted the *Daily Telegraph*'s editorial. That was about right. She visited the war memorial at Islandbridge, the Garden of Remembrance, Croke Park, Trinity College, the Guinness Brewery, the Irish National Stud in Kildare, the Rock of Cashel, Coolmore Stud, the English Market in Cork. On her Cork visit, she went on an unscheduled walkabout.

All told, the trip was an astounding success – and a national tonic. It was impossible not to feel it was a significant event. Despite ourselves, these things sometimes matter. The sense of chapters of history being closed was compounded when Garret FitzGerald – with a deft sense of timing that this much loved 'national granddad' had not always displayed in his political life – died hours after the Queen's speech at the state banquet in Dublin Castle.

Some of the Taoiseach's staff accompanied him when he went to see the Queen off in Cork. They were 'glad to see her leave safely' – their constant terror had been that there would be a security incident during the visit. The preparations were intense and thorough, with constant involvement by the British and Northern Irish authorities. There was, says one official, 'huge British involvement' in the security preparations. As threats from dissident Republican groups, public and otherwise, proliferated in the days before the visit, Downing Street became extremely jumpy, with some officials in Dublin fearing that the visit could be called off at the last minute. 'Cameron almost pulled the plug from COBRA,' one official said, recalling the nervousness of prime minister David Cameron's government. COBRA is the UK government's emergency-response committee, convened to consider matters of national security at home or abroad. 'There was loads of threats. The Brits were very nervous.' If anything had happened to the Queen, Cameron would have had to resign. A pipe-bomb was found on a bus in Maynooth; there were credible bomb warnings in London and Dublin on the eve of the visit. According to people involved, there were new and credible bomb threats made when the Queen's aircraft was actually in the air, and urgent conversations took place between Dublin and London about whether the flight should be turned around, or at least diverted or delayed. In the event, she continued. But the words of one senior British official to Eamon Gilmore's staff in London the previous week were ringing in their ears: Whatever you do, send her back to us in one piece.

There was intermittent criticism of the security arrangements, which – in Dublin anyway – insulated the monarch from any spontaneous contact with the public, but, given the consequences if there had been an incident, few disputed the need for caution to rule the day. In the event the biggest casualty out of the affair was justice minister Alan Shatter's budget: he spent months afterwards engaged in a bitter scrap over who should pay the €24 million bill for all the Garda overtime.

If Queen Elizabeth brought grace and pomp and the timeless allure of royalty, Barack Obama followed on her heels with the unmistakable power of his office and the sheer star wattage of his fame and personality.

The announcement that President Obama was coming had been one of several early boosts for the new administration. It was sealed at a meeting in the Oval Office during the traditional St Patrick's Day visit of the incumbent Taoiseach to Washington. Enda Kenny was barely a week in the job and he was sitting in the epicentre of global political power, shooting the breeze with the president of the United States. Joe Biden was there too. As were treasury secretary Tim Geithner, Dan Rooney, the US ambassador to Dublin, and Bill Daley. The last was Obama's chief-of-staff and son of the famous Chicago mayor and Democratic Party chief Richard J. Daley, whose controversial oversight of voting in Illinois in 1960 reputedly delivered the presidency for Kenny's great hero, John F. Kennedy. It is difficult not to be goggle-eyed in the presence of such power in such a setting; Kenny managed it well enough. It's a photo op certainly, but a long one with plenty of face time with the president. For an avid Americanophile like Kenny, it was a take-your-breath-away start to his premiership.

The Irish delegation included the Washington ambassador Michael Collins, mandarins Martin Fraser and Niall Burgess, Kenny's chief-of-staff Mark Kennelly and press secretary Eoghan Ó Neachtain. The press secretary had been before, with the two previous Taoisigh. But you don't get tired of this stuff.

Like almost all of these affairs, the details had been agreed in advance by the officials, and the Irish delegation had been told about Obama's visit while waiting in the Roosevelt Room. The Oval Office pleasantries, nonetheless, were pretty pleasant. 'Well, we've extended the invitation and you're welcome any time,' Kenny said. 'The good news is I'm coming,' Obama replied.

Now, with the Queen safely dispatched, all attention turned to the imminent arrival of Barack Obama. There is no doubt when the president of the United States is visiting a country – nobody else causes that much fuss, even when the visit is to last just twenty-four hours. The security was overbearing, a lot of the Irish officials thought. They had cooperated closely with the British in the security arrangements for the Queen's visit, but now the Americans just told them what to do. The Irish side thought a lot of it was a bit much. Of all the people who want to kill the Queen in the world, probably 99 per cent of them are in Ireland, they told themselves; of all the people who want to kill Obama, there's probably the smallest proportion in Ireland. But the Secret Service doesn't discuss and doesn't compromise. 'We do this our way,' they said. Among the baggage the president travels with: two armoured-plated limousines, presumably in case one gets stuck – say, on a ramp exiting the US Embassy. Which was exactly what happened, much to everyone's – except the Secret Service's – considerable amusement and delight.

Two months after their first meeting in the Oval Office, Kenny welcomed Obama for a fireside chat, this time in Farmleigh House. The White House released a transcript of the president's remarks after his meeting with the Taoiseach in which he lauded the 'extraordinary traditions of an extraordinary people'. One of those extraordinary traditions is putting a dirty big pint of Guinness in front of every visiting dignitary. Last week the Queen, this week the US president. Unlike the Queen, this guest drank it, joshing with the locals in Ollie Hayes's Bar in Moneygall, from where his great-great-great-grandfather Falmouth Kearney left for the US in the middle of the 1800s. He slugged his pint enthusiastically and appeared at all stages to be thoroughly enjoying himself. Back in Dublin, he barnstormed his way through a speech in front of an audience some 50,000 strong in College Green. Kenny himself had barnstormed his way through an overheated introduction, a part of which, it quickly emerged, was a reprise of a speech given by Obama himself. Deliberate, said his aides. An homage. The press didn't buy it. But outside the media bubble nobody noticed. It was a storm in a teacup.

Obama's visit was cut short by the movement of an Icelandic volcanic-ash cloud that was heading for Irish and UK airspace. Instead of staying overnight, he departed that evening for London, wary of being stranded in Dublin if the ash cloud, as forecast, blew in from the north-west. Insofar as these things can be judged by appearances, Obama seemed genuinely delighted to be in Ireland. But he didn't want to be stuck here either.

The two visits, welcome and all as they were, and important for charging the national mood with some optimism and brightness, were here-today-gone-tomorrow political events. People enjoyed them and the coalition basked in the reflected glow; for some, it was the first time they had felt good about their country in a long time.

But for all the warm words, the coalition knew that they wouldn't change the grim prospects that still faced them. When Air Force One took off, the smiles in Government Buildings turned once more to grimaces. The same set of potentially crushing problems remained. The coalition continued to blame their every woe on Fianna Fáil – and there was plenty of justification for that – but they would soon start making their own mistakes.

Most politicians are extremely concerned with the media coverage of themselves and their work; some are obsessed with it. Enda Kenny is unusually blasé about it; of course, he has people to do that for him nowadays. Perhaps his insouciance stems from his years as leader of the opposition, when his weakness, foibles and failures were endlessly scrutinized. Part of it comes from his character and psychological make-up. Whatever the exact constitution of it, he has a thick skin. Uncharacteristically, then, Kenny was worried about the media's assessments of the government's first 100 days in office.

Kenny knew that a lot of the 100 days thing was his own fault. Two days before the general election, he had issued a plan for his first 100 days with the usual cocktail of pledges to get Ireland working, put manners on the banks, renegotiate the bailout, and so on. The item that caused most hilarity was the one that promised that no Fine Gael ministers would deal with constituency matters for the first 100 days. Well, yes, they thought. When we're in government, we'll have an office full of civil servants to do that for us.

Coming up to the 100 days mark, Kenny was conscious that, while the tone and the mood music were better, actual definable achievements were less obvious. At a Government Buildings press conference, he told reporters that the government had persuaded the Troika to back the jobs initiative, prevented 'the fire-sale of bank assets' and secured 'the restoration of the minimum wage'. It was pretty thin gruel. Gilmore's pugnacious rhetoric ('We will succeed the way the Irish always have: by sheer hard graft and determination') masked an unchanged reality.

The commentators' report cards were mixed. In the *Irish Times* political editor Stephen Collins thought it had been 'roses all the way

for Enda Kenny and his government' (though he qualified his generally upbeat assessment by saying the 'big, hard decisions' had yet to
be made). The same newspaper's economics editor, Dan O'Brien,
thought the new government 'did not inspire confidence', comparing
it unfavourably with the start made by the 1987 government under
Charles Haughey and Ray MacSharry. In the *Sunday Business Post*, I
observed that in the wake of his election, the wave of hope and goodwill that greeted the long overdue change of government, and the
spectacular success of the two visits, Kenny had amassed a vast treasury of political capital. But he seemed not to have a clue what he
wanted to spend it on.

Political capital – a reserve of trust, support, moral authority,
credibility and the confidence all that gives a political leader – is a
perishable commodity. Leaders can't keep it in a bank until they need
it. You've got to use it, or lose it. But Kenny's government was not
going to use it. They were not going to, say, embark on a programme
of immediate reforms and budgetary consolidation. There were no
serious voices in government calling for dramatic departures in government policy. There was no call for a big bang on the public
finances, or welfare, or public sector pay, or relations with the EU
and the Troika. Even on constitutional and political reform, the
approach of the new government was gradual and cautious. Instead,
the leadership of the government decided that they would stick to
the promises of the Programme for Government for at least the first
year and the first budget – no matter what might be forced on them
afterwards.

They would be criticized afterwards for not taking the opportunity afforded by the early months to strike out with bolder reforms,
particularly on public sector pay and welfare. There were arguments
for and against acting boldly. It could be – and was – argued that it
displayed an unwise timidity while the coalition had the fair wind of
a massive mandate behind them. Few believed they would be able to
avoid raising taxes, cutting welfare and reducing public sector pay at
some stage of the government's life – so why not do it early and get
it over with? Against this argument was put the need to stabilize the
governance of the country, a need that experienced politicians from

both sides felt from even before they took office in March. The coalition needed to 'keep its promises and bed down', they felt. No doubt there would be all kinds of unpleasant stuff to come. But there was no sense in going looking for it until the coalition had to.

Once in government, the cautious approach was also partly because those in key positions were so committed to working the bailout, and changing some of the terms of the Troika's memorandum, that the attendant programme of work, reform and governance crowded out any other options. Finally it was because, at its most basic, the government viewed its mission as saving the country economically and politically, rather than revolutionizing it. Compromising on the methods to achieve that salvation was one thing; agreeing on the more profound political questions about the distribution of power and wealth, and the balance to be struck between public and private interests, was another. For all the unity of purpose at the top of the government, nobody involved was in any doubt about the differences between them either.

The coalition's caution expressed itself most visibly in the decision – taken by the EMC around the 100-day mark – that it would stick to its election and Programme for Government pledges not to raise taxes or cut social welfare rates. It was apparent that a decision had been made on it, because suddenly Kenny was out saying taxes would not be increased and Gilmore was simultaneously out saying welfare rates would not be cut. When the latter refrain was taken up by Joan Burton, she was advised to qualify it slightly in the future: there would be no cuts to *core* social welfare rates. That put her on guard immediately.

Privately, Noonan was stressing the necessity that budget adjustments, when they came, had to be substantially weighted towards reductions in expenditure rather than tax increases. 'I remember the 1980s,' Noonan told them. 'We wouldn't cut – it was all on the tax side. And we stagnated for years.' What he was really telling them, Labour thought, was that Labour wouldn't let Fine Gael cut spending in the 1980s and they should let him cut it now. This fundamental policy question was generally accepted to have been settled by a two-to-one ratio, but it was always the subject of budget haggling. And, as the haggling went on, Labour thought that one of the advantages of Brendan Howlin's forthcoming comprehensive review of expenditure was that it would demonstrate to Fine Gael ministers the realities of the cuts that their party favoured. 'We wanted to confront them with the consequences of their own rhetoric.' Labour ministers and advisers suspected that Fine Gael ministers were prone to exhibit what one British commentator has dubbed 'fiscal nimbyism' – cut government spending certainly, just not in my department. The challenge facing them was certainly acute, but it hadn't obliterated the basic differences between the two parties.

It was early to be addressing budgetary matters, even if setting such ground rules served immediate political purposes. The fiscal matters of most concern to the government at this stage would be decided in Brussels and Frankfurt, not in Merrion Street. The economist Jim O'Leary, who had joined the Department of Finance under Brian Lenihan (though he would later return to academia), produced a paper for the EMC that demonstrated that an interest rate cut on Ireland's loans was the most valuable thing that the government could get. Ever since Kenny had been rebuffed on such a cut at the March summit, the coalition had been coming at it another way, pursuing a diplomatic effort to garner support for a reduction.

The groundwork was laid by intensive diplomatic activity by Gilmore and Kenny, and by Irish diplomats in European capitals. The two leaders even went so far as to summon all Irish ambassadors home to Dublin for a pep talk – an exercise that many felt was superfluous, especially when Kenny started telling them how he cried every time he saw Riverdance. A recording of his speech was bandied about for a few days and was the subject of much ribbing. It reminded his handlers of the perils of letting him off unscripted, but it showed that he remained pretty impervious nowadays to the sort of sneering, and occasional justifiable bemusement, that he had attracted when he was in opposition.

At the European summit in June, Ireland received the first sign that substantial movement on the bailout programme was possible. The summit reversed the decision to give preferential creditor status to loans from the proposed new European bailout fund, the European Stability Mechanism (ESM). The preferential-creditor status worried markets because investors were concerned that if a country were to default on its bonds, the ESM would get paid back first, leaving nothing for bondholders. Under such circumstances, few investors would be willing to lend to troubled countries such as Ireland.

Though a bit esoteric, the news was generally welcomed, and certainly hailed by Noonan. The specialist media were more effusive. On the influential irisheconomy.ie website, one poster noted that the finance minister was 'positively purring at this development, almost hinting that it was a result of his negotiation skills'. Noonan wasn't naive enough to think that he alone had pulled it off, but he had certainly pushed for it. He returned to Dublin with the first bit of good news the government had got from Europe for a long time. 'We were able to come home and say, "We got something,"' summarized one official.

Better, much better, was to come. At a special summit in Brussels in late July, European leaders agreed that they would cut the interest rate by 2 per cent on their bailout loans to Greece, Portugal and Ireland – a move breathless government spinners speculated would save the country over €10 billion over the lifetime of the loans, some €800 million a year in interest costs. Whatever the exact number, it clearly transformed the sustainability of Ireland's bailout. Nobody minded that Kenny had actually only sought a 1 per cent cut; nobody minded that Kenny agreed to language committing Ireland to cooperate constructively in discussions on tax cooperation – something suspiciously similar to what Van Rompuy had pressed on him in March, albeit in a different political context. After months of talking about achieving a better deal on the bailout, the coalition finally had something to shout about. It was, the *Irish Independent* proclaimed, an 'historic deal'.

Opposition politicians and some media commentary scoffed a bit at the government's strained attempts to take credit for the interest rate cut – pointing out that Ireland had merely been given what was offered to Greece too. This overlooked the fact that in March, Ireland had not been given what had been offered to Greece. But, as it often does, the concentration on the process obscured the greater matter of the substance of what was decided, and the consequences it would have. The interest rate reduction marked a big breakthrough in the sustainability of the Irish debt arrangements and the programme that governed them. It bore out the incremental approach advocated by Central Bank governor Patrick Honohan soon after the government came together – an approach that relied on the belief that the European authorities would recognize the programme as then constituted could not work, so they would change it. More importantly, it was the first signal to the government and the Economic Management Council that real and substantial changes could be made to the programme that would give Ireland a fighting chance of actually getting out of it.

This was an important signal to them, because for much of the early months on the EMC, nobody knew if the approach they were taking would work. The chances of the conditions of the bailout simply being too onerous to be accepted by the public, and of their just not working to stabilize the national finances anyway – in which case the country would essentially fail in the way Greece seemed destined to – were real and present and palpable. In public they said things like, 'We have made a decisive step on the road to recovery' (Kenny) and 'We have lost no time in rolling up our sleeves, and getting down to the business of getting Ireland working again' (Gilmore). The truth was that between March and July, the leaders of government were not at all clear that the state was financially viable. Members of the EMC looked at one another thinking – and occasionally saying privately – 'We might not make it here.' There were moments – at the news of the most recent downgrade in Ireland's credit rating or something equally negative – when 'things went very quiet in the room.'

According to several people who attended EMC meetings, the interest rate cut was the first moment when the leadership of the country really thought: We might get through this. At the EMC meeting that followed the rate cut, the lifting of the mood was palpable. Afterwards, Gilmore, Howlin and some aides went for dinner in the members' restaurant in Leinster House. Noonan joined them.

The mood was lighter than some previous dinners. 'Do you know,' one of them reflected, 'that's the first meeting when I haven't felt like leaving through the window?'

The interest rate cut also banished any talk of default forever. While the question of a default had not been seriously considered as a voluntary option by the coalition, there were those who believed that events could force them into it. According to one of the architects of the policy, the interest rate cut took 'unilateral pre-emptive action off the table . . . the government was now set on its course.'

After five months of outward, sunny optimism and inward fear and despair, the coalition had finally copped a break – and a big one. But it was also becoming less cowed by its circumstances and by the Troika. For the first time, it began asserting itself a bit with Ireland's lenders.

Though their time must be valuable, a lot of the meetings that the Troika holds are purely for the optics. Maintaining a measure of engagement with the broader political process, and with civil society and interest groups, projects the impression that Ireland's lenders are listening to everyone and taking on board what they say – important if the programme is to be maintained with some level of public acceptance, and 'worked' rather than simply imposed from outside. The extent to which the Troika really listens to what Fr Seán Healy of Social Justice Ireland or the Irish Farmers' Association or the trade unions or the United Left Alliance tells them is a matter its members keep to themselves. But when they emerge to face the media, there's little doubt that the various advocacy groups regard the encounters as being of great significance indeed. But it's hard to see any changes in the nature of the programme as a result of them. The perception of the government, certainly, is that these engagements aren't really that serious.

Because the loans to Ireland are advanced with 'policy conditionality' attached – in other words on condition certain policies are followed – the real business of the Troika is with the government and most of it is done between officials. But the ministerial meetings are important set-pieces. When the Irish government side prepared to meet the Troika for the July review after its first months in office,

Michael Noonan was getting ready to put the boot in. The new government had managed a harmonious transition in Ireland's relations with its lenders but mostly that was because it had simply fulfilled – to the letter – the previous administration's commitments. Noonan felt that things needed to be shaken up a bit. The coalition needed the Troika to move on a few things and he needed to let them know.

At a pre-meeting with Brendan Howlin, Kevin Cardiff and other senior finance and public expenditure officials, Noonan told his colleagues, 'I'm going to have a right go at them. They need to be told a few home truths.' The others stirred a bit. Noonan was famously difficult to read. Where was he going with this? 'I'm fed up being nice to them. This programme's not working. It's too expensive. The debt is too high. I'm going to tell them.'

When the meeting started, the Troika officials gave a glowing account of the progress, praising the Irish side for their 'exemplary' performance. Noonan wasn't having any of it and, as one observer at the meeting put it, he 'lit into them'.

'This is working for you,' he told them. 'But it's not working for us. We're doing everything you say. We've hit every target you've given us. We do everything you ask us to.'

The Troika could hardly dispute that. There had been a rigid discipline in Government Buildings about relations with the Troika – calls returned immediately, emails replied to promptly, absolute transparency in all their dealings. If this seems unremarkable, it was the opposite of what Troika officials were experiencing in Athens, reports – and Commission gossip – suggested. The administration knew it was important from the outset to build up trust and credibility with the lenders. More than one department was subjected to bollockings by Government Buildings for failing to meet a Troika deadline on producing legislation or other promised policy change. 'Don't tell me to go into a room with the Troika and justify your failure to do this pissy legislation when I want to ask them about the interest rate!' one was told. The point of all that was to secure improvements to the deal. There was also a view that there was no point in complaining about everything – the coalition had to pick its battles with the Troika. Well, Noonan was picking one now.

'It's not working for us,' Noonan continued. 'You have to do something for us. There has to be a quid pro quo. We're in the dunce's corner. You have to help us get out of the dunce's corner. Someone has to get out.

'If this is going to work, we need more from your side,' he summarized. His broadside went on for some time. The Troika officials were completely taken aback. But Noonan had another twist. 'Now,' he said, 'it's Friday evening. There's a nice pub on the corner. I'd like to buy you all a drink.'

Back in Howlin's office after the meeting the officials were ecstatic with Noonan's performance, and almost fell over each other complimenting the finance minister. There was a long way to go, but it marked an important moment in the relations between the coalition and the Troika.

If Michael Noonan relished the aggressive theatricality of standing up to the Troika, his boss was about to trump him by launching a remarkable attack on an institution that had been overseeing the Irish for a lot longer than the Troika – the Roman Catholic Church.

Kenny's attack was in response to the report of a Commission of Inquiry into the Cloyne Diocese, the latest in Ireland's seemingly never ending litany of clerical sex abuse. 'The Cloyne report excavates the dysfunction, the disconnection, the elitism that dominate the culture of the Vatican today,' Kenny told an empty but soon to be rapidly filling Dáil. 'The rape and torture of children were downplayed, or managed, to uphold instead the primacy of the institution, its power, its standing and its reputation. Far from listening to evidence of humiliation and betrayal with St Benedict's "ear of the heart", the Vatican's reaction was to parse and analyse it with the gimlet eye of a canon lawyer.'

It was a sensational speech, and it received worldwide attention. In the New York Times, Maureen Dowd hailed a 'breathtaking' intervention which 'thrilled' the country. 'The Irish,' she wrote, 'were taken

aback by the ire of the ordinarily amiable, soft-spoken Kenny.'
Among those taken aback were some of his own colleagues.

Because the media hadn't been tipped off about the speech – 'too
lazy to miss their lunch' scoffed one adviser – a myth arose that the
speech had been delivered almost by accident, without Kenny realizing just how strong it actually was. Among those who doubted
Kenny's comprehension of policy, this suspicion was especially prev-
alent. In fact, it was true that Kenny's aides had not anticipated the
scale of the reaction to the speech – but the Taoiseach had been quite
adamant from the start of the drafting process that he wanted to
make a strong statement of repudiation. Though his speechwriter
Miriam O'Callaghan usually gets the blame or credit for Kenny's
speeches, in fact she works from home and is involved at a relatively
late stage. Her work tends to be on the language, rather than the substance of the speech. When the first drafts appeared, Mark Kennelly
warned him – this is pretty strong stuff. Kenny was entirely happy
with it. Some senior civil servants advised against delivering the
speech in such uncompromising terms, but his own political staff
knew to leave well enough alone.

Kenny's speech was an unprecedented rebuke from the head of
government to a foreign state, much less to the Vatican. But what gave
it its power and significance was that it spoke from the bruised and
disappointed heart of a traditional Irish Catholic, who had always
viewed the Church, for all its faults, as a force for good in the world
and in his life. The abuse scandals had made him question that belief
to its very roots. 'The debate was about Cloyne but the speech was
about everywhere this happened,' says one of his closest advisers.
Some of the assertions made in the speech about the behaviour of the
Vatican per se were later shown to be questionable – a matter that
received little attention. Certainly the Vatican was sufficiently annoyed
to withdraw its Nuncio – an extremely unusual move for a state that
takes diplomacy very seriously indeed. But questions about the details
of Kenny's charges did not lessen the speech's impact. In his questioning and his anger, Kenny was speaking for a whole generation of Irish
people, and of Catholics. Much of what Kenny did in his first year as
Taoiseach was forced upon him by circumstance, or was the result of

the constrained choices his government faced. This was different. There was more to government under the gimlet eye of the Troika than the endless tyranny of the fiscal numbers, after all. Political life continued. So did elections, and there was a big one coming.

Last man standing

It's usually impossible to gauge the significance of an electoral contest, either on the grounds of its outcome or the contest itself, until some time has passed. Mary Robinson's historic defeat of Brian Lenihan in 1990 was a breakthrough for the liberal and secular values that would become ascendant in a rapidly 'modernizing' Ireland, and an explicit rejection of traditional, conservative politics. It was an enormously important event for women in Ireland on many levels, but it also presaged much of the cultural politics of the 1990s. In the same way, Mary McAleese's election became a sort of referendum on whether it was acceptable to be a Northern Catholic and be involved in political life south of the border. Six months before the Good Friday Agreement, the electorate decided that, yes, it was. Partition might well be permanent, they thought, but it should also be porous.

It is a relatively brief remove from the events of September–October 2011, but it is difficult to ascribe any of the same epoch-defining characteristics to the presidential election that sent Michael D. Higgins to Áras an Uachtaráin. It was remarkable in many ways, not least for the media-conducted soap-opera quality of it, but it appears to bear no profound meaning for politics or national life in Ireland.

What it did do was to present the news media with a much greater role than it had ever played in an election before. Because they are about one single contest, not hundreds, because there are a handful of candidates, not thousands, presidential elections are always more 'air war' than 'ground war'. They are fought out in the media, rather than on the doorsteps. But in no election in Irish history did the media play such an influential role. Partly this was because the candidates, for at least the early stages of the contest, seemed engaged in a competition to be as inoffensive as possible, to debate without saying anything of substance, to campaign without alienating a single voter by expressing an opinion with which anyone could take issue. Every one of the candidates was a 'human rights activist' (even Martin McGuinness); every one of them wanted to reach out and make the presidency inclusive; every one had inspiring personal stories to tell. It was a slow bicycle race of empathy. To an increasingly abrasive media, where newspapers competed more and more aggressively for a declining market, there were other, more interesting angles than the vision for an inclusive presidency. But, more importantly, it was because candidates for an office almost completely devoid of real political power have only their character to run on. And it was the media's job to question the characters of the candidates. This is what happens in election campaigns in free democracies.

Each of the candidates was scrutinized, interrogated, turned over and examined by a relentless media – with the possible exception of the eventual winner. Certainly his opponents felt that he had received a softer ride, something most of them ascribed to a soft-left bias among journalists. Whatever about that, it's probably fair to say that if the election had been held solely among people who work in the media, Michael D. Higgins would have won it by a lot more. The media scrutiny effectively destroyed the candidacies of David Norris, Mary Davis, Dana and – very belatedly – Seán Gallagher. The campaigns of Martin McGuinness and Gay Mitchell faltered for different reasons. McGuinness was limited by the reality of his IRA past – partition may be porous, but it is not amnesiac; and Mitchell because he turned out to be a dreadful candidate.

Mitchell won his party's nomination over the disinclination of the party's leadership to back him. He was initially reluctant to stand for the candidacy and would never have done so against John Bruton, if the former Taoiseach could have been persuaded to stand. But, like his predecessor Garret FitzGerald in 1990, Bruton couldn't be. Bruton's *nolle prosequi* meant that there was no outstanding candidate.

With Fine Gael having supplanted Fianna Fáil as the dominant force in Irish politics, many in the party expected the presidency to be the last Fianna Fáil bastion to fall to their advance. They wanted a 'real' Fine Gaeler in the job. Bruton would have been ideal. But Mitchell would do. At the wedding of party organizer Colm Jordan in Donegal in early June, some younger TDs, many ideologically more conservative than older generations of Fine Gael TDs, urged Mitchell to stand. At the funeral of party grandee Declan Costello in early June, as the party's aristocracy gathered in the Sacred Heart Church in Donnybrook, Mitchell was similarly prompted to go for it by an older generation. Within days, he had decided to stand.

The party's actual political leadership wasn't so sure. Attempting to influence the outcome of a vote by leaking findings – or supposed findings – of an opinion poll is hardly the most subtle entry in the book of political tricks, but it's often quite effective. In the days before the Fine Gael selection convention, newspaper stories appeared citing private polling, which apparently suggested that Mitchell would not win the presidential election if selected. The tactic was so transparent that it enraged many Fine Gael TDs. It certainly infuriated Mitchell, who demanded to see the research. Election mastermind Frank Flannery subsequently said on RTÉ radio that, while they had commissioned research on the presidency, they hadn't actually tested the strengths of individual candidates. To put it mildly, this stretched credibility.

But nor was the leadership convinced of the alternatives. Mairead McGuinness had been panting for the party's nomination for months, but, while she had a following among the rural grassroots, some of the party's TDs had never forgiven her for what they saw as her double standards in the heave against Kenny – inciting rebellion and then, when she adjudged its chances of success to be poor, conspicuously trumpeting her loyalty to the leadership. More than a few TDs promised payback if they ever got the chance. Now an opportunity helpfully presented itself. The party leadership made a less emotional decision: they just looked at her numbers and thought, Nah.

Actually, the handlers had another idea. Pat Cox, the former Progressive Democrats TD, independent MEP and president of the European Parliament, had been circling for months. He popped up as a counsellor to the party in its 'transition' period after the election. His name had been tentatively linked with the party's nomination for the presidency. That's how it always starts. On 7 June he applied to join his local branch in Cork. He then went on a pilgrimage – the famous Camino to the shrine of St James in Santiago de Compostela – perhaps to seek the endorsement of the Almighty for his crusade. Wags suggested it would be a conversation of equals.

Fine Gael chose its candidate at a convention of the party's electoral college in the Regency Hotel in Dublin on a glorious day in early July. The sunny weather outside was mirrored in the hall; the delegates were sure that they were choosing the new president of Ireland. Even the Taoiseach, though trying to warn against overconfidence, couldn't contain himself, telling delegates, 'As we speak, the future of Áras an Uachtaráin potentially is being counted in the next room.' Mitchell won handily; Kenny could barely contain his unhappiness at the result. 'Am I supposed to be going around grinning like a Cheshire cat at everything?' he responded, with uncharacteristic sharpness, to a journalist who asked him why he looked so grumpy. Mitchell beamed. But it would be the highpoint of his campaign.

Gay Mitchell was unable to manage the most basic task of a candidate in any election: persuading people to like or admire him and so want to vote for him. This was peculiar. He was a substantial figure whose Christian Democrat views hardly put him at odds with the electorate. He had in the past proved to be a successful vote-getter. He had been Ireland's best MEP by miles. He had won a competitive contest for his party's nomination. Fianna Fáil was not in the field. But, by God, did his campaign bomb.

If the selection of Mitchell demonstrated that there were limits to the leadership's control of the party, the outcome of the election would show that Kenny's machine knew what it was talking about. But it also showed Kenny's reluctance to wield the power of his office; if he had openly backed Cox and told his TDs 'This is my candidate and I want you to select him', it's difficult to see how they could have refused. The unwillingness to take a decision was reminiscent of nobody so much as Bertie Ahern, and Kenny's lack of straightforward leadership allowed a vacuum to develop that was skilfully exploited by Mitchell. He was a tactically astute politician, if hardly a man to sell a vision to the country. The Fine Gael leadership would later be caustic about Mitchell's campaign ('our fucking idiot of a candidate' was how one senior minister referred to him throughout a conversation with me), but in truth they – and Kenny – bore much of the blame for the situation.

It's a testament to the way Fianna Fáil still dominated the political imagination of the country – if no longer its actual politics – that the saga of whether the party would run a candidate garnered so much attention in the months before the presidential campaign actually began. Fianna Fáil was months after an electoral cataclysm, and Micheál Martin was minded to sit it out. He toyed with the idea of running broadcaster Gay Byrne, who initially appeared open to the idea. Byrne entertained a call from Martin to discuss the project at his holiday home in Donegal that August. He had some friends over to dinner that night. Byrne's guests were Frank Flannery, Fine Gael's most important electoral strategist, and his wife. Byrne was tempted, but after much airplay of a story that was a silly-season gift to the media, he was not convinced. That left Fianna Fáil without a candidate. Many in the camp couldn't believe that the grand old party would not run a candidate in a national election, much less for the presidency, which had been a Fianna Fáil possession with the one brief hiatus of the Robinson woman. But not to run a candidate when Sinn Féin was breathing down its neck?

The Sinn Féin threat to Fianna Fáil has always been overemphasized, as the smarter Sinn Féin strategists had long appreciated. The two parties were largely fishing in different pools for their support. In the general election just gone compared to the previous one, Fianna Fáil had lost fully a quarter of all votes cast, dropping from 42 per cent to 17 per cent. Sinn Féin had picked up 3 per cent. Given the obviousness of the numbers, it's remarkable how few people appreciated this. Martin did. He stuck to his guns, and after several half rebellions in his parliamentary party that demonstrated just how shattered the party's sense of itself was, Fianna Fáil sat out the contest.

Independent Oireachtas members and county councils also had, if they were so minded in sufficient numbers, the power of nomination to the contest. They were predictably anxious to assert themselves on the political stage, so the field filled up fast. The Trinity College senator David Norris had been booming about a possible presidential run for months and was now definitely in the field with a campaign team, supporters and a fair media wind. That would turn spectacularly against him when letters begging clemency for his erstwhile partner, facing trial in Israel for the statutory rape of a Palestinian youth, were discovered. Combined with the earlier airing of views that appeared to endorse sexual relationships between adults and youths, the letters destroyed Norris's campaign. Later, egged on by supporters and by the *Sunday Independent*, he re-entered the race at the beginning of September. It was not a wise decision.

Afterwards, Norris was extraordinarily bitter about his experience, and came to believe that there was an organized media conspiracy to bring him down. Instead of time healing the wounds, it appears to have allowed them to fester. He wrote an engaging but exceedingly sour and self-pitying memoir. Norris had fought a long and lonely and incredibly brave fight for the rights of gay Irishmen and women, and the steady achievement of those rights remains his great legacy. Before the presidential election he was widely regarded as an occasionally rather too loud national treasure. Too often during the campaign he came across as a narcissistic old vaudevillian. The sad fact for him was that as the country got to know him better it liked him less, at least as a potential president. Afterwards he was a much diminished figure. That was a tragedy for him, and a pity for the national life he had enlivened, and served well.

Sinn Féin eventually ran Martin McGuinness, seemingly because they could not think of anyone else, and wanted to fill the Fianna Fáil-shaped hole on the ballot paper. Mary Davis, the Special Olympics chief, ran a well-organized and well-funded campaign that turned out to be curiously empty and ultimately pointless. Throughout the campaign, she failed to find a single pithy, convincing answer to the obvious question: Why do you want to be president? Dana Rosemary Scallon flew a pro-life flag but even before her campaign self-combusted in a welter of familial acrimony, which involved allegations of sexual abuse by one of her siblings, her wispy polling numbers demonstrated that, while there are an awful lot of pro-life people in Ireland, there are relatively few who vote on this issue above all others.

But the most intriguing bid was by another independent, Seán Gallagher. An entrepreneur in construction during a construction boom, latterly a minor television personality and – it eventually emerged – a former Fianna Fáil activist, Gallagher was a man who dreamed big dreams, especially about himself. His appeal to optimism and his apparent guilelessness struck a chord with the public, and his campaign built slowly before catching fire, with perfect timing, in the final weeks. By the time the final weekend's polls were published days before the vote, he seemed unstoppable. 'Elections can change in an instant,' I wrote the Sunday before polling, 'and not a vote has been cast yet. The remaining few days of the campaign will no doubt see further acute focus on Gallagher, his business activities and his Fianna Fáil connections. Michael D. Higgins is probably close enough to capitalize if Gallagher stumbles. But . . . it would take something extraordinary to change [the outcome] now.' I had no idea what was about to come.

The final days were an appropriate dénouement to a roller-coaster campaign. Amid a seven-candidate debate on RTÉ's *Frontline* television programme, McGuinness challenged Gallagher about fundraising for Fianna Fáil; a tweet purporting to come from Sinn Féin promised evidence that Gallagher was lying. His halting explanations, fatally, included the words 'If he gave me an envelope . . . If he gave me the cheque it was made out to Fianna Fáil headquarters . . .' From then on, it was a question of how bad the damage would be.

It was fatal. Gallagher dug himself in deeper and deeper, with each explanation and evasion losing tens of thousands more votes. It wasn't just McGuinness's charges either. A *Frontline* audience member, Glenna Lynch, had already asked some pointed questions about his career in business. The next morning on radio, again with Pat Kenny, when Kenny referred to the matters she had raised, Gallagher bristled. 'Who was the businesswoman and what's her background? And where does she come from and what party does she belong to, Pat? I'm tired of people being wheeled out with agendas.' Sensationally, Glenna Lynch rang into the programme, saying that she had no political affiliations and was just an ordinary voter who had concerns about Gallagher's business practices. She then came out with a litany of questions about aspects of his business dealings. Picking through them took the remaining time of his first media appearance after the *Frontline* debate. He was rattled and defensive. Gallagher's team couldn't believe what was happening: their candidate was immolating himself before their eyes. He was destroyed in the final interviews, particularly by RTÉ's Bryan Dobson.

The *Frontline* debate had changed the outcome of the election. Michael D. Higgins, the one candidate who had probably avoided a truly searching examination during the course of the campaign, sailed serenely on.

The presidential campaign was highly entertaining for Ireland's many engaged political spectators. But it mattered little to the business of government in a country that was still deep in an economic crisis and whose political leadership still harboured deep and well-founded doubts about its prospects for exiting that state of crisis. The bald truth is that while Labour was delighted to win the presidential election, and Fine Gael was sorry for Gay Mitchell, neither party leadership thought the election mattered a great deal.

One lesson that the backrooms of each party did draw from it all: negative campaigning works. Outright, personalized, negative campaigning had largely been eschewed in Irish electoral contests, not because of any innate gentility among the native political class, but because its efficacy was highly questionable. Bertie Ahern, who possessed more than any other modern Irish politician an instinctive sense for what voters wanted and would put up with, never allowed it on any significant scale. The presidential election of 2011, however, showed that a candidate could be destroyed by a focus on his or her past mistakes or foibles. In the US presidential election, which was also then taking place, Barack Obama was demonstrating the same thing, with an aggressive campaign against Mitt Romney that effectively sought to disqualify him from the office of the presidency because of his wealth.

There was an important qualification to this, however: attacking opponents also came with a cost to the attacker. Gay Mitchell launched savage attacks on Martin McGuinness, which may have dented McGuinness but following which Mitchell also sank, leading the *Sunday Independent*'s Eoghan Harris to praise Mitchell as having laid down his 'political life' for Ireland. McGuinness himself saw his vote seep away in the final week after his attacks on Gallagher. So that was the other, equally important, part of the lesson: it was better to get the media guys to do the dirty work. Well, the media guys were more than willing to get stuck into that particular task.

12

'The love is gone'

There was a heavy agenda at the cabinet meeting, and the Taoiseach was clipping through it at a reasonable pace. One of the first things he had told his ministers was that he wanted them to 'keep making decisions', and he aimed to set an example at cabinet meetings. The cabinet had been exceptionally unified in the early days: the honeymoon, the feel-good factor of the visits, the solidarity of a great burden shared – they all led to a sense of common purpose that was strongest at the top of government. Now, though, some noticed that an occasional *froideur* had entered into cabinet meetings, a shift in mood that some ministers noticed and commented on privately. 'The love is gone,' one told me. 'Everything is a negotiation now.' That autumn there was less trust between the parties, and more checking up, more trading off. Everything was a deal. 'And you never know if it's your thing that's going to be traded.' Some attributed the change in mood to the upcoming budget process. Some believed officials who told them that this usually happened at some stage in coalition governments. And some pointed to an *Irish Independent* story that appeared on the morning of Labour's September think-in, clearly designed to ruin whatever message-management the party had planned for that day.

'Dithering Gilmore "fails to deliver at cabinet"' the headline had blared over Fionnan Sheahan's front-page story, as Labour TDs, senators and staff headed to the Mount Wolseley Hotel in Tullow, County Carlow, for the annual pre-Dáil term meeting. The piece cited multiple ministers who dismissed Gilmore's contributions at cabinet in the six months since the coalition had been formed in terms such as 'indecisive', 'unsure of himself' and 'quiet'. 'He can't make up his mind about anything without Mark Garrett telling him,' one minister was quoted as saying. Gilmore's performance was contrasted unfavourably with the big beasts of the Labour cabinet – Brendan Howlin, Pat Rabbitte and Ruairi Quinn. By the time Labour representatives arrived in Tullow, it was the story of the day. Often, indeed usually, the story of the day is forgotten by the end of the week. This one wasn't.

Labour responded by pooh-poohing the story in public, and trashing it viciously in private. The paper had an agenda, Labour staffers suggested, and anyway do you really believe the quotes? Gilmore and his aides were not concerned. It was just a bit of mischief-making by the *Independent*. But nobody was buying this studied insouciance, and by the weekend Labour's defence had pivoted. Instead of claiming they disbelieved the story, Labour spinners were now on a different tack. The Sunday papers were briefed that 'Labour strategists' believed that a 'senior Fine Gael figure' was behind the bad-mouthing of Gilmore. Labour sources were content for journalists to believe that it was the environment minister, Phil Hogan.

Actually, other cabinet ministers later confirmed to me that this was also their impression of Gilmore. None of them was Phil Hogan. But Hogan would go on to suspect Mark Garrett of briefing against him. So, senior figures in the coalition were now briefing against one another because they suspected their coalition partners of briefing against them. Normal politics had returned.

But this late-October cabinet meeting was clipping along without any rancour. As with all cabinet meetings, there were several uncontroversial items – promotions in the Defence Forces, annual reports, and so forth – that ministers whizzed through quickly. Eamon Gilmore sought approval for ambassadorial appointments. Everyone assented. Next item. But halfway through the next item, Alan Shatter piped up. He was still reading though the previous memo from the Department of Foreign Affairs on the ambassadors. 'Hey, maybe I'm not the person to raise this, but . . .' Everyone turned to him. He wanted to know: Are we really closing the Irish Embassy in the Vatican?

Gilmore's department had actually notified Kenny's staff of the proposal to shut the Vatican Embassy, though it didn't immediately cause them any alarm. 'I didn't prick my ears up,' says one staffer.

'Perhaps I should have.' Now that the decision had been presented to cabinet, it was impossible to shout it down – it would have been a damaging rebuff to the Tánaiste. Gilmore presented it as a cost-saving move, justified by an internal review. And once it was done, it was done. The government just had to stick by it.

Kenny got serious flak about it at his parliamentary party. Many of his TDs felt that Kenny's Vatican speech was one thing – it was a pointed criticism on one issue (and besides, the public and media reaction was positive) – but shutting the embassy 'was a bit gratuitous'. Fine Gael TDs and some ministers promised reviews and expressed confidence in a future reopening, and a postcard campaign and a wave of representations to their offices made a lot of them feel awkward about it. Gilmore continued to justify the closure on a cost basis, with other ministers and TDs following the party's press office talking points about there being two embassies and two ambassadors in Rome – an unsustainable extravagance in these straitened times. Well, sure. There were also three ambassadors in Brussels, two in Vienna (one at the OSCE), two in Switzerland (one at the Geneva branch of the UN) and two in Paris (one to the OECD). There's a consul (with three staff) and an ambassador (to the UN, with eight staff) in New York. Privately, many diplomats were horrified, especially when Gilmore blithely asserted that the Vatican Embassy produced no 'economic return'. 'If the reason for a diplomatic service is to produce an economic return,' one diplomat complained to me, 'then why do we have embassies all over Africa? Why do we have an aid programme? Why do we have an embassy in Luxembourg?'

Fine Gael read all this stuff, and it rankled. In reality, it was a pretty shameless pandering to Labour's base, and everyone could see it. Still, it wasn't as unpopular with middle Ireland as Fine Gael and many columnists seemed to think. Labour later commissioned a poll showing that while voters were lukewarm on the closure (43 per cent in favour to 35 per cent against), Labour supporters were much more enthusiastic (56 per cent in favour to 18 per cent against). Labour would seek to punctuate government policy with similar nods to its base – a measure of how the leadership constantly felt the need to assert its identity. There were sound political reasons for this, but Fine Gael ministers and senior staff would find it increasingly tiresome. However, the fact was that most voters had bigger things to worry about. Some of those bigger things would soon become the stuff of political debate: the coalition was embarking on its first budget.

Insofar as there is any certainty about these things in politics, Michael Noonan knew that he was going to be the finance minister. When the two parties agreed on the creation of the Department of Public Expenditure, Noonan had expected that Pat Rabbitte would be the appointee and so be his colleague in constructing budgets. Though he knew he could work with Brendan Howlin too, he had been surprised when Howlin was appointed to the new ministry. Now he was surprised at how harmoniously they were working together in putting together their first budget.

If relations between Noonan and Howlin flourished during their first budget process, things were less harmonious when negotiations with the big-spending ministries commenced. There was a spectacularly bad-tempered meeting in early October between Howlin and his officials and Shatter and the team from the Department of Justice, with disagreement centring on – but not limited to – who exactly should pay the €36 million security bill (it cost €24 million in Garda overtime alone) for policing the visits of the Queen and President Obama. The row had simmered on all summer, and with public expenditure now seeking deep cuts in the justice budget, Shatter was making a stand. A few weeks earlier he had complained in the Dáil that he was expected to find €340 million in spending cuts over the next three years. Like every minister facing excruciating budget squeezes, this wasn't how he imagined government would be. The shouting could be heard by officials in the next office.

In fairness to Shatter, the finance and public expenditure officials knew he was fighting his corner. Within the strange and self-contained world of budget negotiations, he was fighting fair. They didn't feel the same about the health and social protection ministers.

Throughout October and November, a series of stories appeared in the newspapers foretelling all sorts of calamities for the infirm, the young, the old, the sick and the indigent in the forthcoming budget.

All budgets are preceded by a process of a negotiation, during which proposed policy actions – cuts or spending in particular areas – are considered. They either stay in or are discarded. Months out, lists of options are circulated and swapped. Leaking details of a measure that's under consideration, in order to generate public opposition and therefore make proceeding with it politically unwise, has been a widely used tactic by ministers since long before the fiscal looseness of the Ahern era encouraged ministers to behave like Augustus Gloop in Willy Wonka's chocolate factory. It wasn't invented in 2011. But until 2011 it had scarcely been more obviously used, nor had it generated as much ill-feeling among cabinet members. One minister says bluntly, 'It was the first time that the government started to lose ground and do itself harm.'

While finance ministers are hardly above leaking to prepare the ground for cuts and tax increases to come, on this occasion it was the judgement of Government Buildings, and the officials who staffed the EMC ministers, that devoting two months to talking about how bad cuts were going to be was political madness. So the leaks, in other words, weren't sanctioned. It was universally believed in government that the sources for the stories were Joan Burton and James Reilly, or more likely people acting with their imprimatur. It was not an unreasonable belief.

Straining under the pressure of constructing a budget that had to raise – as per the Troika's memorandum – some €3.6 billion, Howlin and Noonan were incensed at the leaking from social protection and health. They came to believe that the two departments were engaged in a struggle for resources through the pages of the newspapers. The two finance ministers – and their staff – frequently complained to their colleagues. When Reilly went to a meeting of the Parliamentary Labour Party and warned TDs and senators about the cuts that Howlin was going to impose on him, Government Buildings, particularly the Labour side of it, was incensed. 'He can fuck off if he thinks we are going to leak this stuff for him,' one TD told a senior party official. It was leaked anyway. Noonan thought the whole thing was 'destabilizing'; he could also see that it was making Howlin's job, which was all about slashing spending budgets, harder.

Some officials thought Burton was trying to make Howlin's job impossible. The leaking was also discussed at the EMC, where the two finance ministers asked the Taoiseach and Tánaiste to raise the matter at cabinet. A 'lecture' was duly delivered – 'for all the good it did'. The warnings were 'very pointed', says one minister. They were also very ignored.

In the end, the biggest budget leak didn't come from anyone in the government – not the Irish government anyway. Three weeks before December's budget day, it emerged that the draft proposals for the Irish budget had been circulated to the finance committee of the German Bundestag. It revealed, *inter alia*, that a 2 per cent increase in VAT was on the cards – the sort of sensitive information that would probably have prompted a formal investigation if the leaking had happened in Dublin. There was uproar in the Dáil; a European Commission official said the leaking was 'regrettable', but confirmed that the same draft budget had been sent to all EU finance ministers. A year on from the bailout, this was what 'loss of sovereignty' looked like. Germany shrugged. Well, the Germans thought, we're paying, aren't we? The actual budget itself caused less of a fuss.

Before the budget, the coalition had suffered its first ministerial casualty and its first defeat at the polls. The Labour 'super-junior' minister Willie Penrose, who sat at cabinet even if he was legally not a member of it, resigned over the closure of a military barracks in his hometown of Mullingar as part of a series of budget cuts.

Penrose's departure was a blow to the Labour Party, but, more importantly, it was a reality check – a reminder of the type of thing that would become inevitable as austerity bit deeper and deeper in the coming years. Penrose was a totemic figure in the party, mostly because he commanded a stunningly effective and disciplined local organization that had carved out a secure left-wing seat in a seemingly inhospitable rural three-seater. Indeed, Penrose's was one of the safest Labour seats in the country, and the tightly marshalled platoons of Westmeath delegates that marched into party conferences were very much the envy of many Labour TDs, some of whom were beginning to cast nervous glances over their shoulders at their local organizations. This local strength now impelled Penrose to break with the government: when it came to a choice between local and national, he plumped for the certainty of the hero's welcome in Mullingar. He claimed that Alan Shatter's decision 'was not backed up by facts and figures'. Penrose pressed hard. There's always a way of fixing budget numbers to justify keeping a barracks or a hospital or a Garda station open in the minister's home patch.

Pat Rabbitte tried hard to keep Penrose on board, but the barracks had too much local resonance for him. Howlin tried to help too, but Shatter was adamant. If his budgets in justice and defence were being slashed, he would decide where the cuts were to be made. In fact, Shatter told colleagues that Howlin's department offered him more money if he would keep the barracks open. Howlin's officials produced observations that showed closing the barracks wouldn't save any money. Ministers remember memos being withdrawn from the cabinet agenda at the last minute to try to create space for a deal. When Penrose proposed an alternative plan that would have saved the barracks, Shatter brushed it aside. Several of the Labour ministers thought Shatter could have relented, but he was not for turning. He had to manage all the barracks closures, not just one. Ultimately it was Shatter's gig, and if he insisted, Labour knew it had no option but to back him.

Penrose was extremely bitter towards the Fine Gael minister. He had been unwell and complained to colleagues that Shatter had pressed ahead with plans to close the barracks while he was in hospital. Ultimately, he got sympathy, but not support. When Penrose finally announced his resignation, neither Gilmore nor the rest of the Labour ministers were surprised.

Fine Gael had already suffered a lower-profile defection in the summer. Roscommon TD Denis Naughten lost the party whip after voting for an opposition motion that condemned the closure of an emergency unit at Roscommon Hospital. The future of the local hospital had been a touchstone local issue for years, and needless to say all candidates had promised to save it during the election campaign. Now the government had decided to close the unit, arguing safety standards and the independent advice offered by the government's hospitals inspectorate. Local opinion, as sure in Roscommon as it is in many other parts of the country that central government didn't care about preserving rural communities (sometimes with good reason; sometimes not), was incensed, and simply disbelieved the medical grounds put forward as a reason to proceed with closure. The pressure on the two local Fine Gael TDs, Naughten and Frank Feighan, stoked by a third local independent, TD Luke 'Ming' Flanagan, was intense. They came to different decisions. 'James told us at cabinet that Naughten would be okay – he wouldn't vote against the party,' said one cabinet minister, questioning the health minister's bedside manner. 'So of course he did.'

Naughten's departure was hardly of such import that it affected the coalition's ability to govern. In fact, at senior levels some whispered that it was no harm as a demonstration of the cabinet's resolve. But a recording of the Taoiseach making exactly the same promises about Roscommon as his candidates – preserved by chance by Niamh Connolly of the *Sunday Business Post* – created some embarrassment for Kenny. Despite initial firm denials by Kenny and his staff that he had ever promised anything to Roscommon, Connolly produced the recording of the Taoiseach speaking at a meeting in the town during the election campaign in which he promised to 'protect and defend' the hospital services. 'We are committed to maintaining the services at Roscommon County Hospital.' It was about as much a bang-up job as could be imagined. The paper sought comment from Kenny on the Saturday – the day of the Fine Gael presidential convention – specifically mentioning a tape recording in Roscommon. Amazingly, that afternoon at the post-convention press conference, Kenny continued to deny making any promises in Roscommon. The damage was probably minimal, but it could have been an awful lot worse. It also prompted the question in many people's minds: What else has he promised?

The two resignations demonstrated that even in times of severe austerity, voters expected – and politicians were prepared to promise, even when they had no power to deliver – special treatment for special and local interests. But the economic and fiscal realities couldn't be ignored; the wave of cuts hitting every level of public services was stretching Ireland's hyper-localist politics, in some cases to breaking point. The snapping that periodically interrupted political debate was the sound of political careers ending.

Though Alan Shatter had stuck to his guns over the cuts that led to Penrose's departure, the combative justice and defence minister wasn't quite having everything his own way. On the same day as the presidential election voters had, predictably, endorsed an amendment to the constitution to cut judges' pay. However, they had rejected another amendment that would have strengthened the power of Oireachtas inquiries. The proposal, designed to overturn a Supreme Court judgment limiting of the powers of the Oireachtas to conduct investigations and inquiries, was apparently uncontroversial but brought to the surface one of the most enduring undercurrents of Irish political life: the deep suspicion of central government and of politicians. In a way, it was of a type with the opposition that blew up in Fine Gael's face on the hospital issue in Roscommon. On this occasion, it was awakened by the warnings of several senior lawyers and former attorneys general – including eminences of such vertiginous loftiness as Michael McDowell, Paul Gallagher, Dermot Gleeson and Peter Sutherland – that the referendum would weaken individuals' right to their good name and place too much power in the hands of politicians. As ever, Shatter was unable to pass a gathering of barristers without giving it a kick – he described their intervention as 'nonsense' and 'simply wrong'. Given the choice of believing a politician or anyone else, the public went with option B.

The referendum was narrowly defeated, to the great annoyance of many in government who had planned a lengthy and detailed embarrassment of Fianna Fáil's stewardship of economic and banking matters in an inquiry held under the new, enhanced powers. Inevitably, Shatter (and, to a lesser extent, Howlin, who had drafted the bill establishing the planned new powers of inquiry) was blamed for the defeat. Opposition deputies teased the justice minister about it unmercifully in the Dáil.

Shatter would prove to be a minister of positively hyperactive reforming zeal; he would also turn out to be both a valuable ally and a constant irritant to other ministers. 'You just can't shut him up at cabinet,' complained one, half seriously. 'Even Enda can't shut him up.' His communications with the attorney general were so frequent that she had to secure his agreement that he would not ring her before seven in the morning. There has never been a justice minister so disliked by the legal establishment of the Bar and the Bench – so much so that he would later be involved in an unprecedented public row with senior judges.

Proinsias De Rossa did not like being hung up on. He especially did not like an abrupt termination of a telephone call when he was laying down the law to a parliamentary colleague. So when he found himself speaking into a dead phone halfway – or so he thought – through a conversation with his fellow MEP Nessa Childers about her opposition to the government's nomination of the secretary general of the Department of Finance, Kevin Cardiff, to the European Court of Auditors, he rang back immediately, incensed. Childers did not answer. De Rossa left an angry message. His voicemail expressed his annoyance at being hung up on, asserted that he was the head of the Labour delegation of MEPs (there were three of them) and threatened Childers with expulsion from the group. Childers was taken aback by all this. De Rossa, she later confirmed, 'had used an expletive'.

'It was like being attacked by a pack of wolves,' she said.

If De Rossa was a wolf, he was a greying one. The former Democratic Left leader had departed Dublin for Brussels after the merger with the Labour Party and he was on the last lap of a long and varied political career. His journey had taken him from teenage IRA membership to a remorseless anti-Republicanism, and from the fringes of politics to the cabinet as minister for social welfare in the 1995–7 Rainbow coalition. He had presided over the eventual disappearance as an independent entity of the Workers' Party/Democratic Left strain in Irish politics, which had once punched far above its electoral weight in political influence. Depending on your point of view, it had either disappeared from Irish life, or had taken over the Labour Party. There were more than a few Labour people, some of them in or around the cabinet, who believed the latter.

De Rossa may have been winding towards retirement, but there was still some business to be done, and his view of parliamentary and party discipline contrasted rather vividly with Childers's unstinting conviction that she must do what she believed was right, whatever that happened to be at a given point in time and however inconvenient it might be. De Rossa later apologized, but not in terms that were sufficiently contrite for his colleague. 'With good reason,' Childers later reflected in an interview, 'because he then said I was appalling and populist in front of my colleagues in the Socialist Group.'

Back in Dublin, news of Proinsias's anger and Nessa's wounded dignity was greeted with great amusement – except by the people in Government Buildings, who were trying to fix a thorny political problem: moving Kevin Cardiff out of the top finance job. The cabinet had decided to nominate him to the Court of Auditors – a decision that many government backbenchers and ministers found inexplicable, or at least indefensible. So the last thing the government needed was an MEP – a Labour one at that – making the wrong noises about the suitability of its nominee in Brussels.

Cardiff had been head of banking for several years in the department during a period when the Irish banks committed their collective act of suicide. He was present to offer counsel in Government Buildings on the night of the bank guarantee of 2008. But it was his performance in the briefings to the Fine Gael and Labour negotiators in March of 2011 that really shook the soon-to-be ministers' confidence in him. They could hardly believe it was so bad. The discovery of a government accounting error in the weeks before the appointment, which misstated the state's financial position by a whopping €3.6 billion, didn't make things any easier. Michael Noonan did not want to be going around firing his top officials, though; that's just not the way business is done in the Irish public service. There are good and bad reasons for this. But he did want a change, and when the Court of Auditors opening came up in November, he found a neat way out it.

The trouble was that the politics of appointing a senior civil servant – against whom no personal wrongdoing had ever been suggested, but who had attended at some of the greatest policy disasters ever embarked upon by an Irish government – to a lucrative post in Europe were completely toxic. In a country where ordinary incomes had been ferociously squeezed by a combination of wage cuts and higher taxes – and nowhere were wage cuts felt more keenly than among the journalists who mediated national debate and whose industry was among those hardest hit by the recession – there was a growing fixation with the level of official, political and publicly funded salaries. This had a basis in fact – Irish public sector salaries were hugely generous by comparison with those of most European countries – but it sometimes seemed as if it was the only issue that mattered. Throw into that atmosphere a salary and benefits package for Cardiff topping €300,000 a year, and it was easy to see why the *Liveline* phones were lighting up. And when *Liveline* lights up, backbenchers get worried. Childers's intervention made them edgier still. When Cardiff was initially rejected by a committee of the European Parliament for the post, there was a brief panic in Dublin. After some political muscle was exercised in Brussels, he was confirmed in a subsequent vote of the parliament in mid December.

The whole episode left Labour backbenchers queasy. Privately, many said they were prepared to take flak for all sorts of nasty stuff that the party leadership decided was necessary. But this? The party leadership confined itself to wondering: How did we end up carrying the can for it? It was something that they were going to get increasingly worried by: the tendency of voters to blame Labour for unpleasant things the government did, while Fine Gael remained unaffected. They exaggerated the extent to which the public reacted in this way, but that didn't mean their concern wasn't real. In the months ahead, it would continue to gnaw at Labour.

13

The menace of Denis

It was a day that Fianna Fáil had known was coming for more than a decade. The Flood – later the Mahon – Tribunal had been investigating planning corruption in Dublin since the 1990s. In the middle years of the 2000s, with the scalps of Liam Lawlor, Pádraig Flynn and Ray Burke tied to its spear, as well as scores of minor characters, the tribunal circled inevitably, inexorably, ever more tightly around Bertie Ahern. It eventually destroyed him, not by proving corruption or anything near it, but because he was unable to explain satisfactorily the existence of sums of money in his bank accounts, or when he didn't have a bank account, in his office safe. Ahern's service to the state will almost certainly be more favourably judged by history than by his peers. But when the Mahon Tribunal report was published in March 2012, his own party was ready and waiting: it began the process of expelling him. The former leader of the party, who had dominated Irish politics more completely – electorally anyway – than anyone since De Valera, was now just a prop in another political gesture. Fianna Fáil's paltry twenty seats were as much a part of Ahern's legacy as his three general election wins, but it was still impossible not to see the bathos of it.

The report was more than just the exposure of individuals: it catalogued the systematic privatization of parts of the public realm for individual gain, and the perversion of an entire system of politics to that end. That system was not completely exclusive to Fianna Fáil, but it was a culture endemic in parts of that party. Developer Tom Gilmartin's famous retort during a ministerial-level shakedown for cash – 'You guys make the fucking Mafia look like monks' – still seems appropriate. There was a Mafia-like quality to the planning corruption, complete with its secret networks, its commitment to ensuring the capos wet their beaks, and the pervasive *omertà* that greeted the outside world. It was odd, then, that within a few weeks the fallout from the tribunal's report seemed to have pivoted back to Fine Gael, and focused attention on the party's sometimes controversial relationship with telecoms tycoon Denis O'Brien.

Within days, the Taoiseach was facing questions in the Dáil about his public appearances with O'Brien. How did that happen?

A couple of things drove it. Joan Burton was at the centre of one of them. 'It is perhaps time for the government to reflect on how it should in future interact with people against whom adverse findings have been made by tribunals,' she told the Dáil during a debate on the Mahon report. The reference was a clear one to pictures of Kenny in the company of O'Brien at an event at the New York Stock Exchange the previous week. O'Brien, she noted, had continued to 'pop up at various public events', despite the criticisms levelled at him in the Moriarty Tribunal report a year previously. Kenny insisted he didn't know who was going to be there – a line accepted by most people until it was later reported that his office had specifically been briefed that O'Brien would attend the event. Burton went on to warn about a 'Berlusconi-style, media-political complex . . . undermining the principles of transparent democracy'.

The criticism may have been a solo-run by Burton – she wasn't in the habit of clearing her speeches with Government Buildings – but she was speaking for a genuine unease in Labour about the whole O'Brien–Fine Gael connection. Brendan Howlin also demonstrated it when he suggested that there 'should be a consequence' for people 'against whom adverse findings are adduced by a tribunal of inquiry'. Burton was one thing. But when Howlin entered the fray, the Taoiseach's side of Government Buildings adduced all this as trouble on the way. But there was unease in Fine Gael too – Lucinda Creighton said that O'Brien should not be invited to government events – though such quarters generally adjudged discretion to be the better part of valour. Later, it emerged that Burton herself had actually met O'Brien in New York, an embarrassment that some of her colleagues relished, and joked about privately. But Labour's concern was real. RTÉ's *Prime Time* and the *Irish Times* began wondering what the government might do about the year-old Moriarty findings. Bizarrely, weeks after Mahon reported, it was Moriarty that was making the news.

The O'Brien issue was considered to be pressing by some in Labour because the tycoon was assembling a final push for the takeover of Independent News and Media, publishers of the *Irish Independent*, the *Sunday Independent* and the *Evening Herald*, and Ireland's largest newspaper group by some distance. O'Brien had sunk half a billion euros into the Independent group in an attempt to wrest control of it from the O'Reilly family – a development that seemed inevitable, though the business was now worth a small fraction of O'Brien's gargantuan outlay. At least part of the motivation for O'Brien's investment appeared to be unhappiness with the group's coverage of his business affairs, and of his involvement with the Moriarty Tribunal.

Independent executives, many of whom feared summary execution should O'Brien take over the group, were horrified by the government's apparent lassitude in confronting what they saw as a clear threat to press freedom. The *Sunday Independent*, in particular, began a vocal campaign against O'Brien's prospective ownership of the group, declaring him to be 'not a fit person' to control the newspapers. Some feared an O'Brien regime would publish only fawning coverage of the owners – of which, indeed, the papers had proved so capable during the long O'Reilly era. Others feared direct editorial interference, and their fears were heightened when Leslie Buckley, a director of the company and an ally of O'Brien, was revealed to have questioned the decision to allow Sam Smyth – a veteran reporter whom O'Brien viewed as hostile – to cover the Moriarty Tribunal. The editorial side was further offended when the chairman of the company, James Osborne, revealed that he had been contacted by O'Brien to get an article that mentioned him dropped from the following day's *Sunday Indo*. A clear threat to the freedom of the press, the O'Reilly side howled.

O'Brien was clearly sensitive, but he had some cause too – he pointed out that in one edition of the *Sunday Independent* there were fifteen negative stories about him. In any man's language, that's a campaign against him. The Moriarty report certainly gave just cause for coverage of O'Brien, but observers noted that the *Sunday*

Independent's O'Brien obsession only appeared to really get going when he was threatening a takeover of the group. Any newspaper worth its salt won't shirk from coverage that might embarrass a major shareholder on a matter of public interest. But few have ever waged such a campaign as editor Anne Harris did against O'Brien.

Across town in the *Irish Times*, where, like the rest of the Dublin media, they were watching fascinated, those with long memories recalled the outrage at the Indo group when the *Times* reported on the *Independent*'s attempt to use corporate muscle on the Rainbow government. When O'Reilly's Independent group failed to get what it wanted from the Fine Gael–Labour government – on the then politically sizzling issue of unlicensed television deflectors that provided British channels to large areas of the country – the *Irish Independent* published a front page editorial calling for a vote for Fianna Fáil and the Progressive Democrats at the 1997 election. If the *Indo* had forgotten, Fine Gael and Labour hadn't. Politicians have much longer memories for this sort of thing than journalists. In any event, the law relating to media ownership assumes proprietorial interference – that's why it is intended to restrict the number of media outlets an individual can own, rather than trying to govern the relationship between editors and proprietors.

The situation was complicated by a legal background that was in the process of changing. While media mergers and takeovers were overseen by the Department of Enterprise, where Richard Bruton was minister, the government had agreed legislation that would transfer oversight to Pat Rabbitte's Department of Communications – in other words potentially moving power to approve or reject an O'Brien takeover of the Indo group from Fine Gael to Labour. Bruton's department seemed in no rush to make any progress on the legislation, even as O'Brien gathered his forces in the boardroom. Terror reigned at the Independent among the O'Reilly camp. They went to lobby Rabbitte – chief executive Gavin O'Reilly, another Indo executive Karl Brophy and the journalist Sam Smyth, who had previously spoken to Rabbitte on the issue. The minister was concerned, but he harboured no illusions about the Independent group either.

Others in Labour viewed it as first and foremost a corporate take-over battle, rather than an urgent issue concerning the freedom of the press. Perhaps if it had been anyone other than the *Sunday Independent* making the argument, they might have listened more carefully, but Labour wasn't going to forget what it saw as two decades of spite directed at the party from the pages of the *Sindo*. Labour loathed the *Sunday Independent*, not just on a political level but as a cultural phenomenon, as much for its (actually much diminished) gossipy and trashy tone as for the right-wing politics of many of its columnists. Labour people at all levels could reel off any number of instances when the paper had issued dire warnings about letting Labour anywhere near the levers of power. Forgive us if we don't give a crap if one right-wing media owner replaces another, they thought.

But if they didn't care about the *Sunday Independent*, some in Labour did have a concern about O'Brien. Actually, they had two: one, that he owned too much of the Irish media – he already owned several radio stations, including Newstalk and Today FM – and two, the findings of the Moriarty Tribunal. But they also had a concern not to get drawn in to someone else's row. One senior figure in government told me that Labour was concerned about it, and was pondering what to do. But his main concern, he said, was not to get caught up in it. 'When elephants fight, the grass gets trampled. We'd like to avoid being the grass,' he explained. There were several hopeful stories in the *Sunday Indo* about Labour's concerns about O'Brien. They were based on fact, but the concern never translated into concrete action.

Rabbitte did propose that the media-ownership legislation be transferred to his department so that the new provisions could be enacted immediately, before any O'Brien takeover of the Independent group. Perhaps he would have intervened; perhaps not. In any event, Richard Bruton declined. Perhaps he was protecting O'Brien; perhaps not. It is certainly true that O'Brien gained effective control of the group, and that Bruton neither passed the legislation nor intervened. At the time of writing, the legislation has not been enacted.

O'Brien duly took control of the papers, and though the first casualty was Gavin O'Reilly, he has so far left editorial personnel unmolested, despite O'Brien's lieutenants and supporters having gleefully anticipated the rolling of many heads. A code for journalists has been proposed that would require management sanction for the publication of 'sustained or repeated adversarial material' – such as that published by the *Sunday Indo* about O'Brien – to the consternation of many inside. Those close to O'Brien are said to be enjoying the trepidation among some of their employees as much as actually moving against them – perhaps the anticipation is half the pleasure. In time, O'Brien's newspapers are likely to pay him at least as much deference as Tony O'Reilly's once did. In the meantime, journalists – many of them at present employed by the Independent group – continue to probe the finances of Michael Lowry and whatever influence Denis O'Brien has brought to bear on them. None, O'Brien insists. Quite a bit, says Moriarty. No legal action has been taken against O'Brien or Lowry on foot of the Moriarty report. For her part, *Sunday Independent* editor Anne Harris continues her quixotic but certainly brave campaign against the man who controls the company that owns her newspaper. If nothing else, she has demonstrated that ownership is not always the same thing as control.

Government concern at the media tends to be more related to output than ownership. As all governments do, this one felt it was being unfairly targeted by a hostile media. Environment minister Phil Hogan didn't speak for everyone in government when he called the *Sunday Indo* and the *Daily Mail* 'Knackers' and promised to 'put manners' on them, after they published on the day of the budget pictures of him having a cosy drink with his press secretary in a hotel in Doha. But their general view was that the government was getting an unfairly tough time from the media. The opposition thought the media were buying the government spin. No doubt there were many failings of the political media in covering the government, but they were principally the usual ones – a lack of context, short-termism, a weakness for accepting the conventional wisdom, over-hyping the scandal of the day or the week. It was true that the *Daily Mail*'s establishing of itself in the Irish market, with its considerable investment in political coverage and liking for 'Gotcha' stories, had changed political coverage somewhat, as other papers looked at the competition. This certainly made politicians more uncomfortable with the press, but Irish political journalism had probably been reluctant to pursue such stories in the past.

That wasn't a view, naturally, shared by the subjects of the coverage. Senior civil servants became increasingly worried and frustrated at what they say was the overwhelming negativity of much of the coverage of their departments – 'anti-public sector, anti-government, anti-politics, anti-everything', one of them complained when a group of secretaries general met to discuss what could be done. Some suggested cutting off all cooperation with newspapers that published stories they had been told were false. They knew this was impossible, but it was a measure of how grumpy they were about it all. The *Sunday Independent* was beyond reasoning with. The *Mail* was as bad or worse, they thought. One of the mandarins met with the new editor of the *Irish Independent*, Stephen Rae, to protest at some of its coverage. 'I have a file of stories which are completely wrong, and we told you they were wrong, and you still went ahead and published them,' he was told. Being complained to about the behaviour of your reporters is part of the life of an editor, but it was an unusual step for a civil servant to take. The former owner of the *Independent*, Tony O'Reilly, used to say that all governments felt the press was against them, and all opposition felt the press ignored them. Not much had changed.

14

The cracks begin to show

Many politicians find it hard to be team players. Putting oneself forward for election demands, among other things, a high level of self-regard. But having the necessary level of egotism can militate against keeping personal ambition in check to work in the service of a common goal. To a greater or lesser degree, every cabinet is a team of rivals and therefore hard to manage.

The early period of the Fine Gael–Labour coalition was exceptionally united. But that would not last forever. In 2012 the Labour leader would be faced with two ministers breaking from the united front the government still strove to maintain on all major issues. Both women, both with difficult relationships with the leader, both with significant support behind them in the party. One would stay, and one would go.

The culture of politics, at every level, is one of cutting deals. That's really what the art of compromise means. To Joan Burton it seemed obvious. Europe wanted and perhaps needed Ireland to agree its fiscal compact, and that required a referendum. If the Irish people were to assent, they would want something in return. Cutting the cost of the Irish banking bailout to taxpayers would fit nicely. Many other people in government shared the view. But Burton was the only one who told the *Financial Times* what she thought. A deal on the Anglo Irish Bank promissory notes, she told the paper's Dublin correspondent Jamie Smyth in late February 2012, would be very helpful to the referendum campaign and would be noted by the Irish people. It would, she said, 'emphasize once again the solidarity that Ireland has received from the Eurozone'. Even more controversially, she linked the amount of the annual promissory notes payment to the amount of budget cuts and tax increases that the coalition had to find each year. If Europe wants its treaty, she was saying, give us a break on our budget.

It may have been, as several officials noted, a statement of the bleedin' obvious, but it was one that ministers had been expressly requested not to make. The negotiating strategy being pursued by Michael Noonan specifically eschewed linking concessions on the banking debt to fiscal easing, in the belief that, while the ECB and Germany might be prepared to contemplate restructuring the debt to make it more efficient and sustainable, they would not do so just to give the Irish a break. Now they felt Burton had either carelessly or deliberately undermined that effort. Once again, Government Buildings was furious with Burton. Both Gilmore's and Kenny's staff were furious with the social protection minister. They asked each other if she really wanted to 'sabotage' the country. Advisers often have to take the flak that everyone knows is intended for their bosses. Gilmore's chief economic adviser Colm O'Reardon called Ed Brophy, Burton's adviser, into his office: 'What the hell is going on?' he said. Brophy thought it was like being back at school.

In addition to the private fury, public statements were issued contradicting Burton's comments. The Anglo notes are separate to the fiscal treaty, Noonan told reporters going into a summit of European leaders in Brussels. 'The Irish people are not going to be bribed by anybody.' Those watching in Dublin thought: Chance would be a fine thing. Gilmore authorized his staff to brief against Burton to the newspapers. 'Joan has deliberately created unnecessary difficulties for the government and you would have to wonder what game she is playing,' one of them was quoted as saying in the *Irish Times* lead story. It was as clear a slap-down as any minister in the government had ever been subjected to. Brendan Howlin offered a milder rebuke, but the message was clear.

Gilmore conceived an obvious plan to put manners on Burton: he made her responsible for Labour's campaign on the fiscal treaty referendum. Despite his boss's frequent transgressions in the eyes of the Government Buildings principals, Brophy – a whip-smart lawyer with a keen political sense and a laconic style, who had left a senior associate's berth at blue-chip Dublin solicitors firm Arthur Cox to work as Burton's adviser – managed to maintain good relations with the staff there. Mark Garrett had called Brophy with the idea: What do you think? he asked. At one level, it was a peace offering. But it was a double-edged one. Brophy went to Burton. 'You've no choice,' he said. 'If you don't, they'll brief that you wouldn't take it.'

Burton led the Labour campaign, though Gilmore did a lot of the stumping himself, emerging victorious but with the scars of battle to show for it. It was a bruising few months, coinciding with the stirrings of the first protests against the new household charge, the forerunner to the property tax promised for the following year. Thousands of protestors assembled outside both the Fine Gael and Labour national conferences in Dublin and Galway; and for a time there was acute concern at the centre of government that (as Labour saw it) the clumsiness of the charges introduced by the Department of the Environment was prompting a spread of opposition from the ranks of the habitual protestors to the middle ground. If that happened, they knew, there would be a real political problem. There were some exciting moments at the Labour conference in Galway when charging protestors overcame a threadbare Garda defence line and broke through to the doors of the conference hall. Gilmore had previously warned about having to come to conferences through the ranks of protestors, but he hadn't anticipated that they might find their way inside. Behind the glass walls of the foyer abutting the Bailey Allen Hall in Galway University, there was a good deal of pugnacity among the Labour delegates as the protestors screamed their disapproval outside. 'Let 'em in!' urged one (female) senator, literally rolling up her sleeves. Fortunately for everyone, they did not secure entry.

It was hard to argue for the fiscal treaty; few saw much intrinsic merit in it. The real campaign for it was to point out the consequences of voting against it. A late addition to the treaty establishing the new permanent bailout fund, the European Stability Mechanism, made ratification of the fiscal treaty necessary in order to access this fund for any future bailout. And, while the government insisted that future bailouts would not be necessary, it didn't take a great leap of imagination for voters to adopt the precautionary principle. *Maybe we won't need it; but what if we do?* Despite some alarming polls showing a high proportion of undecideds, and the clearly volatile history of European treaty votes in Ireland, the mood in government throughout was quite confident. Agriculture minister Simon Coveney, who had flourished in his ministerial role to become a truly front-rank politician, ran the Fine Gael campaign. He was assured and impressive throughout. Most crucially, however, nobody on the government side screwed it up, in the way that Brian Cowen and Charlie McCreevy had done in an early European referendum when they admitted to not having read the treaty.

Previous European treaties had been rejected during the era of the great national swagger; the Ireland of May 2012 was a more timorous place. The measure passed comfortably, by 60 per cent to 40 per cent, roughly where most of the polls gauged the race throughout. It hardly counts as one of the coalition's great victories, but it was an important one. If the result had been reversed, it would have precipitated a profound political crisis, and could well have destroyed the coalition.

If Joan Burton chafed at the restrictions Government Buildings sought to place on her occasional strategic solo-runs, at least she exercised considerable autonomy within her own department. Another female Labour minister enjoyed no such freedom. Róisín Shortall was a junior minister in the Department of Health, and she was finding life under the yoke of her Fine Gael minister increasingly difficult.

On the penultimate day of 2011, the *Irish Independent* broke a story that would keep recurring in various forms until its dramatic dénouement nearly ten months later. 'Health minister James Reilly is sometimes not even speaking with his junior minister Róisín Shortall, with the pair reduced to communicating by email,' wrote Fionnan Sheahan. He quoted emails from Shortall to Reilly protesting that the senior minister had declined to do her the courtesy of a conversation. Difficulties between senior ministers and their juniors were commonplace in government; most of the juniors could do little or nothing without the permission of their senior colleague, who was not always willing to give it. Tales of juniors labouring hard on policy only for the cabinet minister to change, dismiss or just take credit for their efforts are not exactly unusual, in this government or in any other one. But the dispute between Reilly and Shortall would go well beyond the quotidian rank-pulling that many politicians are unable to resist. The Reilly–Shortall row would cause the coalition to encounter one of most serious political storms of 2012.

No minister of the government has been involved in as many disputes or controversies as James Reilly. The health minister has been at the centre of some of the most dangerous and damaging rows that have afflicted the coalition. And, while his job as minister for health immediately subjects him to a conveyor-belt of at least low-level controversy and endless budget headaches, Reilly has also managed to generate his own rows and controversies. One Labour minister – who, while professing a *sotto voce* admiration for Reilly, does not have much confidence in him – summarizes, 'James is like a fucking rhinoceros in a conservatory.'

A latecomer to politics, elevated to the deputy leadership because of his support for Enda Kenny during the heave, he has no real political hinterland in Fine Gael. He has no support from his Labour colleagues, many of whom despair of him. He has a constituency of one, the occupant of the Taoiseach's office. So far, that has preserved him.

The *Independent* story about Reilly and Shortall's rocky relationship had been on the money. And relations between the two ministers deteriorated further over the coming months. In March 2011 the coalition had promised that it would, over the life of the government, introduce free access to GP doctor care for all. It set itself a twelve-month deadline for achieving the first instalment, free GP care for people with long-term illnesses. By March 2012 it was nowhere near the target. Shortall formed a private view: Reilly had never been serious about it.

In fact, Shortall was coming to the view that Reilly's interest in any reform of the health service that would disadvantage doctors was deeply qualified. She told colleagues that Reilly often objected to her proposals by saying, 'Oh, Dr So-and-so won't like that!' or 'I want Dr So-and-so in on that – he knows how it works!' Shortall didn't have to convince her Labour colleagues about Reilly. Cabinet ministers – as well as Gilmore's political apparatus – were infuriated when he went to the hospital consultants' annual conference in Killarney and unilaterally set aside a Programme for Government commitment to cut consultants' pay. Brendan Howlin's department could see huge overspends opening up in the health department. But, though her colleagues understood her frustration, Shortall couldn't convince them that doing something about him was more important than a lot of the other things they were doing.

That there was a personality clash between Reilly and Shortall was evident to government insiders, but they were wrong to dismiss it as just that. There were deep policy differences between the two on the most basic approaches to healthcare and the committal of resources. Shortall and her adviser, Maev-Ann Wren, a former *Irish Times* economics journalist who had been influential in drawing up the health policy parts of the Programme for Government, were coming to the conclusion that Reilly was just not interested in the socialized medical model that Labour favoured – reflected in the Programme for Government. Rather he favoured a model with much greater involvement of private-medical interests – a more, as they termed it, 'American' model. They were probably right about Reilly's instincts – he had, after all, become very wealthy himself on the back of his private medical practice. But actually, the great success of the Irish doctors' lobby is to combine the socialized medical system of Europe with the lucrative – for doctors – private aspects of the American system. Doctors' private practices are paid vast sums by the public purse, and the doctors themselves often straddle the two systems. During the years of the Celtic Tiger and its attendant vast increases in public spending, health budgets did even better than other areas of spending. Many of those increases went on pay, and much of that on doctors' pay (though nurses did extremely well too), in part because they had muscular lobby groups such as the one once led by the same Dr Reilly. Despite the huge sums expended on health in those years, there was no profound or lasting structural change. When Nye Bevan founded the NHS in Britain, he said that he had bought the compliance of the medical profession when he 'stuffed their mouths with gold'. In Ireland, government had stuffed the doctors' mouths with gold too, but got little or no reform in return. Shortall came to see Reilly as a representative of the men with mouthfuls of gold.

Though the government was committed to a system of universal health insurance – a policy that remains as far away as ever – it was by no means clear that this would alter the balance between public and private in the Irish system. Insofar as Reilly had a vision he was working towards, it was probably a more efficient – and politically successful – version of what was there already.

As her relationship with Reilly grew steadily worse, Shortall's relationship with Eamon Gilmore was also disintegrating. Although at the time everybody had focused on Joan Burton, Shortall had been infuriated by her omission from a cabinet to which she had fully expected to be appointed. She thought she had done policy, done media, done politics for Gilmore. She consulted the bar staff in Leinster House, whose guru-like status means their wisdom is often deferred to by politicians lowly and mighty alike. She was in, they were sure. The great day came. But the call from the leader did not. At the appointed hour, the new cabinet entered the Dáil and descended the steps in ceremonial procession, to the applause of their peers. Shortall sat and glowered.

The new Tánaiste rang her the next morning. Shortall gave vent to her anger and disappointment at being left out while the boys – Quinn and Penrose – had 'muscled in'. It wasn't possible, he told her; there were a lot of different considerations. He offered her a choice of three junior ministerial jobs, and gave her fifteen minutes to decide.

As Shortall's protests about Reilly became more pointed, Gilmore's people began to detect in them the resurfacing of resentment over her failure to secure a cabinet position, especially when the problem of rank – Reilly was a cabinet minister and she wasn't – became increasingly apparent. She had, after all, been passed over again by Gilmore when Penrose resigned (he appointed Jan O'Sullivan as the 'super-junior'), one cabinet minister reminded people. The Labour hierarchy might have agreed with her on the substance of the issue, but Reilly was the minister, so his was the primary responsibility for policy. Like it or not, Labour wasn't running health. There was another thing too: many Labour ministers wouldn't have appreciated an uppity junior in their own departments. They were also conscious of lots of things they had promised to do, but were having to postpone. They were sympathetic, but that sympathy wasn't endless.

At one stage in the early summer, having been extensively briefed by her, Pat Rabbitte went to see Gilmore to plead Shortall's case. She couldn't get through to Gilmore, she had complained. He had to be told what was happening. She was also being frustrated on alcohol policy, she felt. Rabbitte went to Gilmore's office to see some of his senior staff there. He said he wanted to talk to the Tánaiste about the Shortall situation. 'Hold on, hold on!' replied Gilmore. 'Brendan Howlin has just been in here with the same story and these two men' – he gestured at the aides – 'have been down with her for two hours!'

As far as Shortall was concerned, Reilly was deliberately frustrating her implementation of agreed government policy on primary care – policy inserted into the Programme for Government at Labour's insistence – and she expected political support for that. By July, she was having her doubts if it was going to be forthcoming. She was now completely disparaging of Reilly. When health service executive chief Cathal Magee resigned, Shortall spoke to Gilmore. Reilly, she told him, was unfit for office. She also complained that she had not been informed of Magee's resignation prior to learning about it in the media. Gilmore could appreciate that – he had only heard it on the news too. By now, Reilly's own financial problems were public knowledge: he had been listed in *StubbsGazette* over an unpaid €1.9 million debt he shared with several other investors in a Tipperary nursing home. Most people in Labour didn't think he would survive. Later, Shortall wrote a lengthy memo to Gilmore outlining the problems she was having, including the background to specific issues such as the primary care. He said: 'Take that to the Taoiseach.' The four – Kenny, Gilmore, Reilly and Shortall – met at the end of July for what the Government Buildings people hoped would be a clear-the-air session. But it achieved little. The message, Shortall felt, was 'Go on holidays and come back and get to work together.' She thought Kenny didn't want to talk about policy at all. Both Kenny's and Gilmore's staff thought: How much more time are we going to have to spend on this thing? This is not school. We are not the principal. Behave like grown-ups, for fuck's sake.

The split finally became public over the locations of twenty primary care centres due to be funded by the Department of Health. Shortall's approach was essentially simple: she wanted to put primary care centres in the poor areas that needed them the most. To do this she and her civil servants had developed a complex scoring system, but that was its essence. Reilly wanted to make amendments to her list. Moreover, he knew he *could* make amendments to her list. Questioned in the Dáil, he explained the selection process, during which a number of locations had been added – in his own constituency, in his ally Phil Hogan's constituency, and in the hometown of poor, loyal, threatened Roscommon TD Frank Feighan. 'I have laid it out three or four times to you: the criteria. They're quite extensive criteria and because all of them act in different ways, it's a bit like a multiplier. One and one makes two and two and two make four but four by four makes 16 and not four and four makes eight and so it is with this. It's a logistical, logarithmic progression, so there is nothing, there is nothing simple about it.' As Miriam Lord observed in the *Irish Times* parliamentary sketch, 'You can't beat a university education.' She dubbed the minister 'Dicey Reilly' and it stuck. On television, his cabinet colleague Leo Varadkar – who had more interest than most in Reilly's survival, because he feared being appointed as his replacement – conceded what the entire country could see: that it looked like stroke politics. In any other Western country, Reilly would have had to resign. Labour waited for him to totter over, or for the killer fact that would finally do for him. But it never arrived.

As the media feeding frenzy on Reilly continued, the Labour hierarchy thought that Shortall 'had him by the balls'. He needs her now, they reasoned, and she can use that to win concessions. But Shortall wanted more than concessions. 'She wanted [Gilmore] to go to the Taoiseach and seek Reilly's resignation.' Gilmore discussed it with his most senior staff. The question they couldn't answer was: What then? What if the Taoiseach said no? Were they really going to bring the government down because a minister had interfered in a list one of his junior ministers had drawn up? It was never a serious option.

Gilmore had always sought to learn from the mistakes made by smaller parties in coalition previously. Insiders joked that they wanted to make new ones. One of the things they wanted to avoid was being the moral guardians of Fine Gael ministers. 'Labour doesn't determine who Fine Gael ministers are and vice versa,' a senior Labour figure told me at the time. The truth was this: there were situations where Gilmore would have no choice but to go to the Taoiseach and demand a resignation of a Fine Gael minister to save the government. But this wasn't one of them. Gilmore told Shortall bluntly: I am not bringing down the government on this.

The opposition would have been remiss had they not put down a motion to flush out Shortall, and they duly did. As colleagues watched anxiously, Shortall delivered a speech that did not mention Reilly once but clearly warned about the direction in which his stewardship was taking the health service. 'A key question arises for us all: Who will bear the burden of the cuts? Do we increase prescription charges for medical patients, for example, or instead reduce the drugs bill? Do we cut public health nurses, or instead collect money owed by insurance companies? Do we cut home help services, or instead impose a cap on consultants' pay?'

This was actually devastating stuff. In all cases, Reilly had taken the option not favoured by Labour backbenchers – or indeed, by government policy. Closing, Shortall warned, 'Decisions taken by government over the next few months will determine the shape of the future healthcare system. That will determine the shape of the system for years to come.'

If it was a coded warning to Gilmore, it wasn't a very difficult code to crack. What Shortall was saying was that Reilly was tearing apart the public health service. Had she pursued her rebellion there and then, it would surely have spread and perhaps broken Reilly. But she then went and voted confidence in the minister. The Irish parliament has a long history of people participating in empty formulas, but talking principle and voting pragmatism hurt Shortall's credibility and diminished the power of her resignation a week later.

The day after the speech and the vote, Shortall met with Gilmore. The speech had been a mistake, he told her. The familiar argument was rehearsed again. 'He's screwing the Labour Party,' she protested. 'You'll have to leave that with me,' he said. In public, she wouldn't express confidence in Reilly. The following day, Labour's executive council met, and Gilmore expressed his full support for Shortall. But Fine Gael was incensed at her speech, and when reporters inevitably asked Gilmore the obvious questions, he expressed support for Reilly too. This is where microphones become dangerous. Labour ministers were caught in a bind: they had to back their cabinet colleague, but the party organization was solidly behind the junior minister. Now a new voice entered the fray: Labour Party chairman Colm Keaveney told the *Irish Times* he had been 'inundated' with calls from members praising Shortall's speech. 'They're telling me she delivered her message with dignity, honesty and self-criticism and that she was faithful to her values.' That last bit was intended to wound, and it did. For his part, Reilly was practically teasing her, pointing out to reporters that she had voted confidence in him. 'Actions speak louder than words,' he grinned.

In a final attempt to re-establish working relations between the two warring ministers, a meeting was set up in Leinster House the following Tuesday. It descended into bad-tempered exchanges. The resignation came the following day, 26 September. Gilmore was in New York at the United Nations, as the *Irish Independent* jibed, talking about world peace. Back home, the Labour Party was at war.

The abandoning of Shortall was brutal politics. Gilmore wanted to keep her on board, and agreed with much of what she said. He thought Reilly was a disgrace. But he was not willing to rock – and possibly destroy – the government by backing her. All governing is a matter of choices. The Shortall affair demonstrated Gilmore would make some bloody ones.

15

Budget battles

It was less than a week to go before the budget, and the process was stuck. The Tánaiste faced the Taoiseach in a crisis meeting. 'I need the 3 per cent and I'm not sure I can deliver support for the budget without it,' Gilmore said. Kenny exhaled and replied, 'I can't give it to you.'

Both men agreed to talk again later. Their officials had been working furiously for weeks now, and the two parties were as far apart as ever. The sticking point was Labour's demand for a 3 per cent increase in the universal social charge for employees earning over €100,000 a year (the self-employed were already paying at this level, something that was seldom mentioned). It was fundamentally a political, rather than an economic or budgetary, issue. The measure would raise about €70 million, the Department of Finance estimated – a significant but not material amount of money in a budget that was going to raise, between new taxes and spending cuts, some €3.5 billion. But the USC increase had come to attain huge political significance. Fine Gael thought this was a breach of the Programme for Government promises not to raise income taxes and argued that if it were to give up its tax pledge, Labour would have to give up its pledge not to cut social welfare. It proposed a 3 per cent across-the-board cut in social welfare rates, excluding pensions. This was out of the question for Labour. It had a few days, and no more, to agree a budget and save the coalition. Budget day was less than a week away – on Wednesday, 5 December. Budgets can't be fudged or postponed. If a government can't agree a budget, it can't govern. The clock was ticking.

Budget discussions had been ongoing for months between the Department of Public Expenditure – or PER, as it's known in official circles – and the other 'spending' departments. Since its foundation when the government was formed, the new department had been

wrestling with the conundrum of cutting public spending while trying to maintain services provided by the state. This was the time of
the year when the emphasis was on the former, and PER had been
crunching budgets for months. Tax, the other component of the
budget day package, is the responsibility of the minister for finance.
Offsetting revenue and expenditure elements of the country's budget
is a delicate balancing act, requiring cooperation and agreement
between the two ministers responsible. In a coalition government, of
course, the budget also requires agreement between the two parties.
That agreement seemed further away than ever.

The stalemate went to the very apex of the administration. If PER
is in the front line of the budget battles, the generals are in the EMC,
the inner cabinet of Taoiseach, Tánaiste, public expenditure and
finance ministers, and their officials and advisers. There had been a
series of EMC meetings during November at which the pros and
cons of setting out spending and tax plans for three years, rather than
one, in the forthcoming budget was discussed. This would have been
a revolutionary move that – while effectively tying the government's
fiscal hands for the remainder of its time in office – would have enabled ministers to say, 'These taxes and no more; these cuts and no
more.' Such certainty would promote stability, those in favour of a
three-year deal argued, and stability should help with consumer confidence. They all knew that if consumers could be persuaded to spend
a little more and save a little less, it would give the domestic economy
a huge shot in the arm. It would also eliminate the centrality of a
budget 'big bang' in the political and economic year, of which Howlin was becoming increasingly critical. A 'big bang' budget is great if
you have money to give away, like Fianna Fáil's Charlie McCreevy
used to have; when you are delivering hairshirt budgets, it becomes
an enormous political problem to manage. But to agree a three-year
deal meant that the unsustainable pledges of the Croke Park public
service pay deal, and on tax and on welfare, would almost certainly
have to be abandoned. It would be a massive gamble.

Meanwhile, PER had delayed its bilateral meetings with the big
spending departments – health, education and social protection –
until well into November. This was specifically to avoid the leaking

that had punctuated the previous year's budget season. Sooner or later, all governments become paranoid about leaking. For this one, it was sooner. The leaders of the two parties believed that Joan Burton and James Reilly had been more or less negotiating through the media before the coalition's first budget, a process they thought hugely damaging to the coalition, and they were determined to avoid a repeat. Research by Labour in the spring of 2012 had found that the party and the coalition were being blamed for measures that had been leaked the previous November – specifically to get them taken out of the budget – but that had never actually been implemented. 'For fuck's sake!' exclaimed one aide when he learned of the research. 'It's bad enough being blamed for the stuff we actually do!'

For the coalition's second budget, the leaders on the EMC and their advisers decided that they would keep the budget discussions essentially among themselves. Contacts were between officials in the spending departments and PER on specific items, and no overall budget discussion took place at cabinet. People hammered away at their own details, but nobody outside the EMC had a grasp of the bigger picture. Every week throughout October and November, when the government press secretary and his deputy (the former a Fine Gael appointment, the latter Labour) met the political correspondents for the weekly post-cabinet briefing, they were asked the same question: Was the budget discussed? Every week the answer came back: No, not this week. Incredibly, the budget was not discussed by the full cabinet until less than a week before it was due to be delivered. One senior aide explained: 'Because the EMC doesn't leak.' He might have added: 'Until it's in our interest to do so.'

The taps that had so gushed with advance budget information the previous year were kept firmly shut off by this EMC-centric process – something that its members and the staff who supported them were quietly very pleased about. Ministers outside the process, especially Burton, railed against it. Her frustration boiled over at a bad-tempered bilateral meeting to agree her budgets with Howlin and his officials. The delegation from social protection had been in contact with PER and had already had a preliminary meeting a week previously. PER, like its predecessor the Department of Finance, has a team of officials who monitor the social protection budgets, effectively 'marking' the department. Officials had been exchanging documents since September. The documents were lists, essentially, of possible cuts. On the basis of agreed options papers, Burton and her team had made their choices on where the cuts were to be made. Individual items came and went over the process. The bereavement grant of €850 – paid to the next of kin of deceased persons, regardless of income – was on the list to be cut, then off, then on again. Then off again, finally. At one stage, the proposed cut to child benefit was €20 a month; it came in at €10. This is the budget process; this is the sausage-making.

Now, very late in the day, Howlin indicated that his department had its own suggestions about the final list. The good news was that he had secured another €150 million for Burton's department from Noonan; the bad news was that he wanted to decide how at least some of it was to be spent. A document outlining PER's ideas was sent to Burton and her aides half an hour before the meeting was due to start.

When she went into the room in Merrion Street, Burton tore into Howlin, castigating him and his officials. Howlin tried to calm her, saying, 'Joan, Joan, I implore you . . .' but Burton was furious. 'I object to this!' she thundered. Not alone was she being denied any input into wider budget strategy, but now her authority to decide how her own department spent its resources was being undermined. Give and take on budget measures was part of the budget process, but Burton thought this latest intervention went way beyond what was acceptable. Ronan O'Brien, Howlin's special adviser, bridled at her disregard for the fact that PER had scrapped and scraped for her to get an extra €150 million, reducing her cut from €540 million to €390 million. 'What do you want us to do?' he barked. 'Go back to a €540 million cut, is that what you want?' The meeting ended badly, and without agreement.

The following day, the aides tried to patch things up. Ed Brophy, Burton's adviser, received a call from Mark Garrett. The Fine Gael side had got wind of the row, he said. 'Why is something that should have been a good news story now sounding like a bad news story?' he asked.

Gilmore and Howlin had been well aware of increasing dissent among the Labour ministers about the closed-door nature of the budget process, but they weren't too worried about it. They were focused on doing a deal at the EMC. There was a series of politician-only EMC meetings, with the officials and advisers excluded, while the four men who made the key decisions of government tried to agree a deal themselves. Many of them took place at nine or ten o'clock at night, when the participants were all tired, which didn't help things. It makes the aides and civil servants nervous when the politicians disappear into a room by themselves, but it has always been a feature of budget deal-making. Irish politics has always stressed the primacy of the people who are directly chosen by the voters, and most Irish politicians prefer it like that. The politicians are the ones with the mandate, and they are the ones whose necks are on the line.

The Labour side got word from the room: Noonan had agreed the 3 per cent USC hike. There was no mention of welfare cuts. The line was fed out to the parliamentary party and from there to the media, where it appeared as informed speculation in a number of reports. The Labour proposal had been ventilated as far back as October: the *Sunday Times* reported that junior minister Sean Sherlock had proposed the measure at a meeting of the parliamentary party, to wide acclaim among backbenchers. Labour was now cock-a-hoop: it was on. There was only one problem. As far as Fine Gael was concerned, it hadn't agreed any such thing. Labour briefed that a USC hike 'could circumvent the government's commitment not to increase income tax in the budget, as the USC is not strictly an income tax'. Bullshit, thought the Fine Gaelers.

When the matter came up at the next EMC meeting, Noonan insisted there was no agreement on a unilateral tax hike. Only if Labour agreed a welfare cut could the tax hike be on the cards. Labour thought he was going back on his word. This is what happens, reflected one civil servant only half in jest, when you let the politicians do things on their own. The disagreement would bring the coalition to the brink of failure.

*

With a week to go before budget day, the regular Tuesday cabinet meeting was given over to non-budget items, with proceedings being dominated by discussion of the report of the expert group on abortion, commissioned by the government at the beginning of the year and overdue since July. The issue had exploded with the news that a young Indian woman, Savita Halappanavar, had died in Galway University Hospital while miscarrying seventeen weeks into her pregnancy. The reports said she had asked for an abortion but been refused before her death. It was not yet clear if the report of the expert group on abortion now before the government was relevant to her case, but political reality had already conflated the two. A row flared briefly when health minister James Reilly – whose department was responsible for managing the government's response to the tragedy – suggested that a decision on the expert group report should be postponed. Gilmore reacted angrily. The Labour leader had sat on his pro-choice backbenchers all year, promising them action on the abortion issue. Some of them had even threatened to publish their own legislation if the government didn't act. Reilly was five months late publishing the expert group's report, and only did so then in the wake of the Savita story, and now he wanted to postpone again. Labour had run out of patience.

Gilmore's prickly reaction signalled two things: one was the by now well-established Labour belief that Reilly was simply not in control of his brief and not up to the job. Ruairi Quinn confirmed as much to Labour backbenchers the following day in comments that were quickly leaked to the newspapers. In public, they tut-tutted, but Labour sources inside and adjacent to the cabinet had been saying the same for months. This time, Quinn didn't even bother to deny it. But the skirmish also revealed something else that nobody noticed at the time: it showed that tensions between the two parties on the budget had escalated considerably.

The following day's – Wednesday's – cabinet meeting was devoted entirely to the budget. Both public expenditure minister Brendan Howlin and finance minister Michael Noonan briefed their colleagues on their respective tax and spending plans, but, still conscious of the threat of leaks, they omitted many of the specifics.

The meeting didn't reach any conclusion on the budget package as a whole, but it wasn't really expected to. Important elements of it had been agreed between the public expenditure department and the line departments. All the smaller departments had long since been done, and now the big spenders – health, education and social welfare – had recently agreed their packages.

Crucially, the health and education squeezes had been eased by the extra €150 million found for each department, to be funded mostly from extra taxation measures. Government spokespeople said that another meeting was arranged for the Thursday. Again, that meeting didn't reach a conclusion on the package, and another meeting was arranged for Saturday. To the outside world, it seemed pretty run-of-the-mill budget foreplay.

On the inside, it was a very different story. Ministers with sharp antennae and with networks around government had known since early in the week that there was a big problem emerging with agreeing the budget. To the rest, it became clear on Thursday. Fine Gael had dug in its heels: Labour's demand that the universal social charge be increased by 3 per cent for those earning over €100,000, which much of the party thought was a *fait accompli*, would only be agreed if there was a corresponding cut of 3 per cent in all social welfare payments, excluding old age pensions. Reports continued to suggest that the 3 per cent hike was as good as agreed, interpreted by Fine Gael as an attempt to create 'facts on the ground'; Fine Gael had countered by leaking that any tax increase would have to be matched by a welfare cut.

All budget negotiations feature a lot of things that don't end up in the final document. Some are put on the table for negotiating purposes (especially in coalitions), and some are really intended as part of the budget. Some things, in other words, are more on the table than others. Labour thought that its USC hike was really on the table, but that Fine Gael's welfare cut wasn't all that serious. But that was very far from the case. 'We had an understanding we were going in that [the USC hike] direction,' one of the Labour participants said. But one of the Fine Gael architects of the budget was adamant. 'Is it really likely,' he told me, 'that we would be willing to ditch our promise on income tax without Labour doing something on welfare?' Frustration was becoming evident on both sides: there were angry exchanges at one of the EMC meetings, especially between Noonan and Gilmore. 'Neither party was minded to back off,' said another person involved in the process.

A series of budget stories was now leaked to the newspapers – among them was one in the *Irish Independent*, telling its readers how much they would be paying on the property tax. Partly the leaking was from the centre of government and calculated to distract attention from the growing gulf at the epicentre of the administration. Partly it was because ministers at last had been given briefings on the contents of the budget outside their own departments. And partly it was because the first casualty when relations break down is discipline. 'The real worry,' one of the participants told me, 'was that the dynamic between the two sides was now bad.' That hadn't happened before.

Labour sources targeted much of their ire at Andrew McDowell, the Taoiseach's highly influential economic adviser. McDowell had been pushing the Fine Gael line all week in talks with Labour that were becoming increasingly difficult as the clock ticked down towards the budget. Very often people complain about advisers when they really want to complain about the principals, but can't. McDowell wasn't on a solo-run; he was just pushing the Fine Gael line.

The cabinet on Thursday – which was interrupted for leader's questions in the Dáil chamber – ended without confronting the issue head on. Gilmore and Howlin and their advisers went into a series of rolling meetings all day, at which they frankly discussed the prospect of leaving government if there was no agreement on the budget. Gilmore told his aides that he believed it was a good government, that he had a good relationship with Kenny and that they hadn't yet come across a problem that they couldn't get over. But if this couldn't be sorted, he said, they would have to 'go to the country'. There was some black humour about inquiring about the price of corriboard (on which election posters are printed), but not much; generally the mood was gloomy.

A meeting of the EMC was arranged for that night. In the afternoon,

Colm O'Reardon called McDowell and asked to see him. They both knew that if there was to be a solution to the problem, they would probably have to find it. Each left his office to walk to the other's, and they met at the central stairs, both laughing at the over-the-top symbolism of meeting halfway.

Before the EMC met that evening, the Taoiseach and Tánaiste went alone to Kenny's office. The staff waited outside in the Taoiseach's dining room, adjacent to his office. Eventually, the Taoiseach emerged and asked O'Reardon and McDowell to come in. 'We have an impasse,' he told them, 'but we want to move forward. Can you try to come up with some proposals to fix this?' It wasn't a breakthrough, but it might be the path to one. The two advisers now arranged a series of meetings on Friday with key officials from PER and finance to sketch out ways of squaring the circle.

By Friday morning it was becoming evident across government that the budget difficulty was escalating, though officially the cabinet was still in the dark about it. Burton's adviser Ed Brophy received a call from Ronan O'Brien. Despite their bosses' clashes, the two were on good terms. 'The blueshirts want a 3 per cent welfare cut across the board,' O'Brien told him. 'That's just mad,' Brophy replied. 'I know. Things are really bad.' Burton was furious, telling people she wouldn't move on her settlement, which she regarded as closed. To her, it underlined the shambles that the EMC had made of the budget process.

Fine Gael insisted that the 3 per cent proposed cut in all social welfare rates would raise €600 million; Burton's officials crunched the numbers on Friday and said that the number was actually €265 million. Burton's department produced a note that it circulated to the negotiators listing all the sensitive social welfare payments that would have to be hatcheted under the Fine Gael plan. It would involve cuts to thirty-one separate schemes, including the widow's pension, the deserted wife's benefit, the disability allowance, the carer's allowance, the blind pension and the one-parent family allowance. The politics of such an across-the-board cut weren't too hard to see. No way could Labour stand over it. What was driving them crazy was that they didn't believe Fine Gael wanted to do it either.

Phones rang and beeped across the government all Saturday morning as the lower ranks of officials and advisers began to get wind of something very wrong. Political advisers always have a slightly higher stake than career civil servants in the fortunes of a government in one simple but important respect; if it falls, they're out of a job. 'People were ringing me and saying the government was in danger on this,' one official told me. 'People were really, really worried. It got completely out of hand.' Another received a call from Government Buildings to tell him, 'I don't know if the government is going to survive. It's really serious.'

The Labour EMC people – Gilmore, Howlin, O'Brien, O'Reardon – and Garrett met in Howlin's office at 11 a.m. They discussed the basic questions of Labour's role in government and what the parliamentary party could live with. As always in these moments, it was partly soul-searching and partly an exercise in political calculation. The Labour leadership had more or less told its TDs that they were getting a tax increase on the rich; but the price of delivering it was too high for Gilmore. 'I want the 3 per cent,' he said. 'But I'm not prepared to trade welfare cuts for it. There is no moral equivalence.' The papers drawn up by O'Reardon and McDowell had demonstrated that there could be a way of increasing taxes on the rich without hitting income tax or the USC.

After lunch in Doheny & Nesbitt's pub near by, Gilmore reconvened the meeting, clarified the decision and the strategy, and went to the Taoiseach's office. Kenny was sure they could come to a compromise, earlier telling one of his most senior civil servants, 'I want you to know, the government is not going to fall on this.' The bones of the agreement were appearing now. There would be no income tax increases or welfare cuts, but capital-gains and capital-acquisitions taxes (mostly covering inheritances) – generally paid by the better off – could be increased. In addition, there would be reductions in the pension tax relief for the wealthy – though most of these elements wouldn't come into operation for another year. The property tax would be tweaked to ensure that those in houses worth over a million euros paid at a higher rate, and also to ensure that Labour could talk about a 'mansion tax'. Labour had got a package of tax measures on the wealthier all right, though Gilmore and his aides also knew that other changes to come were deeply regressive.

By mid afternoon word had begun to reach both Fine Gael and Labour of the following day's Red C/*Sunday Business Post* poll. For Fine Gael, the shock of a six-point drop in support – to its lowest level since 2008 – stiffened its desire to hold its line on election promises not to raise income taxes. 'We've got to hold the line on the tax stuff,' one minister told me that afternoon. This was always Fine Gael's objection to the USC hike: that voters would not buy the sophistry that it wasn't really an income-tax increase. Labour also thought the *Business Post* numbers would make things more difficult. 'They had a bad poll that showed them out of touch on abortion and it spooked them,' one Labour figure said. For Labour, the poll's explicit findings that voters preferred tax hikes on the wealthy to social welfare cuts only strengthened its arguments. Cabinet members on both sides prepared for a difficult meeting. But at leaders' and EMC level, where the decisions were really made, the deal was well on its way to being done.

Ministers gathered in Government Buildings before 5 p.m. on the Saturday evening, hovering around the cabinet room and the small ante-room where teas and coffees are served before meetings. But there was no sign of the Taoiseach or Tánaiste. In fact, Gilmore was upstairs in his office, having returned from the Taoiseach's office with the offer in principle of the tax hikes. He thought that if Labour were to resile from its 3 per cent demand, all the Labour ministers should agree to that. He was also watching his back. Colm O'Reardon and Brendan Howlin went downstairs to summon the Labour ministers; Fine Gael looked on in alarm. 'Don't worry,' O'Reardon joked to Paul Kehoe. 'It's not a walkout.' But they all knew it pretty much looked like one. The Labour contingent trooped out of the cabinet room, as the Fine Gael ministers watched in silence. Even if the danger of the coalition falling apart had been at its greatest the day before and a compromise was now on the way, the withdrawal of the Labour ministers from the cabinet room was the most dramatic moment to date in the short life of the coalition.

Gilmore briefed his colleagues on the events of recent days and the proposed solution. The Labour ministers backed his decision – in reality, they had little choice. Kenny, Gilmore, Noonan and a handful of senior officials – Andrew McDowell, Colm O'Reardon and secretary to the government, Martin Fraser – now adjourned to the Taoiseach's office to finalize the details of the agreement. Howlin later joined them. They were gone for almost two hours. The rest of the government waited, in various states of confidence, nervousness and anticipation. Ministers lolled around, some having coffee, some on the phone, some shooting the breeze. One minister thought the whole thing was pretty relaxed; others thought it was too relaxed. Most were just wondering, What the fuck is going on?

Somewhere between 8.30 and 8.45 p.m., the party leaders returned. The cabinet meeting concluded quickly, within a half an hour, underlining its role as a rubber stamp in a budget process that had seen all the major decisions reached by the EMC. Even the big rows were at the EMC, not the cabinet. Most of the Fine Gael ministers went across the road to the Merrion Hotel for a drink. Some were wary about being spotted; a few years previously, Brian Cowen had famously been observed by a reporter while drinking late into one budget night in a nearby bar. The Merrion is Dublin's poshest hotel – a five-star hotel that famously accommodates the IMF and ECB delegations which supervise Ireland's bailout – and the politicians were aware of the PR perils in being seen there. But they were tired and thirsty and they wanted a drink. Someone suggested they avoid the more public Cellar Bar and instead go to the hotel's quieter ground-floor bar, where the large Georgian windows looked across the street to the floodlit Government Buildings. Stress released, the conversation flowed. If some of the hotel's predominantly American guests wondered who all these middle-aged men attacking their pints with relieved looks on their faces were, they didn't ring the *Daily Mail* about it. 'It was good craic,' recalled one minister. Politicians are normally good company over a drink. A few of the Labour ministers went to O'Reilly's Bar near by. Their mood was quieter. It had been a long few days.

16

'Fianna Fáil have stolen my speech'

Few things undermined the credibility of the late Brian Lenihan more than his repeated declarations that the country had 'turned the corner', or was in recovery. These repeated insistences continued right up to the denials that a bailout was in preparation when IMF and EU officials were already in Dublin; a lie that, though understandable, was hugely politically damaging for the beleaguered Fianna Fáil–Green government. Often Lenihan's pronouncements came as part of budget speeches – like his 'turned the corner' assertion and his earlier 'call to patriotic action' wheeze – that also contained billions of euros in cuts to public services and tax increases. That probably didn't help his case. But it underlined the fact that budgets are one of the very few times of the year when the public follows politics as closely as do those in the political-media bubble around Dublin 2. What the minister for finance says on budget day, and how he says it, matters. If one of the key insights that any politician can have is to realize just how little attention people pay to politicians a lot of the time, it's just as important to realize when people *are* paying attention. How many times of the year do the bookies publish odds on what colour tie a minister will be wearing? When else does anyone notice?

'Budget day is a good day for taking stock of where we are, so let us take stock,' began the finance minister when he rose before a packed chamber shortly after 2.30 p.m. on Wednesday, 5 December. Noonan's speech was cautious but optimistic. His special adviser, Eoin Dorgan, a brilliant young career civil servant, had served as Lenihan's press officer and had learned from Lenihan's mistakes: there was no bombast and there were no hostages to fortune. 'There are manifest signs,' Noonan said, 'that the country is emerging from the worst of the crisis and that the efforts of the Irish people, despite the hardship, are leading to success.' Happy days are here again, it was not.

Journalists watched the Labour backbenchers for any twitch that might signify that a backbench rebellion was fermenting. Interpreting the body language of TDs and ministers in the chamber is an entertaining and frequent chore of the watching political correspondents; it is also, alas, fraught with difficulty. But, looking at the Labour deputies listening to first Michael Noonan and then Brendan Howlin, it was impossible to assume anything other than disgruntlement on their part. Concluding his speech, Howlin tried to strike an optimistic note. 'When I took office last year,' he said, 'I could not be certain that we could make it through this crisis. I no longer hold this fear.' All right, thought some of the Labour backbenchers. But will Labour make it through this crisis? Ominously, the party chairman Colm Keaveney muttered that evening: 'Fianna Fáil have stolen my speech.'

It's one of the apparent laws of coalition government in Ireland – and, seemingly, in our nearest neighbour – that the smaller party takes the greater part of the flak for unpopular actions of the government. Labour always expected that, and its expectations were not confounded. No budget that extracts €3.5 billion from citizens is likely to be acclaimed, but the regressive nature of some of the tax changes and cuts opened up Labour's flank where it was most sensitive. Predictably, Labour's pre-election Tesco-style ads – warning of Fine Gael cuts to child benefit and new taxes on wine, on savings, on the family car, on water ('Look what Fine Gael have in store for you') – were dug out and republished on the web hours before the following morning's newspapers could give them the full treatment. A few Fine Gaelers allowed themselves a smirk at that. They also suspected that the late addition of a euro in excise on to a bottle of wine – explicitly warned about by Labour before the election and which excited a large degree of howling on social media sites – was contrived by Noonan as a calculated 'Screw you' to Labour. Some of the cabinet were uneasy about it; the backbenchers were less concerned about their partners' sensitivities.

Gilmore's defence was that the budget had introduced half a billion euros of taxes on the wealthy. Labour quickly published briefing notes showing 'significant fairness measures in this budget totalling over €500 million'. A quick reading of the budget documents, however, showed that half of this wouldn't come into operation until 2014. The Labour backbenchers floundered.

'Broad swathe of taxes and cuts hits almost every adult in State' declared the *Irish Times* of the coalition's second budget on the morning after. The *Indo* was more pointed: 'We've no more to give: Most savage austerity budget yet takes €1,000 a year from most family incomes'. For the *Daily Mail* it was 'hard pressed working families', instead of the very wealthy or those on welfare, who were 'squeezed and squeezed again'.

But all the reports noted one thing on the day after the budget: the frequently predicted Labour backbench revolt against another austerity budget had failed to materialize. The backbenchers were far from happy, but they were still onside. Róisín Shortall had voted against the budget, but her fellow travellers still within the parliamentary party had stayed on board. That, thought Gilmore's aides, was the real test. We got through it.

Not quite. Party chairman Colm Keaveney had long been identified as one of the chief flight risks. A few ingredients were mixed together in his cocktail of disaffection: a long-standing antagonism with the party leader, who had tried to block his election as party chairman the previous March; a genuine opposition to the nature of the budget measures; and a constituency revision that did him no favours. If Keaveney thought that the prospects for an independent candidate in the revised Galway East might be better than those for a Labour candidate at the next election – though he testily dismissed that interpretation – he wasn't the only one who had come to that conclusion. The other parties thought so anyway. On the night before the budget, Gilmore had summoned Keaveney to his office in Government Buildings. Earlier, Keaveney had been vocal at a parliamentary party meeting, looking for details and warning about welfare cuts. He also met Brendan Howlin privately, again seeking details. 'I can't tell you, I'd lose my job,' Howlin told him.

The meeting with Gilmore was no more conclusive. 'Big day tomorrow, Colm,' Gilmore told him. 'Big day for the Labour Party.

Big day for leadership – for me, party leader, and you, party chair-man.' Keaveney looked for details, referring to his own budget spreadsheets, where he had compared the effects of various possible budgetary measures. Gilmore spoke in generalities, without revealing any of the details of the package. Keaveney continued to press him, eventually exclaiming, 'I'm been told fucking nothing here!' Gilmore repeatedly told him that there would be 'counter-balancing measures'. Trust me on this, Gilmore said, there will be counter-balancing meas-ures. Keaveney asked about cuts to child benefit. Gilmore was non-committal, asking only, 'Would that be a stumbling block for you?' Keaveney told Gilmore what he already knew – that they had all campaigned against it. 'You're not with me, are you?' the Tánaiste asked. During the budget debate, Keaveney sat disconsolately on the backbenches. One of his colleagues sat beside him. 'Fuck it,' she said ruefully. 'You were right.'

One of the dangers of leaking budgets before they are announced is that media attention after the big event then tends to fixate on indi-vidual measures – often involving relatively trivial sums in the greater scheme of things – that have *not* been flagged in advance. The con-stant demand of editors everywhere is for something new. Though budget 2013 had been kept secret throughout the lengthy process of its preparation, there was a flurry of leaks and previews in the final couple of days. Now attention began to focus on a cut announced in the budget to respite grants for carers. This was a special one-off pay-ment made to those who cared for sick or elderly members of their families, in addition to their carer's allowance. It was intended to pro-vide them with an opportunity for a break from the incessant responsibilities of looking after relatives in difficult and stressful situations, though in many cases it simply became part of the house-hold budget. Like a lot of such payments, the respite grant had rocketed during the years of plenty. Budget 2013 chopped it from €1,700 to €1,375. The measure would save a measly €27 million. The airwaves fairly wailed. 'They're making it harder and harder,' sobbed Ann, a carer to her thirty-year-old daughter, who has been disabled since birth, on Joe Duffy's *Liveline*. There were many others. Such stories highlighted the problem with implementing cuts to Ireland's scattergun welfare payments system: people in difficult circumstances often found themselves on the receiving end of several cuts at once.

After every budget in the age of austerity, there's a blame game. A year previously, Ruairí Quinn had been in the firing line because of cuts to the special budgets for disadvantaged schools. After a brief panic, the government did a U-turn; but this time there would be no U-turn. The budget had been too difficult to put together, and neither party was prepared to open it up again. High-level contacts between the two sides in Government Buildings confirmed it: this year, there was no turning back. Labour TDs openly blamed Fine Gael for 'protecting the rich', while they pleaded that they had sought to protect the poor and those struggling as best they could. This intensely annoyed a lot of people in Fine Gael. One minister ranted at great length about Labour's attempts to weasel out of responsibility for the budget by blaming all the tough stuff on Fine Gael. When I asked him if he would be quoted by name, he initially assented, then paused and asked for time to consider. Later he called back, having consulted with Noonan. His comments were all off the record. 'They're under a lot of pressure,' he conceded. He didn't want to make things worse.

For many Labour TDs and senators, the real test wasn't the budget votes – few of them were going to object to the hikes in excise and capital taxes, after all – but the votes on the social welfare bill a week later. They had, after all, gone around knocking on doors promising not to cut child benefit. Government Buildings knew that Colm Keaveney was still wobbling – the weekend papers had made that much clear. Gilmore dispatched Joan Burton to 'mind' him; Keaveney was known as an admirer of the social protection minister.

Burton went to Keaveney's Dáil office and spoke with him for a good two hours. She filled in the party chairman on the back-and-forth negotiations over the previous months – everyone could see what they had cut, but she wanted to tell him about the cuts they had avoided. There were a few extra spending initiatives in the social protection vote, and Burton told Keaveney he was welcome to take credit for them. Then she tried another tack. She told him that a rebellion now would only help Gilmore in the long run. If he stayed as an internal critic in the parliamentary party, it would give him a lot more clout in the longer term. If he ignored the whip, he would be throwing away the power of his chairmanship of the party. Keaveney wouldn't commit one way or the other. He listed his complaints against the leader, the constituency rows, the snub at the party's centenary celebrations in Clonmel the previous Sunday. He believed he had been sidelined at the event, later complaining that he had been 'asked to introduce the band'. He said that Garrett had briefed the media against him, and was responsible for a *Daily Mail* story that revealed he had employed his wife as his parliamentary assistant. The grievances came pouring out.

But, for all the personal nature of some of Keaveney's problems with Gilmore, he was rebelling now on an issue of substance – the content of the budget. He had sent 1,400 emails to Labour members and the replies had come flooding back, confirming his view that the party grassroots were becoming deeply disillusioned. He was also acutely aware of the hanging rope: a cut in child benefit was something that Labour had explicitly fought the election and entered government to avoid. Sure, it hadn't been specifically mentioned in the Programme for Government, but TDs were aware that 'Everyone knows that's just bullshit.' After all, Labour candidates had repeated it often enough in the final days of the campaign. 'You've walked us into the last-chance saloon,' he had told Gilmore in front of a parliamentary party meeting that day. Frantically, Keaveney sought backbench allies, but none were forthcoming. 'Shut the fuck up and take the pain,' Eric Byrne implored him. 'We're soldiers in a war.' After meeting Burton, Keaveney went to RTÉ to be part of a radio panel on the *Late Debate* programme. The UCD history professor Diarmaid Ferriter was also on the panel. Ferriter is a man of forthright views. He asked: 'I just wonder what Labour is actually for now?' Keaveney found it excruciating. Every time he said 'This is a progressive budget', he thought it was a lie. The following day his mother phoned him. She had seen a woman at the checkout in front of her literally run out of money to pay for her groceries. People are really suffering, she told him.

On the first day of the social welfare bill debates, the party chairman duly, if reluctantly, voted with the government, gnomically tweeting *Alea iacta est* – 'The die is cast', reprising Julius Caesar's famous declaration, as he crossed the border into Italy, that a war for ascendancy in Rome was about to begin. But Caesar had signalled his intention to start a war; Keaveney had conspicuously stepped back from conflict.

Only until the following day, Thursday, 13 December. Shortly after lunch, the news exploded out of Leinster House: Keaveney had voted against the government. The man himself again announced his move via a tweet in Latin: *Acta non verba* – 'Actions not words'. Walking through the division lobby, hard-left TD Richard Boyd Barrett complimented him. Gerry Adams did too. 'This too will pass,' Adams told him. His now fellow Labour rebel Róisín Shortall approached him. 'You did the right thing,' she said. Jesus, thought Keaveney. So this is the company I'm in now. In a statement, he said he had been working to 'overturn the more odious aspects of this budget'. His votes in favour were merely to buy time for those efforts. He praised his fellow Labour TDs, 'the finest group of people that I have had the honour to work with' and insisted on his loyalty to the party's values 'and the values of its membership' – values, the heavy implication was, no longer practised by the leadership. Keaveney attacked Fine Gael for seeking to become an 'Irish Tory Party'. This interpretation was shared by a lot of Labour backbenchers; indeed, it was once shared by Eamon Gilmore, who told people after the 2007 general election that new Fine Gael TDs such as Leo Varadkar and Lucinda Creighton were 'Tories'. Keaveney had been quietly telling people for months that Gilmore's leadership would not survive. Now, he sought to strike a blow as part of that process.

The reaction from Government Buildings was immediate and furious. Behind closed doors there was unrestrained anger at Keaveney's treachery; in public, though, the line was more restrained. 'He was always going to go,' said one of Gilmore's aides. 'I think Joan was minding him.' Gilmore himself said he presumed that Keaveney would resign the party chairmanship, a call echoed by several other TDs. Later, Gilmore gave a 'barnstorming' performance at an emergency meeting of the parliamentary party that evening, putting 'fire in the belly' of bruised TDs, according to those present.

The pushback against Keaveney was savage. Pat Rabbitte monstered him on *Morning Ireland* the following day, decrying his 'political narcissism' and his 'pirouetting on the plinth . . . saying "Watch me now as I agonize about this decision"'. Even for someone with Rabbitte's finely tuned ear for a soundbite, this was catchy stuff. But some Labour TDs thought it was getting up the noses of their grassroots supporters, among whom there was a fair degree of sympathy with Keaveney. They, after all, were the ones that had put up the posters promising not to cut child benefit.

Gilmore's advisers believed that you sometimes define yourself by your enemies in your own party. Like political operators all over the world, they were in awe of the political skills employed to deliver Tony Blair three majorities, and they remembered how he moved his own party to the right, almost against its will, with the promise of power. Keaveney had made himself an internal enemy, and a campaign was immediately started against him. Some TDs, who had grown tired of Keaveney's grandstanding, thought: Fuck him. Good riddance. Others reflected: He's right. We did promise not to cut child benefit. 'Most politicians have big egos,' said one special adviser to his colleagues during one of the many post-mortems. 'But Colm, he's operatic.'

For days afterwards, Labour spinners continued to question Keaveney's motivation. His differences over constituency matters with the leadership were reaired; he was said to be 'obsessed' with Gilmore's chief aide Mark Garrett over clashes when both were student politicians. He was annoyed that an invitation to attend the British Labour Party conference was not passed on to him. And there was the perceived sidelining at the celebrations for Labour's foundation. There was some truth to at least most of these things. But all the spinning couldn't gloss over the fact that Labour was doing things in government it had promised not to do. Try as they might, Labour spinners couldn't gainsay that point.

When a few Labour senators began to wrestle publicly with their consciences that weekend, threatening to vote against the social welfare bill in the Seanad the following week, the party could barely summon the emotional energy to fight on another front.

The senators met Gilmore and Burton; wearily they were told that the cuts couldn't be reversed, but they could have whatever watery assurances about fairness they needed. In the end, just one senator, James Heffernan from Limerick, of whom few outside his constituency and Leinster House had ever heard, joined the ranks of the rebels. 'Who the fuck is he?' sneered Labour spinners. But Heffernan's reasons for his vote were wounding all the same. 'A solemn pledge was made not long ago as I was travelling door to door and meeting people in my own area of Kilfinane, Kilmallock, Bruff and all areas throughout my constituency and the county of Limerick,' Heffernan told a quiet Senate chamber. 'My party said we would not cut child benefit. That pledge is now broken and in good conscience I cannot be party to that.' It was easy to dismiss Heffernan. The truth was that Labour spinners had a point: few people actually had heard of him as a national politician. It was less easy to dismiss what he said.

Labour's reaction to the defections illustrated the central political problem for the coalition: the basic unpopularity of depriving people of benefits that they had acquired during the boom years – no matter how unsustainable their payment might be. The basic grounding principle of Irish politics during the years of economic growth – that the fruits of that economic growth should be spread among voters in return for re-electing Fianna Fáil-led governments – hadn't suddenly become unstuck once prosperity evaporated and budgets were squeezed. It had left Ireland with a politics that was itself wholly unsuited to the new economic order. For the past decade and a half, and maybe for much longer, the Irish people had been electing politicians on the promise and delivery of resources to them, their families, their communities and the country. During the years of the boom, the state's largesse crossed all ages, classes and geographical areas. Once the goodies were taken away, neither voters nor politicians knew what to expect of each other.

17

Prom night

Newspapers might be a sunset industry (or they might not), but no politician has yet delivered an important speech on Twitter or Facebook. However, they regularly turn to the op-ed pages of newspapers to stake out policy positions, signal new directions or otherwise give notice of their intentions. Eamon Gilmore began the new year of 2013 as an op-ed contributor to nine of Europe's leading newspapers. His thoughts – under the headline 'Ireland out of the crisis' – appeared in the *Frankfurter Allgemeine Zeitung* in Germany and also in *El Pais* in Spain, *Politiken* in Denmark, as well as newspapers in Poland, the Czech Republic, Italy and Sweden. The Irish ambassadors had worked the Christmas-party circuit well. Gilmore had a simple message: Ireland needs a deal on its bank debt. Irish taxpayers, he said, cannot be left to 'bear the weight' of supporting the European financial system on their own. His target was not just the readers of the esteemed organs carrying his words; it was also the policy-making elite of Europe. A new and more aggressive phase in Ireland's campaign to get some relief from its Sisyphean burden had begun. A pretty antsy month lay ahead.

No single issue featured more prominently in the nightmares of government ministers than Ireland's bank debt. It was not just that the Cowen government's salvation of the catastrophically busted Irish banks had prompted the most wounding, and largely justified, political charge in modern Irish history, now transferred to the Fine Gael–Labour coalition – that of bailing out the banks while imposing brutal austerity on the country – it was that it had saddled future governments with a crushing load of debt. The financially literate ministers knew that some alleviation of the debt was vital if the country was ever to recover economically and emerge from the bailout. Barely a few weeks in office one senior minister was already confiding, 'It can't be done. Four and a half million people just can't shoulder this level of debt. Just can't be done.' The efforts to take some of the debt off the hard-pressed shoulders of the Irish taxpayers would lead to some of the most fraught moments in the coalition's existence.

Twice the Irish government had come up against the ECB in its efforts to alleviate the burden of historic banking debt on Ireland's crushed public finances; twice it had been rebuffed. Michael Noonan's plan to burn Anglo Irish Bank bondholders in the first weeks of the coalition's life had perished against the granite rock of Jean-Claude Trichet's immovable resolve – and his threat to withdraw ECB funding for Irish banks. A year later, Noonan tried again, but his requests to a change to the promissory notes scheme – with its politically and fiscally murderous €3 billion payment by the Irish government every March – again fell on deaf ears. The small group of officials and politicians who between them made the vital decisions about the country's financial future resolved that when it came to the third time, they would not fail again.

Since the second March failure, in 2012, the Irish side had awaited a 'technical paper' from the Troika on the options for dealing with the promissory notes issue. For a time, this gave everyone some space, but officials soon began to suspect that they might never see it – or at least that they would never see 'anything meaningful in it'. Anyway, the view was hardening that the problem hadn't been 'technical', but political.

In the summer of 2012, with the first flush of office long behind them, most of the people involved thought about it in the same way as they thought about the entire undertaking of government: a slog through adversity to a better, though highly uncertain, future. Encouragement came from an unusual source: from the belly of the beast itself. In July, Noonan led a team of officials, including Andrew McDowell, John Moran and Jim O'Brien, to Frankfurt for a bilateral meeting with the ECB president Mario Draghi, who had replaced Trichet the previous November. The change in the president's office had been exhaustively analysed and dissected. What might it mean for ECB policy? So far, Draghi had been cautiously moving towards a more catholic view of the bank's role – with an eye on the European economy as a whole, rather than solely on the level of inflation, or 'price stability', as Trichet had endlessly cited. Dry analysis is one thing; but sitting across the table from people and looking into the whites of their eyes is how politicians figure out if they can do business. Eamon Gilmore had once airily dismissed Trichet as a mere 'civil servant'; in fact, he was an orthodox, if conservative central banker. The Irish side was hoping that his successor was more of a politician. Given the ECB's enormous funding commitment to Irish banks, the bailout programme and the extent to which the Irish economy was exposed to events in Europe, few of Draghi's visitors had as much hope invested in him as the Irish did.

The delegation found the atmosphere in the ECB's headquarters entirely more congenial than relations between Dublin and Frankfurt would have suggested. Draghi greeted them warmly and proceeded to shower them with praise about the implementation of the programme. The meeting was, if not quite convivial, certainly considerably better humoured than a lot of Ireland's previous exchanges with officials from the ECB. The Irish side presented its take on the history of the programme, the causes of the crash, the damage sustained by the sovereign when the Irish banks were saved and the need for some alleviation of the burden, as much for political reasons as for financial ones. Draghi was receptive, expansive, political, engaging. Afterwards, the Irish team thought that this was as much to send a message to his own side about the necessity to do a deal with Ireland on the promissory notes as anything.

Klaus Masuch was also part of the ECB delegation. Masuch had been the ECB's representative on Ireland, part of the original triumvirate of top officials – along with Istvan Szekely of the European Commission and Ajai Chopra of the IMF – who were the face of the ECB/EU/IMF Troika in Ireland. While Ireland had – to his amazement – warmed to Chopra during his time here, to the extent that people greeted him by his first name and complimented him when they met him, Masuch had frequently found himself playing bad cop, reminding the public and the government of the ECB's support for Irish banks, emphasizing the need to close the deficit and consistently restating the belief that it was Ireland that had got itself into all this trouble in the first place. The European elements of the Troika – the ECB and the European Commission – both found it amazing that they were regarded as Ireland's oppressors, while they thought they were Ireland's saviours, but few officials professed the thought as plainly as Masuch. He delivered lectures on these themes not just to politicians and officials, but also to the media, until the Troika – perhaps wisely – abandoned the practice of giving press conferences after their quarterly reviews. The decision to stop the press conferences followed a number of lively confrontations between Masuch and journalists, with Vincent Browne especially prominent in questioning the Troika representatives on a few occasions. The hard line also earned Masuch a certain notoriety in official circles. At an economic conference in Kenmare in 2011, attended by Chopra (who charmed all present with his affability and apparently genuine concern for Ireland), one influential economist revealed his view of the Troika, a view that was widely shared in policy-making circles. 'The IMF are all right,' he told me. 'The Commission guys, they're all right. But the fucking ECB are fucking cunts.' If Masuch was in any way put out by having to be the one to take a tough line, he certainly didn't show it. In fact, some observers of the process felt that he secretly might relish it. In any event, Masuch's tour of duty in Ireland had come to an end; he had been posted to Greece as head of the ECB's mission.

Though he was no longer part of the ECB's Irish team, Masuch sat beside Draghi for the meeting in Frankfurt, and the Irish side noticed that he had a document he was trying to bring to Draghi's attention. Masuch repeatedly pushed the document in front of Draghi; the Italian, becoming a bit irritated, the Irish thought, repeatedly pushed it back. But Masuch was insistent; back the document would go to Draghi. Soon the Irish delegation was hardly noticing what Draghi was saying, they were all so engrossed in what was happening with Masuch and his document. Eventually, the president stopped abruptly. 'What is it, Klaus?' The meeting froze. Draghi was a bit exasperated, but his demeanour was more theatrical than genuinely annoyed. Masuch nudged the document again. 'Oh, yes, my very diligent friend Klaus has something he wants me to say.' He picked up the document and waved it about. 'I note here,' he said, peering at Masuch's pages, 'that Irish public service pay is twice the level of public service pay in Greece!' The Irish side didn't think Draghi appeared to be too out-raged by the revelation. Now he addressed Masuch: 'Is that it, Klaus? Did I get that right? Okay? Okay?' He turned back to the Irish side. 'Now. I have made the point that Klaus wanted me to make.'

A smiling Noonan intervened. 'Ah, now, Mario. Sure that's why we asked for Klaus to be transferred to Greece.'

The ECB side of the table exploded in laughter. When it died down, Masuch shot back: 'Ah, Mr Noonan, but it is the Greeks who are complaining about it!'

The Irish side enjoyed the Masuch put-down – if that was really what it was; they liked to think so – enormously. But they took a far more important meaning out of the meeting back to Dublin with them. The change at the top of the ECB was a significant one for Ireland. The bank debt, and in particular the promissory notes arrangement, was back on the agenda.

The key difference, the Irish side believed, was that they were now involved in a process that was at least partly political. The ECB retained its independence certainly, and would jealously defend it. But a subtle, though hugely important, shift had occurred. The lead-ership of the bank was now reacting to the political context. Noonan and his officials reckoned that this gave them something to work with. That September, they got going.

There is a rhythm to the political year everywhere, and September is always a busy month, when politicians and civil servants return from their August holidays for the commencement of the autumn political term, which runs until Christmas. Following a series of pre-paratory meetings at which finance and Central Bank officials had met their European counterparts, Noonan took himself to Paris and Berlin to press the case for a debt deal for Ireland. At the Berlin meet-ing with the German finance minister Wolfgang Schäuble, Noonan discussed the attitude of the ECB to the deal. Schäuble told him he should meet the German ECB executive board member Jörg Asmus-sen, who had previously served as Schäuble's chief-of-staff. Asmussen would be attending a meeting of EU finance ministers in Cyprus, then holders of the European presidency, a few days later. Noonan agreed, and asked Schäuble to come to the meeting too. He assented. After the Cyprus meetings, Noonan told reporters, the ECB was 'more eager now to move forward'.

One of the blessings and the curses of the Troika programme is that it brought a greater level of transparency to the national finances, and to the government's budgetary plans, than had ever been seen before. So the Troika's review documents were quite clear a long time in advance about how much each budget would have to raise. The number for the 2013 budget, to be announced in late 2012, was €3.5 billion – rather uncomfortably similar to the €3.1 billion that government was going to have to pay over on the promissory notes the following March. There were technical differences, of course, but that didn't mean the politics of it were any less troublesome. In a polity where the single most important question was 'What is the public's tolerance for austerity?' the political importance of the promissory notes deal actually outweighed its fiscal and economic significance. And that was saying something.

Throughout the autumn, official contacts between the Irish government – with teams from the Department of Finance, the Central Bank and the National Treasury Management Agency forming the core of Dublin's efforts – and the ECB intensified. In a parallel process, diplomatic activity intensified with the Irish embassies in Berlin, Paris, and the other Eurozone countries both lobbying and absorbing as much information as possible from their local finance ministries and central banks. Every week, a conference call between the ambassadors and senior officials in Dublin was conducted in Iveagh House, the Department of Foreign Affairs headquarters on St Stephen's Green. The top-secret project was given the codename 'Project Red'. Actually, 'Project Red' was the term for the planned liquidation of Anglo Irish Bank that would accompany the promissory notes deal; the wider effort to secure a deal on the promissory notes was called 'Project Dawn'. But the guys in the Department of Finance liked the 'Project Red' tag – partly, said one, 'because it sounded so fucking ridiculous'.

On a couple of occasions, ministers thought they were on the verge of clinching the deal, but each time agreement failed to materialize.

There were knockbacks too. Ireland was hanging at least some of its hopes on the declaration by European leaders at its June summit that the European Stability Mechanism – the common bailout fund set up in the wake of the Greek, Irish and Portuguese crashes – could rescue banks directly, without going through the national governments, and thus lifting the burden of debt from the shaky sovereigns. Crucially for Ireland, European leaders had apparently agreed that the same terms could be applied retrospectively to previous bailouts, raising the prospect of the Irish government actually getting back some of the billions of euros of taxpayers' cash ploughed into the Irish banking sector. As ever with the European response to the financial crisis, though, it was two steps forward and at least one back. In September, the German, Dutch and Finnish finance ministers – all substantial donors to the new fund – seemed to rule out 'legacy assets' being included in the direct recapitalization plan. More worryingly for Ireland, the German chancellor Angela Merkel appeared to agree with them. After the October summit, she told reporters, 'There will be no retroactive recapitalization.' Irish political debate often ignores inconvenient things said in Brussels, but there was no ignoring this.

Kenny now weighed in for favours from his supposed political friend and ally. Fine Gael had trumpeted Kenny's closeness to Merkel when he was in opposition, and made political hay during the election campaign when he went to visit her. Presumably in an attempt to highlight this relationship, the public relations consultant Terry Prone, whose business had provided media coaching to Kenny and other Fine Gael ministers, once advised Kenny's wife Fionnuala on radio that there was no need to worry, the two leaders were just good friends. History does not record if Fionnuala Kenny ever feared being supplanted in her husband's affections by the German leader, but if so, she must have been reassured when one of Merkel's first acts after Kenny became Taoiseach was to try to strongarm him into conceding on Ireland's corporation tax. It was true that they got on, and it is not true that in politics there are no friendships. But interests usually trump them.

Irish officials now played the card that it was in the EU's – and therefore Germany's – interests that Ireland should have a viable path to exiting the bailout, thus illuminating that path to others. Officials in Dublin wheeled with their German counterparts. The Irish ambassador in Berlin, Dan Mulhall, ran down every one of his contacts. Eventually a statement was agreed, and Kenny travelled from Mayo on a Sunday to seal its delivery. After a half-hour call, a joint statement was released by the two governments, acknowledging that Ireland was a 'special case'. According to a senior civil servant, it was really the only time that Kenny used his political capital with Merkel on the banking debt issue, and he used it to good effect. After a fraught few days, the game was back on, the officials thought.

The shape of the eventual agreement was clear to those involved, but agreeing the final details was proving maddeningly elusive. Then, to the horror of Government Buildings, the story almost broke.

On 4 November, the *Sunday Business Post* published a story by Ian Kehoe and Cliff Taylor revealing that an 'early closure' of IBRC, the former Anglo Irish Bank, was one of the options being considered by government as part of a proposed deal with the ECB on the promissory notes. The story caused consternation in the Department of Finance and the Taoiseach's department among those who were in the loop on 'Red'. One senior official was at a wedding in Cork that weekend, and only got to bed at 6 a.m. At 7 a.m. he was woken by another official about the story. If word of a planned Anglo liquidation leaked into the market, the bank's creditors would move immediately to protect their assets as best they could. The entire plan could be frustrated by legal actions.

In the event, the story did not use the word 'liquidation'. Nonetheless, finance was terrified the newspaper would follow up on the story the next week and firm up the liquidation angle, or that others would do so in the week that followed. To their relief, the story excited no interest elsewhere, but they still faced the prospect of further revelations the following weekend. The emergency legislation was by now ready to go. The EMC decided that if the newspaper followed up the story and used the word 'liquidation' – now being referred to in the Department of Finance as 'the L word' – the following week, the government would recall the Dáil that Sunday and pass the emergency legislation overnight. Preparations were made for the dramatic move of an immediate meeting of the Dáil.

Officials did a good job of not betraying their anxiety to the newspaper. They got their copies on Saturday night. No liquidation story appeared. 'We got a serious fright before Christmas, we thought the thing had broken,' Noonan later said. That, he said, would have left him 'halfway across the river' – with no ECB deal, and no paddle either.

As Christmas approached, frustration was building at cabinet over the glacial pace of progress and Noonan's unwillingness to provide information about the process. Noonan wasn't just wary of leaks in the normal course of these things; he was operating on the assumption that if he briefed the cabinet, it would be leaked, and a leak would derail the Anglo plan, and probably the promissory notes deal. 'Of course I can brief you. I can provide you all with a full briefing if that's what you want. But it will be on the front page of the *Irish Times* tomorrow,' he told his fellow ministers on one occasion. He reiterated the same view a number of times. It was an astonishing lack of trust in his colleagues, but it explained to some extent the growing tendency of the leadership of the government to do business at the EMC, and not at the full cabinet.

At one meeting before Christmas, tensions boiled over, with Rabbitte and Noonan angrily clashing about the lack of progress. Rabbitte had said on RTÉ that the government wouldn't pay the €3 billion due in March, and Noonan was fretful that loose talk could derail his delicate strategy. Words were exchanged, and the *Sunday Independent* duly got wind of it. '"Rabbitte, keep your nose out of prom note" rages Noonan' roared the headline, above a story that gave a blow-by-blow account of a pretty serious bust-up. The two men spoke later, and Rabbitte got a full explanation of where the finance minister thought progress was at. Rabbitte remained uneasy that the deal would be done in time. He was hyper-aware of the potential political fallout of having to pay the €3 billion in March – and of a government division over whether it should be paid. The row was quickly patched up, but it was about substantial things, not a personality clash. Experienced politicians know that those are the most serious kind of rows.

Rabbitte's comments on RTÉ demonstrated that the poisonous

politics of the Anglo notes couldn't be ignored either. Noonan and the others knew they couldn't force a decision from the ECB by March. And if negotiations were still proceeding at the same snail's pace – what then? In fact, both ministers and officials believed they couldn't even wait until March. Running right down to the deadline would weaken their hand. The St Patrick's Day exodus of ministers also meant that by the time they returned, there would be only a week until the payment date. They became convinced that they needed a deal in February.

But January was turning out to be even more frustrating. 'We were getting lots of "We want to help" and "You are doing the right things", but there was still no sign of a deal,' says one person involved throughout the process. There wasn't an explicit decision by the EMC, but the line from Dublin began to get a lot tougher. Gilmore and his aides had decided to 'cut up rough'.

At the end of January, Gilmore attended an EU–Latin American summit in Santiago, Chile, where he met a number of European leaders, including the German chancellor Angela Merkel. 'He didn't go to see the Latin Americans,' an aide later observed. Gilmore warned Merkel of the 'serious consequences' for his government if a deal with the ECB couldn't be done in the coming weeks. When the chancellor wants to block something at European level, she rarely simply says 'no'. She says, 'I cannot get this through my parliament.' Gilmore told her that before the March payment date, there was sure to be a vote on the promissory notes in the Dáil. 'I am not sure I can get that through my parliament,' he told her. The story was leaked to me, which I reported as Labour figures worrying that failure to achieve a deal could spell the end of the coalition. Privately, I was told repeatedly by people completely familiar with Gilmore's thinking: If this deal doesn't happen, then the government is finished. Labour can't stand over the payment of the promissory notes' €3 billion at the end of March, they insisted. I thought it was an extraordinary gamble. 'You've bet the farm on getting this deal,' I observed to one senior figure over breakfast. The Labour leadership believed it had no option. 'The farm has kind of been bet for us,' he replied.

But if Dublin was upping the pressure abroad, the tension was also beginning to tell at home. Labour frustration with Noonan's sphinx-like demeanour on the negotiations was beginning to build, while Fine Gael thought Labour was getting too jumpy. Neither side liked the consequences of a deal not being reached, but many in Labour thought they were more serious for the smaller party. The talking up of the possible end of the coalition wasn't just to put pressure on Merkel and the ECB; it was to send a message to Noonan about the need to pull out all the stops. 'It'll be okay,' insisted one senior official on Kenny's staff to me at the time. He thought that Kenny had Merkel onside, and 'Merkel gets what she wants.' 'They just need to calm down,' another senior Fine Gael person in the administration told me, tut-tutting at Labour's public fretting. 'They're completely obsessed with themselves,' he said.

The truth was that nobody knew if they would conclude a deal in time. There was an agreed strategy at EMC level, but different ministers reflected it differently. When Gilmore warned about the 'catastrophic' consequences of not achieving a deal, Noonan issued a pointed rebuff a few days later. Taking the unusual step of summoning reporters in Limerick on a Monday (ministers normally travel to Dublin on Monday evenings), he said: 'I don't understand why people are getting so excited.' He went on to say that linking the promissory notes negotiations with the future of the government – as Gilmore had been very publicly doing – was wrong. 'I don't put the two issues together at all,' he said. 'I don't see any threat to the coalition government.' What he was really saying was: *Gilmore! Keep your mouth shut! It's not helping!*

One of the great advantages of the EMC, its participants thought, was that the two parties didn't have to talk to one another through the media. Now they were. Briefing the political correspondents at the weekly post-cabinet session the following day, the government press secretary Feargal Purcell and his deputy Cathy Madden (one representative from each of the coalition parties) tried their best to insist there was no division among the parties, using the phrase 'on the same page' three times, plus several other euphemisms. But it was clear that they were only on the same page if the chapter concluded with a deal on the promissory notes. Otherwise, the story could have a pretty sticky ending.

But things were moving on. At its meeting in late January, the ECB discussed the Irish situation, though no agreement was reached. A few days after the discussion in Frankfurt, Reuters reported that the ECB had rejected the Irish proposal to swap the promissory notes for long-term government bonds 'and agreed that it amounted to "monetary financing" of the Irish government, banned under Article 123 of the EU Treaty'. This wasn't entirely true. The bank hadn't quite rejected the Irish bid, but it hadn't accepted it either. The report caused an enormous flap in Dublin, and it was immediately rubbished by Government Buildings. The various sides to the argument (and there was more than one camp in the ECB) suspected the others of leaking the news tactically. But by now the Irish side knew that Frankfurt could probably live with some version of the notes-for-bonds plan. The bank issued a statement a day later, saying discussions were ongoing. Noonan maintained an inscrutable silence. Labour's fretting jumped a few notches – senior figures knew the party couldn't walk itself back from the position it had adopted. That nobody outside of a few senior ministers and officials knew what was going on added to the atmosphere of nervous uncertainty.

It was expected that the bank's governors would discuss the subject at its next meeting on 6–7 February. Officials in Dublin were in daily contact with Frankfurt now. Privately, some on the Irish side thought, It's now or never. When Patrick Honohan left Dublin for the meeting, they figured, he might very well have the fate of the coalition in his hands.

When calls from the news agencies Bloomberg and Reuters came into the Department of Finance's press office on the afternoon of Wednesday, 6 February, the civil servants present knew the game was up. When journalists are chasing a story, they seek information. When they have the story, they seek comment. These calls weren't fishing expeditions, seeking information: they were looking for the department's reaction to a story they were going to run on the planned liquidation of the former Anglo Irish Bank as part of the deal between the Irish government and the ECB on the Anglo promissory notes.

The department had been fielding calls from the agencies for the previous few days, and had simply been refusing to comment. The press office knew that was the way a lot of reporters worked: gradually chipping away at a story, coming and going with them, until they were satisfied they could run it. So far, the agencies hadn't been sufficiently sure of the liquidation story to run it. Now they were. The minister needed to be told, and told now.

That afternoon, as on so many occasions in recent months, the council was discussing the prospects for a deal with the ECB on the promissory notes. But this time it was different. This wasn't an abstract discussion of strategy, or a briefing on the technical design of a package. This was the time to make or lose the deal. Honohan was already in Frankfurt. Having played a long game of poker for months and months, the government was playing its last hand now.

The Irish side had run up against deadlines with the ECB before over the past two years, and government officials reckoned that delay was one of Frankfurt's standard tactics. Keep putting off a decision until a deadline has passed. Whether that was true or not, the Irish were determined there was going to be a resolution of the promissory notes issue in February. That left this meeting or the next one. No time like the present, they thought. In any event, matters were about to be taken out of their hands.

The EMC was meeting that afternoon. Senior finance official Ann Nolan briefed those present on the state of play, the procedure for pushing ahead, and the dangers if no agreement was forthcoming from the ECB. When she was finished, Noonan summarized. 'So there you are now. You've heard what Ann says. I'm happy to be guided by you,' he told the council. 'I'm in your hands.' Noonan had brought the negotiations as far as he could. He wanted the final pushing of the button to be a decision of the entire leadership of the government. Kenny sought opinions. Gilmore was bullish, very aggressive. Howlin let his secretary general Robert Watt follow him. 'Fuck it, let's do it,' Watt said. 'We have to show them we're serious.'

The press office in the Department of Finance is at the front of Government Buildings, overlooking Merrion Street. The EMC was meeting in the Sycamore Room, at the far side of the quadrangle. Paul Bolger, the department's press officer, made the journey as quickly as he could. He entered the Sycamore Room and asked Noonan to step out. He briefed him about the Bloomberg and Reuters stories, expected to break that evening. It was not long after 3 p.m. Noonan went back in and broke the news to the other EMC members.

It wasn't completely unexpected. The agencies had been in constant contact with the Department of Finance on the promissory notes issue in recent weeks, and the finance officials knew that both Reuters and Bloomberg had alerted their reporters in Frankfurt and in European capitals to shake down their sources about the Anglo/IBRC story. At a meeting the previous night, Tuesday, the EMC had explicitly discussed what it should do if the story leaked. One of the lessons the civil service has learned from the collapse of the Fianna Fáil–Green government is that it should have contingency plans for all eventualities. Everyone knew the story could leak, and they knew they needed a plan to deal with it. That moment had now arrived. 'It's a market moving event,' said one source of the Anglo/IBRC liquidation story when it began to leak out that afternoon. 'It's flashed up on every trader's screen.'

Noonan now outlined the immediate plans to the EMC. Under the legislation that had nationalized Anglo, he could appoint an officer to take over the powers of the board of the bank. The orders had been prepared months before. Officials produced them immediately, and Noonan signed them. After all the Technicolor drama that had surrounded Anglo Irish Bank since it first began to totter on the dizzy heights to which it had ascended on the pile of borrowed money it could never repay, this was the low-key death sentence for the bank. Its board and executives had no forewarning. Noonan nominated KPMG as liquidators. Anglo was dead.

KPMG had produced a plan for the winding down, or liquidation, of Anglo for Brian Lenihan in 2010. The blueprint had languished in a drawer until the previous autumn, when the accountants received a call from the Department of Finance. They were asked if the plans could be updated, and made ready to go at a moment's notice. That Wednesday afternoon, KPMG received another call from the Department of Finance, with the message: It's on.

But the appointment of a liquidator only 'bought them a few

hours', according to someone involved in the discussions. Officials had decided they needed powers for a special kind of liquidation to take account of IBRC's particular circumstances and to achieve what they wanted with the promissory notes. It involved wide-ranging new powers for the finance minister in the liquidation process. The fifty-page bill had been drawn up in the autumn and a plan formulated for its enactment overnight as emergency legislation. 'The government cannot introduce legislation until it receives a stamped copy from the attorney general,' Noonan would tell the Senate early on Thursday morning. 'I have had a stamped copy in my possession for several months.'

With the news agencies perhaps only minutes away from publication, the ministers decided the emergency legislation had to go ahead. However, they knew they were ordering the liquidation without having had any word from the ECB on the deal to restructure the €28 billion in promissory notes. This was the other element of the plan – and the one where the political problems really lay. Anglo was a constant irritation certainly, but it was the promissory notes arrangement that necessitated the €3 billion payments every March. Liquidating the bank was welcome, but without a deal in place on the prom notes, it would force liability immediately upon the government. Killing off Anglo was only half the plan.

The governing board of the bank was meeting in Frankfurt, but the news had filtered back from Patrick Honohan: there would be no agreement on the Irish deal that evening. 'Weidmann [Jens Weidmann, president of the Bundesbank] wants to sleep on it,' one senior official was told. There wasn't even a guarantee that it would be signed off at the following day's meeting. As the whips sent out notification to TDs to stay around Leinster House for the evening, the government was faced with a massive uncertainty. What if Frankfurt's feet didn't warm up? They all figured they had a deal in principle, but they needed one in practice. Tempers rose. Some on the Labour side complained furiously that Honohan was not keeping them informed, but he was in constant contact with the Taoiseach's office.

By 6 p.m. on Wednesday, the Leinster House rumour machine –

which had been in full flow all afternoon – had been overtaken by reporting. RTÉ's *Six One News* was reporting that the emergency legislation to allow for the IBRC liquidation would be put before the Dáil that night. President Michael D. Higgins was in Rome and, while the constitution allows for a commission to sign legislation in his absence, ministers thought he should be brought back. Two finance officials were dispatched to Rome to brief the president and accompany him home.

Meanwhile, in Dublin, word had come through from Frankfurt that there could be roadblocks to a deal in the morning. By 8 p.m. there was confusion, with the Department of Finance unable to say even if the legislation would be passed that night. Inside the department, officials joked that the two lads would be flying out to Rome to tell Michael D. Higgins he wouldn't be needed after all. At a tension-filled meeting of the EMC, Kenny, Gilmore, Noonan and Howlin decided: they had to proceed with the Anglo liquidation, hope for the ECB's approval in the morning and deal with it then if no deal was forthcoming. It was high-wire stuff. The whips were told that the legislation was going ahead, and the Dáil would sit to begin debating it at 10.30 p.m. #promnight, as Twitter had dubbed it – no event in the age of social media is truly significant without its own hashtag – was on.

At 8.45 p.m. the cabinet met to formally approve the legislation. Oireachtas clerks worked furiously to produce copies of the bill and associated documents. There was no going back now. TDs filed into the Dáil at 10.30 p.m., but the chief whip, Paul Kehoe, appeared to request an adjournment until 11 p.m. A scattering of TDs remained in the Dáil, though few of them read the copies of the bill. At 11.02 p.m. the Taoiseach and Tánaiste led the cabinet in procession into the Dáil chamber. Fianna Fáil leader Micheál Martin and other opposition leaders appealed for more time to study the bill, having only been briefed about its contents less than an hour before. Government TDs were giddy and loud, howling down the Sinn Féin leader Gerry Adams when he advised the Ceann Comhairle: 'If you want some order from government TDs, you should close the Dáil bar.' (On this very point, a smart Freedom of Information request from the *Sunday Independent* several weeks later discovered that the members' bar in Leinster House sold 200 drinks that night. Given that there are 226 members of the Oireachtas, it was hardly bacchanalian. Indeed, to those of us who favour the consumption of a moderate amount of alcohol prior to making important decisions, it seems a little on the light side of what is advisable.)

At midnight, Michael Noonan rose and began reading his prepared script to a packed House. 'I would have preferred to be introducing this bill as part of a broader agreement with the ECB,' he told them, 'but the ECB will continue to consider our proposals tomorrow.' So that was it: the deal was still up in the air. 'We can't vote for this if we don't know the other parts of the package!' thundered Shane Ross. But, as of now, there was no other part of the package. Ross was right: in the absence of a confirmed deal with the ECB, the Dáil didn't know what it was voting for. Ministers didn't even know what was going to happen the next day. What if the ECB didn't budge? Would the government act unilaterally on the promissory notes? Labour sources subsequently claimed the coalition had decided to proceed the next day and restructure the notes even if Frankfurt couldn't make its mind up. Others present are certain no such decision had been taken on the Wednesday night. It's clear that in the absence of a go-ahead from Frankfurt, the coalition would have been plunged into a potentially life-ending crisis.

By 12.40 a.m. the Dáil was getting rowdy. 'This is the last time I'll ask you to keep quiet!' the Ceann Comhairle warned. 'The next time you'll be going out that door!' Then, looking around, 'Or that door, whichever.' Thousands were watching live on television or on the internet, while Twitter throbbed with observations, declarations of treason and the usual competition with one-liners. 'Is this the Gathering?' asked the comedian Dara Ó Briain.

By 3 a.m. the debate was done, and the government suffered no defections. Fianna Fáil supported the bill, which passed by 113 votes to 35. Noonan made his way to the other side of Leinster House, where bleary-eyed senators went through the same process, and the same arguments. Key officials were sent home to bed – tomorrow would be another hectic day. 'Though I didn't sleep very well,' said one. The Senate passed the bill at 6 a.m. on Thursday morning, whereupon a dispatch rider brought it to Áras an Uachtaráin. The president signed it into law shortly before 7 a.m.

The next day Mario Draghi entered the press room in the ECB's headquarters in Frankfurt a couple of minutes after 2.30 p.m. local time. Irish eyes were upon him. It had been an anxious morning in Dublin. A group of senior officials met for a long breakfast after a short night's sleep; there was confidence, but more than a touch of nerves. But still the toing and froing with Frankfurt continued. A small amendment was proposed by the ECB side over the eventual disposal of the bonds by the Irish Central Bank, so Dublin ran the numbers: Yes, that could work. Could that do it? Could it really do it? At about midday, the Department of Finance got word from Honohan: *Yes!* The Taoiseach rang the Tánaiste to report that the deal was done. My breakfasting source texted: 'The farm is safe.'

At the press conference, Draghi wittered on about inflation and financial stability. They were watching in Merrion Street, but in celebration, not concern. First question from the press pack when he finally finished: 'What about the Irish deal?' 'We unanimously took note of the Irish operation,' he pronounced. Central bankers speak their own language. To those who could speak it, this was the affirmation; to the rest, confusion. 'It's very concerning that he only noted it,' Eddie Hobbs told RTÉ's *Liveline*. They are not great fans of Eddie's in the Department of Finance and they fairly hooted their delight when he failed – understandably, given Draghi's almost oracular circumlocutions – to comprehend that the deal was done. 'What the fuck does "unanimously note" mean?' they joshed in the Department of Finance. 'What would "not unanimously note" mean?' asked someone. 'Would that mean someone was asleep?' After the weeks of tension and the legislative all-nighter, the release of stress was enormous.

The Taoiseach, as he often does, went around congratulating people. 'You've done a great job,' he told the officials in finance. The cabinet met in high good humour to approve the deal. A short while later, before 3 p.m., the Taoiseach rose in the Dáil: 'I wish,' he began, 'to make an important announcement for the information of the House.' Pat Rabbitte grinned like a Cheshire cat. For all the talk of progress, government TDs had had precious little to cheer about since they first took their seats two years earlier. But this was a good day for them, and the throaty hear-hears testified to it. 'The annual promissory notes payments,' the Taoiseach explained, 'are gone.'

The promissory notes deal was one of the most significant events – perhaps the most significant – of the government's first two years. While the political dividends at the polls were anaemic (to several ministers' vocal disappointment), and the immediate financial effects would almost cause as many problems as they would solve, as ministers, union leaders and interest groups soon targeted the €1 billion in savings, the real significance of the deal was that it opened the way to an exit from the bailout later in the year. It represented a concrete, tangible achievement; it enabled the coalition to credibly argue that it was making progress on what was certainly a difficult path, but one that led to a better future. It was like switching on the lights on a runway at night – suddenly the path ahead becomes clear.

For a government that had largely lost its narrative in its second year, this represented a vitally important breakthrough. If the coalition is ultimately to be a success, the prom night battle may turn out to be the turning point of the war.

It also demonstrated that the government was apparently willing to gamble its future to secure such an outcome. Improbably, the chief gambler appeared to be Eamon Gilmore. In January he and his aides had figured that Labour could not be part of a government that would continue to pay the promissory notes bills. 'I am absolutely clear that we would not have paid, and Labour would not have been part of a government that did continue paying,' said someone who knows the Tánaiste's thinking.

Would Labour have demanded unilateral action if the ECB had continued to stall? And would Gilmore have walked if Fine Gael had refused? We will never know. Perhaps the Tánaiste himself does not know what he might have done when faced with the question at five minutes to midnight. The government, after all, had previously baulked at entering direct confrontation with the ECB. And Gilmore, only the previous December, had abandoned a key budget demand when the future of the coalition appeared to be on the line.

Even before the coalition took office, its leadership had accepted what seemed to them to be Ireland's financial realities and the weakness of their position when negotiating with Ireland's funders. Prom night, and the tense weeks that preceded it, didn't completely redraw that picture. But it did change it significantly. The coalition asserted itself more than it had ever done, and that produced a signal success. 'The ECB had never had hardball from Dublin,' reflected one of the architects of the deal in the immediate aftermath. 'Now it was getting hardball.' But it was not without cost. For all the coalition's joint jubilation at their achievement, the episode had accentuated the differences at the top of government. The prom night partners might have been dancing together, but the romance was under pressure.

18

Labour's way

When Conor Brady became editor of the *Irish Times* in 1986 following the retirement of Douglas Gageby, that grand old man of Irish journalism, it was against the wishes of most of the editorial staff who favoured a different candidate, James Downey. So when Brady held his first meeting with the representatives of the paper's journalists, he anticipated an awkward encounter. An office politician supreme, Brady quickly disarmed them, *Phoenix* magazine reported. 'Well, it could have been worse,' he told his visitors. 'It could have been Vincent Browne.'

Twenty-six years later, Browne was the country's most celebrated and highest-profile journalist. He would never edit the *Irish Times*, but he wrote a weekly column for the newspaper, as well as presenting a nightly political discussion show on TV3. Though lampooned as a professional grump, Browne's shows would sometimes surprise viewers with unusual reporting pieces. On Wednesday, 14 November 2012, Browne took his camera crew into the Tara Street offices of the *Irish Times* to observe and report on a day in the life of the newspaper – to watch as it was put together, to observe both the mechanics and the decision-making processes, and to follow its path from editorial and story conferences, through page make-up, and on to the printing of the finished product.

Give me lucky generals, said Napoleon. The day Browne chose to follow and film was also the day when the newspaper published one of its most significant stories for years. As Browne and his cameras gazed on, the page-one headline on that morning's edition was this: 'Woman "denied a termination" dies in hospital'.

The crucial paragraphs in Kitty Holland's *Irish Times* story read as follows:

'He [Savita's husband, Praveen Halappanavar] says that, having been told she was miscarrying, and after one day in severe pain, Ms Halappanavar asked for a medical termination.

'This was refused, he says, because the foetal heartbeat was still present and they were told, "this is a Catholic country".

'She spent a further 2½ days "in agony" until the foetal heartbeat stopped.

'The dead foetus was removed and Savita was taken to the high dependency unit and then the intensive care unit, where she died of septicaemia on the 28th.'

The story, also carried in that day's *Independent*, flashed around the world: Catholic Ireland had refused a woman an abortion and, as a consequence, she had died. The story would turn out to be more complicated, but that is what many people heard and understood. The country was about to be plunged once more into one of its periodic bouts of self-flagellation on abortion.

The reaction was immediate, heartfelt and outraged. A candlelit vigil outside Leinster House that night drew 3,000 people; there was another in Cork. At a demonstration outside the Irish Embassy in London, protestors held placards suggesting Ireland's pro-life beliefs killed Savita. Social media exploded in a welter of fury and sympathy. The *Daily Mail* contacted Savita's mother in India. Its black-bordered front page the following day shouted: 'My daughter did not die, she was killed'. Inevitably, politicians served the role most frequently allocated to them: to be the focus of public anger. But on this occasion, many politicians were angry too.

As the storm gathered force, pro-life groups feared the public anger at the fate of Savita would lead to the overturning of Ireland's restrictive abortion laws. Damn right, thought pro-choice activists. In the *Irish Independent*, leading conservative commentator David Quinn warned, 'We must not allow ourselves to be conditioned by ceaseless one-sided propaganda into thinking our law on abortion is inhumane or unjust.' On the facing page, former Labour minister Liz McManus argued, 'Abortion is still a significant part of Irish life. We just don't talk about it . . . The government can seize this chance to prove we are facing up to our responsibilities.' The battle lines were clear; they had been drawn many times before.

*

The government had already decided it had to confront the issue of abortion in Ireland. For many TDs and ministers, especially in Labour, the terrible news about the death of the young woman underscored their determination to introduce legislation – which would, at the very least, offer legal protection and clarity to the limited abortion regime sanctioned by the Supreme Court in the X case twenty years earlier. In 1992 the court had ruled that a suicidal pregnant teenage girl – X – was legally entitled to an abortion because of the risk to her life.

The trigger for finally legislating for the 1992 ruling – planned long before the Savita case – was the report of an expert group set up to consider a 2010 decision of the European Court of Human Rights in Strasbourg on the case of an Irish-resident Lithuanian woman. The woman – C – had become pregnant while in remission from cancer. She had sought advice on the advisability of continuing her pregnancy, but she had not been able to get sufficient information due, she alleged, to the deficiencies of the Irish legal position on abortion. While the ECHR had always upheld the entitlement of each country to write its own laws on abortion, and rejected arguments that there is a right to abortion under the European Convention on Human Rights, it found in her case that the lack of clarity over whether she was legally entitled to an abortion or not had violated her human rights. Under the X case interpretation of the 1983 pro-life amendment to the constitution, which acknowledges the equal rights to life of the mother and the unborn, the Supreme Court had ruled that where a woman's life is threatened by her pregnancy – including by her own hand – she has the right to an abortion in Ireland. The state, the ECHR found, had not sufficiently vindicated that right.

The ECHR judgment was delivered in the dying days of the Fianna Fáil–Green government. After the general election Enda Kenny and Eamon Gilmore knew they had to reconcile their parties' deeply differing views and cultures if the abortion issue wasn't to detonate under their government at some point in the future. Abortion was one of the issues Programme for Government negotiators 'kicked upstairs' to be resolved by the party leaders. At their pre-coalition talks, the leaders agreed that an expert group would be set up to consider the ECHR judgment and to advise the government on a response. It was, they knew, likely to be a minimalist response. Both men were pretty sure they wouldn't be having another abortion referendum. They felt they had enough to be dealing with.

The expert group on abortion was appointed in January 2012. It comprised medical experts, lawyers and Department of Health officials. Its work was conducted under the ambit of the Department of Health and therefore also under the ambit of the coalition's most accident-prone minister, James Reilly – the minister in whom Labour had least faith or trust. From the very beginning, Labour resolved to watch the matter like hawks. The group's report was due in July, then September. Coming up to mid November there was still no sign of it. Labour was concerned, but not agitated – officials knew that the report had been delayed by an illness. Then they got word: the report had been delivered to Reilly. He got it just as the *Irish Times* was preparing to break the Savita story. On the Wednesday morning, both the *Times* and the expert group report were on the minister's desk.

Reilly sat on the report for a few days. Two days after receiving it, he told reporters that he had given it 'a quick glance', but had not had time to study it closely. When he had done so, he said, it would be given to the cabinet and published. Some in government wondered if the dog might eat his homework before he presented it to cabinet. Other people wanted things to move a little more quickly than that. A few days before it was due for publication, I received a call from a senior government source. Come out to meet me, he said. I walked around from Harcourt Street to Camden Street, where he approached me on the street. He produced a copy of the report. Tearing off its cover sheet, he handed it to me. 'You didn't get that from me,' he said.

As Labour had envisaged, the report of the expert group offered a road-map for legislating for the X case. The government was obliged to provide clarity in those instances when abortion was legal, and to provide facilities where they might take place. It said there would have to be a 'procedure for determining entitlement and access to termination of pregnancy'. The test to be applied was quite simple: it was the one that the Supreme Court had laid down in the X case. Doctors would have to decide as a matter of probability whether (1) there was a real and substantial risk to the life of the mother, including by suicide; and (2) this risk could be averted only by the termination of the pregnancy.

This test was actually a straightforward question, the report suggested. 'Although medical decisions may be difficult in particular cases, the complexities will not arise from the words of the test but from diagnostic and treatment issues. Implementing the test, therefore, does not require another definition of the test . . .'

If the government followed the expert group report, the question it faced was not *whether* the X case should be legislated for, it was *how* it should be legislated for.

The timing of the release of the expert group report – 27 November, barely two weeks after the Savita story became public – aroused immediate suspicion among anti-abortion groups. 'It's a fucking conspiracy!' one prominent pro-life voice insisted to me when I met him on Grafton Street. 'It's a fucking conspiracy between the *Irish Times* and the Labour Party and they are using that poor woman's death to do it!'

The reaction to the publication of the expert group within Fine Gael was less hysterical, but equally concerned. At a parliamentary party meeting, several TDs expressed their concerns that they were being 'press-ganged' into moving too quickly on the issue. From the start, one of the most vocal opponents was the European Affairs minister Lucinda Creighton, who argued that Fine Gael had 'no mandate' to proceed with legislation on abortion. Other TDs feared that the introduction of threatened suicide as grounds for abortion would 'open the floodgates' and lead to 'abortion on demand'. These phrases would be heard again and again as Fine Gael agonized over the issue. 'Critical voices heard at FG party meeting' reported the *Irish Times*. Characteristically, the *Indo* put it more bluntly. 'Fine Gael tearing itself apart over abortion law' blared its front page.

Kenny knew that the government would have to legislate. But now he did what politicians do when caught by any issue where they are unsure of the political ground: he tried to stall for time. But Gilmore pressed and pressed. The Dáil private members' motions on the issue earlier in the year, urging the government to legislate for the X case, had been reluctantly voted down by Labour TDs only on the promise that the government would act on the expert group report when it was finished. It was plain that the issue was too important to Labour to long-finger it indefinitely. In addition, Kenny's health minister had made it clear that the government would deal with the issue in the lifetime of the parliament. Indeed, there was also a liberal wing on the issue in Fine Gael, which was just as perplexed as anyone else by the famous contribution of Mayo TD Michelle Mulherin to the private members' debate, when she essayed that 'fornication . . . is probably the single most likely cause of unwanted pregnancies in this country'.

After the expert group delivered its report, Labour was in a far stronger position. Labour officials had worked carefully and discreetly on the terms of reference for the expert group with a view towards ending up with exactly the sort of report that the group ultimately produced. According to one person who was closely involved in the process at all times, 'Getting the terms of reference we wanted was absolutely critical. In many respects that was the key battle.' The direction given to the group largely determined its eventual findings. Reilly had admitted as much months earlier in a letter to Fine Gael TDs in which he suggested that he would legislate to provide procedures to determine whether women could have abortions or not. The letter was leaked to the *Irish Catholic*, which ran an outraged report headlined 'Fine Gael push to introduce abortion'. The health minister's staff rubbished the report, but it had made elements of the party nervous.

But it wasn't Reilly who would be the crucial actor in Fine Gael. It was Enda Kenny. What was Kenny's own view? He had constantly reassured his TDs that he himself was as pro-life as any of them but would have to act to take account of the expert group report and the Strasbourg judgment.

In reality, it wasn't the judgment of the court in Strasbourg that would eventually shape the government's response on abortion; it was his partners in government. Kenny was reasonably comfortable with this. He was broadly pro-life, but not dogmatically so. His mental make-up allowed him to hold certain principles, but also to admit exceptions to them. If that was philosophically untenable, it was a contradiction shared by half the country. In this, as in much else, he was always guided as much by his instincts as his intellect.

His biographer, the journalist John Downing, writing in the *Irish Independent*, described Kenny as a 'mildly liberal inbetweener'. Downing quoted an old Fine Gael hand who remembered Kenny in the days of the fights in the party over the liberal agenda: 'There were broadly three groups in Fine Gael . . . the "urban liberal wing" who favoured change, the "traditional wing" who strongly resisted change; and then there were the "inbetweeners". These were generally from outside Dublin, many of them sympathetic to change, but very aware of the political problems associated with being seen as "too radical" or "too modern". Enda Kenny was always an inbetweener.'

Perhaps the characteristic Irish politicians most share is their disinclination to be disagreeable to anyone. Many think of votes as lost by disagreement, rather than won by argument, or by taking a stand with which voters might agree. With a few exceptions, they are conflict averse. On those occasions when a politician finds himself in a position where he must take a decision that significant numbers of people will find disagreeable, he will usually plead that he has no choice – that someone or something is making him do it. The C case judgment would fulfil this function for Kenny. The 'inbetweener' was caught between Labour's demands for action and his own party's conservatism, but the expert group report would provide Kenny with a way out.

If many Fine Gael TDs were hyper-allergic to liberalizing Ireland's abortion regime, it wasn't just because they held strong pro-life views – though they did – but because they had given explicit promises not to legislate for abortion in advance of the general election.

By international standards, Ireland remains a very anti-abortion country, and there is nothing like the majority support for access to abortion that there is in many comparable countries. It is arguable that this position is facilitated by Ireland's proximity to Britain – every year about 4,500 women providing Irish addresses use its extensive abortion services. But the number of people who believe that abortion is the most important issue for politicians is relatively small. Candidates running primarily on a pro-life ticket have been trying to get elected to the Dáil for more than two decades, without a single success. This lack of a popular electoral mandate has combined with a loss of the lobbying clout once enjoyed by conservative Catholic organizations such as the Society for the Protection of Unborn Children, the Pro-Life Campaign and the Knights of Columbanus – the 'Masterminds of the Right', as journalist Emily O'Reilly dubbed such groups in her eponymous 1992 book. In addition, the political influence of the Catholic hierarchy has almost entirely diminished. There was a time when these lay groups and the bishops could bring huge influence to bear on the politics and government of Ireland – the 1983 pro-life amendment of the constitution remains their outstanding monument – but their power is largely gone.

Some of these groups – or their successors – have realized this and sought to promote their points of view and their political agenda in a more low-key fashion, mostly by lobbying candidates who are standing for election. Ireland has a small electorate, a lot of politicians and an electoral arithmetic that places a comparably large value on each individual vote. Irish voters are consequently more powerful than their counterparts in many polities. They are very often fully aware of this, and seek to utilize this power. And many politicians will promise anything to help themselves get elected. So, while individual pro-life candidates have not mustered enough votes to be elected, the few hundred votes – or perhaps few thousand, depending on where – that the lobby commands in each constituency is of potentially enormous value to candidates in an electoral system where the difference between success and failure is often no more than a handful of votes. It gives them influence, if not representation.

As the parties prepared for and fought the general election campaign of February 2011, pro-life groups sought assurances from candidates that they would not vote in the Dáil to allow abortion in Ireland. And many candidates were willing to give them. A letter from Fianna Fáil headquarters issued to pro-life organizations and campaigners said that the party's position on abortion 'remained unchanged' – Fianna Fáil, it said, 'will maintain Ireland's ban on abortion'. It went on to promise, 'Fianna Fáil will uphold the right of the Irish people, and the Irish people alone, to decide on Ireland's abortion laws.'

That was fine as far as it went. But the pro-life lobby could read the political runes as much as anyone else. They knew Fianna Fáil wouldn't be in government. So it was Fine Gael candidates they targeted most energetically. In response, Fine Gael candidates were authorized by party headquarters to issue letters to any constituents who sought them. The letter began: 'Fine Gael is opposed to the legalization of abortion.' It went on to promise that an all-party Oireachtas committee would consider the judgment in the European Court of Human Rights. The letter, signed by director of elections Phil Hogan, also said that Fine Gael would 'bring to the all-party committee a clear commitment that women in pregnancy will receive whatever treatments are necessary to safeguard their lives, and the duty of care to preserve the life of the baby will also be upheld'. The letters were seized upon by pro-life campaign groups as a pledge not to legislate for the X case. Not surprisingly, they now started to produce their letters. This was entirely predictable. Did Fine Gael really think that pro-lifers would forget about them?

For many Fine Gael TDs the Savita case and the expert group report created a new context for the abortion discussion. Several admitted to having their minds changed by the Savita case. But it was a slow process, and Fine Gael constantly told Labour that it couldn't be rushed. Many were still under ferocious pressure from pro-life lobbyists. Gilmore was not insensitive to their situation. Months earlier, when he had told Labour TDs to back off on supporting private members' motions brought by left-wing TDs seeking legislation for the X case, he asked them to allow him the time to bring the Taoiseach around gradually. He needed Kenny to be willing to impose the whip on Fine Gael TDs when the time came to vote on the legislation that would, he anticipated, arise out of the report of the expert group. And, although Kenny had little enthusiasm for the task, this was what he was planning to do. He just wanted to do it at his own pace.

Labour appreciated this, but it kept the pressure on. When Reilly suggested at cabinet that there was no need to rush into legislation,

Gilmore reacted furiously. When the cabinet had agreed to the publishing of the expert group report, it had also agreed a timetable for making decisions of substance on the issue and set the end of the year as the deadline for deciding on a course of action. Gilmore was determined that they stick to that plan.

A week before Christmas, at the final cabinet meeting of 2012, Labour got its way. The Fine Gael leadership knew Gilmore was under pressure from his own side over the budget. If we're going to legislate next year, we might as well say so now, they reasoned. So the cabinet agreed to proceed to legislate for the X case along the lines of the expert group report. It also decided that the Oireachtas health committee would hold a series of hearings on the legislation in the new year.

Following the cabinet decision, the government announced that legislation would be passed by the summer of 2013. The package of measures would include detailed regulations to follow primary legislation. Crucially, while the government statement made no mention of the risk of suicide being the basis for a termination, Reilly confirmed that the legislation would cover the area of suicide, as it was 'very clear' that the Supreme Court judgment in the X case included suicide as grounds for abortion.

For Labour, that cabinet decision was perhaps the vital step. The expert group report had certainly been important in signposting the way – but how many previous reports had been left languishing on shelves in government departments? However, with a cabinet decision to legislate in place, the health minister had to deliver something. Labour TDs, beset by a hostile reaction from their own grassroots to another austerity budget, and still reeling a bit from the rebellion of party chairman Colm Keaveney, now had something they could point to as a concrete Labour achievement in government. This, they were able to say credibly, would not be happening if we weren't here.

The Oireachtas health committee convened for three days in early January, meeting in the Senate chamber, chaired by a self-consciously authoritarian Jerry Buttimer, the Cork Fine Gael TD. Buttimer was a bit of a hooligan in the Dáil chamber and took especial delight in heckling his constituency colleague, Fianna Fáil minister Micheál Martin. But in his new role he was efficient, even-handed and determined to brook no dissent or disruption. He received many compliments about his chairmanship, and he was delighted.

It rapidly became clear that suicide was the key concern for the anti-abortion campaigners, and for many Fine Gael TDs. The pro-life lobby received some comfort from the perinatal psychiatrists who gave evidence. Dr John Sheehan of the Rotunda maternity hospital said, 'I refer to the question on whether we, as perinatal psychiatrists, have ever seen a situation in that termination of pregnancy has been the treatment for a suicidal woman. To reiterate our statement, with more than forty years of clinical experience between us, we have not seen one clinical situation in that this is the case.' However, Dr Anthony McCarthy of the National Maternity Hospital at Holles Street added an important qualification: he said that pregnant women who are suicidal would still go to Britain for a termination, because of the restrictions.

Dr Rhona Mahony, master of National Maternity Hospital, complained of the lack of clarity behind the current guidelines on when practitioners can terminate a pregnancy: 'I want to know that I will not go to jail and I want to know that she [the woman being treated] will not go to jail.' She said there had been three terminations in her hospital the previous year where the woman's life was at risk and the foetus was not at a viable stage. On a national scale, she estimated that between ten and twenty abortions are carried out each year in Ireland. On suicide, she said that two women in Ireland took their own lives while pregnant between 2009 and 2011.

The evidence of Mahony and other obstetricians – including her predecessor as master at Holles Street, Dr Peter Boylan, who favoured a change in the law – was highly influential with a number of wavering Fine Gael TDs. The doctors hardly seemed like raving abortionists; rather, they were compassionate professionals trying to do their best for mothers and for their babies. Even if Mahony's fear of imprisonment was pretty unlikely to be realized, they were saying there was a 'grey area' in the law and they were asking the politicians to fix it.

The committee hearings were widely praised for the generally calm and civilized manner in which they were conducted. But they also demonstrated that the pro-life activists were not minded to accept any compromise on the legislation. Once suicide was included as grounds for a termination, they would oppose it.

Whatever about expert evidence from interested and disinterested parties at the committee, this was now a political process. The most intractable politics is that which is rooted in culture, and culturally Fine Gael and Labour were miles apart. Since the inclusion of suicide was what most alarmed the pro-life lobby, some Fine Gael TDs started laying down markers on it. Meanwhile, Labour TDs pointed out that legislating for the X case meant, de facto, legislating for suicide; there was no way around it.

But compromise is the business of politics, especially in a coalition government. The compromise that the original cabinet decision had arrived at was that legislation would proceed and would include provision for abortion in cases of threatened suicide, but that it would be tightly controlled. The argument now became about exactly how 'tight' the suicide test should be.

The general concerns of the pro-life groups about mental health grounds for abortion were well founded. The experience of several other jurisdictions – including Britain, where almost all Irish abortions take place – has been that apparently restrictive mental health grounds lead over time to a regime where there are practically no restrictions on abortion, at least in the first six months of pregnancy. But the Irish situation was never going to be about simple 'mental health' grounds. The pro-life amendment of 1983 meant that the unborn life could be ended only if it constituted a threat to the *life* – and not just to the *health* – of the woman. That's why the threat had to be suicide. All sides agreed that it concerned just a tiny number of cases. Nonetheless, pro-lifers worried that once doctors were entitled to carry out abortions, on whatever grounds, that is exactly what they would do.

Labour may have got the decision to legislate, but Fine Gael was going to make it as restrictive as possible. Labour knew this, so while the preparation of the bill fell to Reilly's Department of Health,

Labour insisted that a group that included Labour junior ministers Alex White and Kathleen Lynch should oversee the process. The group met in the aftermath of the committee reports, and agreed that procedures that would facilitate abortions would be restrictive and formalized, though Labour stressed that they could not be so restrictive as to act as a deterrent to the exercise of a woman's constitutional right to abortion.

A key aim of the Fine Gael side became making sure that the matter wasn't just handed over to an individual doctor. There had to be a rigorous process involving multiple doctors. This soon became 'the more the better'. Proposals involving panels of two to three doctors were discussed. Ostensibly, there was no progress for several weeks. The attention of Government Buildings was focused on the promissory notes negotiations and eventual deal.

In the meantime, the inquest into the death of Savita Halappanavar took place in Galway. It was a huge media event, directing further attention to the forthcoming legislative proposals. The inquest revealed a catalogue of medical errors, yet many people – including her husband – believed that Ireland's restrictive abortion laws also played a role in her death. It was impossible to say if Savita would have survived had she been granted an abortion when she sought one, but Peter Boylan, the obstetrician acting as an expert witness to the inquest, certainly believed she would have. In any case, without a better diagnosis of her condition, any of the proposed changes to the abortion regime would not have enabled Savita Halappanavar to secure a termination in Ireland. Unless, of course, she was suicidal.

The temperature continued to rise in the Fine Gael parliamentary party as a group of TDs and senators became more and more vocal about their opposition to legislating for suicide. The former Taoiseach John Bruton argued strongly against legislating for the X case, on the oft-rehearsed pro-life grounds that the Supreme Court's verdict in the X case was mistaken. Bruton knew that his pleas to ignore the Supreme Court and the ECHR would cut no ice with the government – he was appealing directly to the backbenchers and the grassroots, effectively inciting rebellion against the leadership. Leadership insiders were scathing about one of their former heroes.

The lobbying from pro-life activists became more intense, ranging from well mannered but insistent to abusive. Several Fine Gael TDs took exception to the more aggressive lobbying, and some complained to the Garda. Government Buildings just asked TDs to hold off until they saw the legislation, and most complied. But, as they awaited publication of the draft heads of the bill, nerves were put on edge in late April when the *Sunday Independent* published transcripts of secretly recorded conversations with two Labour TDs, Anne Ferris and Aodhán Ó Ríordáin. The two TDs had been recorded while speaking to a third-level student who was posing as a pro-choice activist. Both spoke about Labour's plans to coax Fine Gael into implementing abortion legislation. 'We need to get 76-odd Fine Gael TDs who are very anti-abortion to walk into Leinster House and vote for it,' Ó Ríordáin told her. A lot of the 76-odd Fine Gael TDs were pretty annoyed when they read that. Ó Ríordáin was pilloried, even by his own. The fact that his brother Colm was Gilmore's chief economic adviser added spice to some of the internal criticisms. Sure it was a sting operation; but nobody made him say it. It made Fine Gael even jumpier.

Two days later, the *Daily Mail*'s page-one headline asserted that 'Fine Gael chiefs' were 'prepared for loss of 26 TDs'. If it was true, it meant that the abortion legislation was finished. Kenny could not push anything through over the objections of a third of his TDs. But it wasn't true. If the hard-line pro-life lobby in Fine Gael had over twenty TDs, they would have marched them out on to the plinth on Leinster House immediately, and that would have been that.

In fact, there were two points of view within Fine Gael. One faction was opposed to establishing suicide as a basis for abortion on moral grounds, and believed its case was strengthened by the evidence before the committee. The other, much larger group consisted of TDs and senators who reluctantly accepted the need to legislate for the X case, but were concerned that the legislation should not open the doors to a much more liberal regime. In other words, they wanted the suicide test to be as tight as possible. It was the second group that Kenny and his officials worked on. Trust me, he told them. I'm one of you.

Mindful of the Fine Gael view that the more doctors who had to examine an apparently suicidal woman the better, Reilly produced a new draft of the heads of the bill in mid April that included a two-stage process to be undergone when a woman sought an abortion on the grounds of suicidality. The heads are not the legislation itself, but rather a description and explanation of what each section will do when drafted. But this document was unusually detailed. Under the first draft of the heads of the bill, a case of threatened suicide would have to be assessed by two three-doctor panels.

Labour was enraged. 'Reilly has lied, lied and lied again on the abortion legislation,' texted a senior adviser. In fact, under Reilly's proposals, if a woman wanted to appeal a refusal from the six doctors, her case would have to be evaluated by three further doctors. That made nine all in. Fine Gael spin-doctors were insisting that the abortion bill would be tabled at the following week's cabinet meeting; Labour sources said 'no way'. The six-doctor story was leaked to the *Sunday Times*. 'Labour rejects "unworkable" abortion bill', it reported. All hell broke loose.

As Labour TDs vented their fury in public and in private, Anthony McCarthy, one of the psychiatrists who had given evidence to the health committee in January, described it on *Morning Ireland* as 'a sick joke'. Reilly emerged to insist that a suicidal woman would not have to be 'interviewed' in person by six doctors, though that was not what had been reported.

Despairing of Reilly's surprises, Labour sources said there was no way they would agree to such a proposal. The cabinet got a briefing from Reilly that Tuesday that only left Labour ministers even more annoyed. The Taoiseach and Tánaiste were sufficiently concerned to convene a meeting of several senior ministers later that evening to find a way forward.

But tensions were also rising in Fine Gael. Its TDs were facing up to the fact that the coalition was going to push ahead with a suicide clause – as, really, they should have understood since December. Their constituency offices were coming under huge pressure from pro-life activists. There were several angry exchanges at the parliamentary party, but Kenny stood his ground. Waterford TD John

Deasy – a long-time opponent of Kenny – fairly pointed out that TDs had been promised a say in this decision, but were being frozen out, and were about to be presented with a *fait accompli*. He was right. That was exactly what was going to happen. Kenny dismissed calls for a free vote, angrily telling Dublin South TD Peter Mathews that he didn't know what he was talking about: a free vote would put even more pressure on TDs, Kenny said. He had long since had enough of Mathews, who frequently tested the patience of meetings with lengthy, if informed, critiques of the banks and banking policy. He would later declare his opposition to the legislation. Lucinda Creighton objected to the bartering of policy concessions on abortion with Labour. It was appalling, she said, to be saying to Labour, 'You let us impose pay cuts and we'll give you abortion.'

Privately, several more TDs warned that it would be 'very difficult' to support a suicide clause. Others told journalists that rebel TDs could break away and form a new party, speculation carried in several newspaper reports. Kenny's people monitored dissent through their excellent networks in the party, but they remained phlegmatic. They knew there was strength in numbers: if there were enough TDs prepared to break, they would come out and say so. One TD noted that Kenny had expertly separated the 'floodgates' people – who were concerned that legislation could have unintended consequences – from the hardliners, who were opposed to any legislation that included suicide. The latter were much fewer in number. The TD was right: it was a skilful piece of politics by Kenny.

The next week was taken up with increasingly fraught negotiating and drafting of the final heads of the bill. Reilly removed his second tier of assessment for threatened suicide, and the proposals reverted to a shape much closer to Labour's wishes, though with a tight suicide test. By Monday night the two parties had a draft they were happy with, and prepared to put it to cabinet the next morning. It was draft 43 of the heads of the bill.

The following morning at cabinet, Reilly walked in with version 45. Labour immediately objected, demanding to know what the changes were. The discussions were postponed, and only resumed at a special cabinet meeting that evening at 5.30 p.m. Early-evening news bulletins reported that ministers were still trying to reach agreement on a draft. In fact, Reilly and the Labour minister Alex White were alternating at the computer in the Taoiseach's private secretary's office, typing up amendments to the legislation. Kenny and Mark Kennelly hovered near by. Advisers and ministers came in and out. Some used the opportunity to lobby their colleagues for places on state boards for party supporters. 'It's fucking chaos here,' texted one insider. 'Like Fianna Fáil never left.' Shortly before 9 p.m., and nicely in time for the evening news, the cabinet signed off on the heads of the Protection of Life during Pregnancy Bill. The final document was marked 'draft 51'.

After 8 a.m. the next morning, government press officer Tom McLoughlin peered out at the assembled journalists in the Press Centre in Government Buildings, checking his watch frequently. If it was early for a press officer, it was very early for the journalists. But government spinners had carefully considered the choreography of this. Getting out early didn't just make sure that the government's interpretation of the bill was the first that most people heard; putting the press conference live on *Morning Ireland* enabled Enda Kenny to speak to middle Ireland directly and unmediated. Kenny was notoriously tardy, but RTÉ was calling the shots for this one. He would have to be on time.

Pale and appearing tired, the Taoiseach took to the podium and repeated his core message: We are not changing the law on abortion, he reassured. It wasn't quite 'nothing to see here', but it did seem incongruous given the tortuous negotiating and politicking that had preceded the publication of the heads. But Gilmore did not contradict him, saying it was already legal in Ireland to end a pregnancy when there is a risk to the life of the mother.

In private, and very possibly with full awareness of the other's position, both party leaderships were claiming entirely opposite interpretations for the legislation. Fine Gael TDs were told it would be implemented in as conservative a way as possible; Labour that it represented a significant liberalizing of the position. With regard to Kenny's assertions that the law was not changing, the Labour leadership quietly explained that they had to allow him the latitude to say this to his own people and to the nervous conservatives in the country at large. But, they insisted, it was not true. The law was being changed. 'Ah, come on,' one senior figure told me, when I put Kenny's words to him. 'It's the biggest change since 1983.' Because of the nature of the issue, Labour did not claim victory. But that is how it was regarded inside the inner circle. In the words of one insider, it was 'an outstanding political achievement'.

When Labour insisted it wanted the abortion legislation in place before the Dáil adjourned for the summer break, it was deadly serious about hitting that deadline. That meant the Dáil would have to pass the bill by the middle of July, to give the Seanad time to pass it by the end of the month. 'If we have to,' promised one Labour figure, 'we'll keep them in there until the middle of August.'

On 20 June, James Reilly rose to propose the second reading of the Protection of Life in Pregnancy Bill. 'I stand before the House today fully aware of the sensitive and complex nature of the matter we are about to deal with,' he began. It was, he continued, the beginning of a difficult debate. He was only half right. The Dáil exchanges would be polarized all right, but what followed wasn't really a debate – it was a series of statements. Nobody's mind would be changed by any of them, not least the leadership of the coalition. If Bismarck compared making laws to making sausages – saying that nobody should watch either being done – horse-trading is a more apt comparison for law-making in a coalition government. However, when it came to the abortion bill, by the time it reached the Dáil, the process resembled nothing as messy as sausage-making or horse-trading; instead, it was like a military campaign, and it was time to make sure that the foot soldiers followed orders. But one of the officers was preparing for mutiny.

If Lucinda Creighton had been surprised when Enda Kenny pulled her aside at the celebrations on the night he became Taoiseach and told her, 'I will be giving you a call tomorrow', then she certainly didn't expect to be handed one of the two most prestigious junior ministerial posts, European Affairs (the other being given to Brian

Hayes, another rebel). Yet she had seized the opportunity and earned the respect of politicians and officials at home and abroad, especially during Ireland's presidency of the European Union in the first half of 2013.

But as early as the previous December – as they were driven to a European Council meeting in Brussels – Creighton had let the Taoiseach know her strong anti-abortion views. After their conversation, she thought Kenny had no intention of legislating for abortion in the case of threatened suicide. So she was horrified when the legislation was announced the following week. *Gilmore's got what he wanted*, she thought. She was right.

Months later, she sought a meeting with Kenny to discuss the issue; it was weeks before he found a slot in his diary. She laid out her objections; Kenny responded using the vocabulary that would become familiar in the debate: *This is about saving lives*, and so on. *What is he talking about?* she thought. Later, when she tried to argue that introducing the legislation would be electorally disastrous, Creighton learned from a high-ranking party official that both the bill, and the language that Kenny and the ministers were using, had been run through focus groups to ensure maximum public acceptability. As ever, Kenny's machine was leaving little to chance.

In the time leading up to the Dáil debate, there had been a lot of overheated speculation about the number and nature of Fine Gael defections. But as the debate ran its course, the question seemed to become reduced to this: *What will Lucinda do?* Most in the political and media bubble around Leinster House were unable to process her apparent willingness to sacrifice her ministerial position on a matter of principle. *What was she really at? What was the angle? What complicated political manoeuvre was this?* In fact, though she was in a minority inside and outside the party in her interpretation of the abortion bill, Creighton simply proposed to do exactly what she had always indicated she would do.

In the hope that she would be able to effect amendments at the later stages, Creighton voted with the government in the early stages of the bill. Yet she already knew she had little hope of getting amendments through. On 1 July, she had made a strong speech, attacking the bill. Later that day, she travelled to Strasbourg with Kenny. Though his advisers were frosty, Kenny, as ever, was friendly and made small talk. 'Look,' she said, 'I want to talk to you about abortion.' She told him James Reilly would accept no amendments or compromises. But Kenny knew that already. And Creighton knew he knew. Earlier a cabinet minister had texted her: *You're wasting your time with these amendments – the deal is done.* In truth, it had been done a long time ago.

On the final weekend before the vote, ministers worked the phones in an attempt to keep down the number of defectors. Leo Varadkar rang one TD and embarked on small talk. Leo, he said, bemused, you've nothing to worry about; I think the legislation doesn't go far enough. The conversation was repeated all over the country. For TDs who were strongly pro-life – and there were several – it was difficult. For the rest of them, it just wasn't something the public was that exercised about.

In the final days, as those in the Dáil endlessly rehearsed their positions on the bill, groups of pro-life and pro-choice supporters gathered outside, the former maintaining a three-night, two-day vigil. The pro-life demonstration was mostly, but not exclusively, religious in character; much to the delight of the pro-choice people, who taunted them mercilessly.

In an ill-judged attempt by Government Buildings to get things wrapped up, the Dáil sat until 5 a.m. on the Thursday morning, 11 July. TDs were allowed to say as much as they wanted to. The session resumed twelve hours later, but it soon became apparent that the fight was going out of the anti-abortion TDs in the chamber.

Then Creighton's moment came. Shortly after 8.45 p.m., the first group of amendments – including one proposed by Creighton – was put to a vote. The division bells rang and TDs trickled in. Creighton sat in her allotted seat at the front of the chamber. The Taoiseach was conspicuously engaged in amicable conversation with Cork TD Áine Collins, who had been pulled into a controversy – via fellow TD Tom Barry's lap – much earlier that day. Creighton chatted to Fergus O'Dowd. She looked nervous. When the question was put, Brian Hayes leaned over towards her and asked her a question. She nodded

once. The light denoting her seat on the monitors blinked red, surrounded by a sea of green dots. Creighton looked deflated and rueful.

After the vote, she sat on the steps beside Kenny. 'I'm sorry it has
come to this,' she said. He returned the pleasantries. And then: 'Will
you write me a letter of resignation? I'd have to convene the cabinet
to dismiss you.' After the next vote, he saw her again. 'I saw you on
Prime Time, well done,' he said, 'I'll talk to you about your future
again.' Creighton was a bit taken aback. Then Kenny pressed her:
'Can I have that letter by the next vote?'

Creighton's vote was strangely cathartic. The debate picked up
pace. There would be no changes to the bill, beyond the minor ones
the government had already conceded. At 12.25 a.m., on Friday
morning, 12 July, the final vote was taken: 127 votes to 31, a massive
level of parliamentary consensus. 'It's done,' Labour TD Aodhán Ó
Ríordáin tweeted. The legislation moved to the Seanad the following week. It passed there, with less fuss, but considerably more
acrimony. Then to President Michael D. Higgins, for his signature.
And then inevitably, in one way or another, to the courts.

19

'Falling bond yields butter no parsnips'

Anyone who has given a speech to a hostile audience knows how much easier it is when the crowd is on your side. Eamon Gilmore is no different. The Labour leader is not a natural orator (few Irish politicians are), but he can be a powerful speaker when his subject connects with the mood of his audience. And he has rarely faced a more supportive audience than he did at the O'Reilly Hall in UCD, on Sunday, 6 March 2011, as Labour delegates gathered to discuss the leadership's motion to join a coalition government with Fine Gael.

True, the notion of 'Gilmore for Taoiseach' had been washed away by a combination of its own one-dimensional appeal and Fine Gael's carefully prepared assaults on Labour's tax policy. Yes, Labour had flirted with utter disaster, at one stage falling behind Fianna Fáil in the party's private polls. And it was now clear that any government would have a significant Fine Gael bias. But the Labour campaign had finished on an upward trajectory, and the team that scores last to secure a draw is always happier than the one that has conceded, even if they have both attained the same result. The mood was jubilant and determined. Everyone knew that the conference would vote to join the government – with Labour having asked for and been granted late-deciding votes to deny Fine Gael an overall majority, it could hardly do otherwise – but Gilmore's speech still gave them a thrill, and they cheered him to the rafters. Whatever the rejectionistas on the left of the party might say, mainstream political parties exist to attain and use power, and now, after a long, long time, Labour was on its way back into government.

Wisely, the Labour leader warned the delegates of the hard times ahead. Be prepared, he told them, to walk through 'forests of placards'. By the summer of 2013, almost halfway through the government's

term of office, they understood well what he had meant. The forests
had grown quickly.

In early 2012 I sat opposite a Labour adviser in his office in the
Government Buildings complex. He leaned back in his chair, took a
long drink from his cup of coffee and stretched. There were piles of
paperwork on the desk. A hockey stick stood in the corner of the
office. I wondered idly what exactly it was used for. Not to play
hockey, I thought. His mind was firmly on the longer term. 'Look,' he
said. 'If in four years' time, people believe things have got better under
us and they are optimistic about the future, then we'll be re-elected.' In
December of that year, Gilmore gave an interview to the *Irish Times*.
By the end of 2013, he said, we would be in a 'post-recession' Ireland,
and Labour would see a political dividend from that.

The comments reflected the Labour leadership's long-term view
of the coalition government, and of its political fortunes within it.
That it viewed economic recovery as its route to political success
meant that, for the time being anyway, the interests of the country
were aligned with the interests of the party. This was in direct contrast to the latter period of Fianna Fáil in government under Bertie
Ahern, when the re-election prospects of Ahern demanded short-
term and ultimately disastrous economic policies by his government.
The coincidence of the economic and political cycles had changed,
and would change again – but for now, Labour hoped, they were
aligned. And that gave the governing core of Labour a clear medium-
and long-term focus. The problem is that being in government
– especially during an economic crisis – is like being under fire from
a machine gun spitting out short-term problems.

The Labour leader faced pressure from events, from a fractious and
nervy parliamentary party, from an organization fearful of facing
voters and from a deputy leader who was following a careful and
deliberate strategy to position herself as an alternative to his leadership. The forest of placards outside would be the least of his worries.
The bigger threats came from closer to home.

Twenty-four months after Gilmore's UCD speech, on 6 March 2013,
the leaders of the government parties came together to mark two

years of their coalition. 'We are not looking for claps on the back or credit,' the Taoiseach said. Sometimes we require politicians to tell us the most ridiculous lies. The Tánaiste nodded gravely. 'No one is claiming victory,' he said. The day before, the Taoiseach had moved the writ for the Meath East by-election, indicating a short campaign that would end on 27 March. When it came to the by-election, it was just as well Gilmore had said he wasn't feeling victorious.

Labour's candidate was massacred in Meath, by a margin so great that it sent shockwaves throughout the party and rocked Gilmore's leadership in the days that followed. All this was a massive overreaction – 'for God's sake, we got 6 per cent in a presidential election and we didn't lose our heads', complained a senior Fine Gael figure – but such overreactions are part of the dynamic of politics. It was entirely predictable.

Nobody expected the Labour candidate, Eoin Holmes, to be elected, and he seemed determined to fulfil those expectations. The two issues that he appeared to most identify with were legislation for the X case and the legalization of gay marriage. Though important to elements of the Labour base, to say they did not resonate with the voters on the ground on this occasion was an understatement. It required either remarkable chutzpah or political blindness for a candidate to have himself pictured toasting gay marriage legislation while running for election during the worst recession in the history of the state, in a constituency split between a commuter-belt south decimated by the economic crash and a largely culturally conservative rural north. As the conservative commentator John McGuirk tweeted sarcastically, 'Still cannot believe the Eoin Holmes/Ivana Bacik gay marriage photocall didn't boost the Labour vote in Nobber.' There was nothing stronger than water in their glasses, but that hardly mattered. The image of him making a toast with Labour's leading social issues liberal told the story of much of the campaign. Toast was right.

Actually, councillors (as Holmes was and is) and TDs are a good deal more 'in touch' than most commentators. This is one of the reasons why they find it hard to make decisions that people don't like, irrespective of their necessity. But Holmes wasn't running this type of campaign because he was 'out of touch'; he was running it because he had a bad political strategy.

The leadership was happy for him to beat the drum about social issues as a message to Labour's base everywhere outside Meath East. He was a sort of political suicide bomber, sacrificing himself to a greater end. The level of media admiration the candidate attracted may have made strapping on the explosives vest a bit easier – he was widely described in reports as an excellent candidate by journalists who related easily to a jeans-wearing, left-wing film producer and café owner, who wished for, in his own words, a 'more modern, liberal and tolerant Ireland'. In fairness, most reports acknowledged that, despite this excellence, his appeal was not catching on the ground. 'He's the ideal by-election candidate,' said one. 'Sadly it's not the ideal by-election.' It may have been more accurate to say that Holmes was an excellent individual, but a poor candidate.

Not satisfied with an epic flameout, Holmes's campaign then targeted Labour's partners in government for some gratuitous abuse in the final days before the vote. He published a leaflet depicting Taoiseach Enda Kenny as welcoming every possible outcome of the by-election campaign – a Sinn Féin win, a Fianna Fáil win, a Fine Gael win – with a cheery 'Grand so. No change in government', via speech bubbles imposed on doctored photos. Only a Labour victory – meaning 'more power to Labour' – elicted a 'Drat!' from the Taoiseach. Most politicians have a broad tolerance for election stunts like this. The reaction in Fine Gael ranged from widespread anger at a constituency level to bemusement among the leadership. Why bother to assault your coalition partners in a contest you had already lost?

When the result of the first count was announced, Holmes's performance in winning just over 1,000 votes and less than 5 per cent of the vote received the ultimate insult from his opponents' supporters: many burst out laughing. The candidate himself appeared briefly in the count centre but then hightailed it out of there. You could hardly blame him, but it looked dreadful. 'The childish behaviour of the Labour Party candidate Eoin Holmes in throwing a sulk at the count centre in Ashbourne last night provided a vivid image of the party's calamity,' scolded Fionnan Sheahan in the *Irish Independent*.

Labour ministers – many of whom were out of the country on St Patrick's Day trips for a period in the middle of the campaign – were shocked by the extent of the defeat. Labour TDs saw an intimation of their own mortality. Labour councillors shuddered at the thought of facing the same voters in just over a year's time. Maybe everyone expected to lose, but nobody expected to lose so badly. As news of the tallies emerged from Ashbourne, alarmed calls and texts flew non-stop around the Labour political apparatus. 'Why are we concentrating on the 10 per cent issues?' asked one senior staffer of the candidate's advocacy of gay marriage and abortion law reform. Later, he texted: 'On balance, I'd take 10 per cent now.'

Pat Rabbitte fronted up and agreed to a request from local TD Dominic Hannigan to go to Meath to face the music at the count. Labour's former leader can take it as well as give it; he has the hide of a rhinoceros. 'Falling bond yields,' he observed, 'butter no parsnips'. Gilmore stayed away. The following day, the Tánaiste recruited a few backbenchers to stand supportively behind him as he ran with one of the oldest political tropes: We are listening and we hear the message. 'I don't intend to ignore it, I don't intend to ignore what we have heard from the people in Meath and we will address it.'

He was not, however, so keen on what he was hearing from some of his own party. A scattering of councillors surfaced in the Sunday papers calling for his head, with some favouring his replacement by Joan Burton. In the *Sunday Business Post*, a Meath councillor declared, 'The public have lost faith in Gilmore.' Semi-detached party chairman Colm Keaveney weighed in with an op-ed piece decrying a 'failure of nerve' by the party leadership, who were failing to 'defend Labour's values'. There was an orgy of 'What now for Labour?' coverage. All parties react to media coverage. Labour tends to react more than others. 'It's just the type of people in our party,' sighs a senior adviser. 'What the fuck was riding on this? Nothing!' bemoaned one minister.

But it had been a mistake to pay the campaign so little attention. The five Labour cabinet members meet before the cabinet proper for discussions every week. They never once discussed Meath. 'I don't believe that Eamon Gilmore was involved in one serious discussion about the Meath by-election,' says one of those. That wasn't quite true, but there is no question that the contest was far down the list of the Tánaiste's priorities, and those of his key staff. Though they didn't admit it publicly, they now realized that was an error. And they had to deal with the consequences. Having created the mess – or at least been complacent while the mess happened – they had to clean it up.

'The trusty old listening exercise. Malcolm [Tucker] would be proud!' A government adviser was texting his amusement at Gilmore's efforts to reach out to his TDs after the Meath disaster. Less charming, more wearily cynical, more scathing and certainly more foul-mouthed in its treatment of British politics than its *Yes Minister* predecessor, Armando Iannucci's scatological television satire *The Thick of It* nonetheless reminds some people in government that the public face of politics is often, very often, the direct opposite of what is happening in private. While the level of incivility practised by Iannucci's communications adviser character Malcolm Tucker is not completely unheard of in Irish politics, it is unusual; people are not usually so eye-wateringly abusive. But the show's depiction of the basic tactics of political management – such as the 'listening exercise' – is true to life.

While Gilmore's public response was to listen humbly and engage with his backbenchers in a conversation about the state of the party and the future of the government, in private he worked to minimize the fallout and put the sorry episode behind him. No amount of listening to his backbenchers was going to change his political strategy. That strategy had been evolving since the formation of the government, and it had for months past been focused on asserting a more independent and recognizably 'Labour' stance for Labour in the coalition. It sought to project the smaller party's identity as a distinct part of the government that achieved identifiable things. This was not dreamed up as a response to Meath East. Gilmore and his staff didn't think the result that significant. But the by-election disaster certainly gave the strategy more impetus. Within weeks, however, the Tánaiste and his party would be faced with another, potentially more serious reversal.

Who won and who lost in the battles that preceded the 2013 budget is still discussed at all levels of government. Certainly, Labour's climb-down on its public demands (made public by itself, of course) for a 3 per cent increase in the universal social charge for higher earners lent weight to the claim – often heard from Labour people, actually – that Fine Gael had 'won' the budget battles. Fine Gaelers acknowledged that, but they pointed to other concessions on tax, particularly on taxes aimed at the wealthier, as evidence of what they had conceded. Neither side wanted to claim outright victory in public, as they knew there would be a resumption of hostilities the following year. But it is true that the perception that Fine Gael had 'won' was felt much more in Labour than vice versa.

In fact, while Fine Gael had been determined to beat back Labour's USC demands, it had conceded quite a lot on tax. This was a product of two things. One was Michael Noonan's belief that the more certainty he could give on the taxation horizon the better, and he conceded several moves on tax (such as on pensions tax breaks for the wealthy) that would not come into operation until 2014, to allow people to plan confidently for the future. The second was the undertaking Noonan got from Labour to cut the public sector pay bill.

Not surprisingly, nobody trumpeted this from the rooftops at the time. But, according to Fine Gael people who were closely involved at every stage of the construction of the budget in November/ December 2012, Labour's agreement to move on the public sector pay bill was a vital part of the architecture of the budget deal. Labour points out that Brendan Howlin had been engaged for months already on the pay-bill issue through his efforts to squeeze public service allowances and overtime. The fact is, the pay reductions were in the budget numbers. It's understandable that at the time of the budget nobody broadcast that Labour had agreed to cut public service pay; as it was, Labour backbenchers had a tough enough time voting for cuts to child benefit. But that's what happened. And early in the new year Howlin invited the trade unions to renegotiate the Croke Park deal with the aim of saving €300 million.

Up to this point, Howlin had been the star performer among the Labour cabinet members. He had reduced spending in line with commitments to the Troika while maintaining – just about – public acquiescence with the programme. He had supervised the continuing reduction of numbers in the public sector, instituted under the first Croke Park deal, while maintaining industrial peace. He had kept the parliamentary party on board. He had haggled and horse-traded at budget time for social welfare and health budgets. But it was a juggling act, and he knew it. Now, the need (which Labour acknowledged) to cut the public sector pay bill would throw another ball into the air for him to keep up. It would be one too many.

Actually, Howlin had been struggling with two directly competing imperatives since the previous summer. He had to reduce the public sector pay bill, but he wanted to keep the trade unions on board and avoid strikes by public servants that he and others feared could pull the coalition asunder. That, at its most basic, was his dilemma. In preparation, he had commissioned a review of all allowances and premium payments in the public sector with a view to making substantial savings in an annual bill for salary add-ons that ran to €1.5 billion a year. Over the years, a Byzantine system of allowances and special payments had evolved in the public service as a way of giving extra pay to people without increasing the headline salary amounts. When the substantial pay increases of the Celtic Tiger years arrived, the allowances system remained in place. It followed the first rule of public sector budgeting – when there's money there, it gets spent.

The result was almost a shadow system of public sector pay that topped up the modest pay of many lower- and middle-income public servants. There were some 1,100 different allowances across the public sector. Some areas were positively bulging with them. Teachers could get them for all sorts of duties – such as yard duty – which many parents regarded as part of the job. The total cost of teachers' allowances was over €600 million. Prison officers received an average of fourteen different allowances. The Garda pay bill featured payment of more than 100 allowances.

The squeeze that many journalists were feeling on their own incomes gave them a heightened interest in all stories about public sector pay, and the allowances report was built up into a major development. Allowances such as the one for eating a sandwich at your desk were splayed across front pages for the consideration and outrage of the public. Then, in September 2012, Howlin finally announced that just one of the existing allowances for existing public servants would be scrapped. For the first time since he took the job, he was utterly savaged.

In public, Howlin pooh-poohed the criticism as 'crude' and 'simple'. At cabinet, he 'complained bitterly of the scars on his back' from the allowances débâcle, recalled one person at the table. At the EMC, however, he told colleagues that he was putting together the basis for a new public sector pay deal that could make significant savings while locking in the public sector unions for the remainder of the government. There was as much support for this on the Fine Gael side as there was with his Labour colleagues. 'If we can do it,' said one Fine Gael minister then, 'it will dwarf any savings we might have made from the allowances.' Enda Kenny laid down covering fire in public, asking all departments to report back to him on how they could 'sweat' the Croke Park Agreement for more savings. Back at cabinet, several ministers didn't know what to make of Howlin's strategy. Joan Burton, who had excellent relations with the trade unions, was nonplussed. She didn't know what Howlin was at. She wasn't sure he knew either. Whatever it was, Howlin wasn't telling them.

Howlin didn't just ship criticism from the media. While Fine Gael ministers were cautiously on board for his plans for a wider deal with the unions, Fine Gael backbenchers – as usual kept out of the loop – were angry that the government appeared to have caved in rather than taken on the public sector unions. They were furious when a *Sunday Business Post* survey that summer demonstrated that many public servants had seen the impact of the 2009 pay cuts eliminated or at least mitigated by the payment of annual increments to their salaries since then. The feeling was especially strong among a cadre of younger TDs, who became known as the 'Five-a-Side Club', as they had played indoor soccer together. They weren't really rebels, but they were frustrated. Leinster House is a hard place to keep a secret, though in truth they weren't especially secretive, and they had already come to the attention of the Taoiseach and his chief whip Paul Kehoe, who had suggested they disband forthwith. The place, the Taoiseach intimated, for any discussions about government policy was at the parliamentary party. Where, as the group knew well, such discussions never happened in any meaningful way.

They continued to meet, albeit a bit more surreptitiously. But when – as they saw it – Howlin ran up the white flag to the unions on the allowances issue, they were spurred into action. Eight of them published a joint op-ed article in the *Irish Examiner* calling for allowances and increments to be frozen. Labour went bananas, accusing them of an 'anti-public sector agenda'. Louth TD Ged Nash likened them to the elite Oxford University dining society, the Bullingdon Club, whose former members included George Osborne and David Cameron. The comparison was preposterous. Having pints and talking politics in Buswells Hotel is not that rarefied an outing. But it demonstrated the prickliness between the two parties outside ministerial level. Several ticking-offs were duly delivered to the Five-a-Siders by the chief whip, who summoned each of them in turn to his office by text message. 'We know all about you,' one of them was told. He thought the Gestapo charade idiotic. Kenny criticized the eight publicly.

Howlin wondered if the young TDs had been put up to it by Noonan. In public, Howlin was airily dismissive of the Five-a-Siders; in private, he was furious. Months later, he would have an angry confrontation with one of its leading members, Dublin South East TD Eoghan Murphy, outside a committee room. In front of onlookers, it finished with Howlin demanding, 'What did you say to me?' Murphy replied, 'Excuse me for expecting better.'

But Howlin's suspicions about them were incorrect: the Five-a-Siders had always acted on their own initiative. At leadership level at least, Fine Gael was prepared to back him. The quid pro quo was that he had to produce results. So when, after weeks of negotiation, an agreement on a new public pay deal that included pay cuts was struck with the unions in the early hours of Monday, 25 February, Howlin thought he had squared the circle. But it wouldn't be quite so easy.

The deal was due to be accepted or rejected by the union memberships by the middle of April. The basic belief of the government was that the union members would have to agree, because the alternative was pay cuts imposed by legislation. Government confidence that the public sector trade unions would sign up to the pay reductions under Croke Park II steadily diminished as the deadline for ratification by their members approached. As the date neared, Howlin grew more and more explicit in his warnings about this. In the days before the SIPTU ballot was due, he wrote an op-ed in the *Irish Independent* warning of across-the-board pay cuts of up to 7 per cent if the deal went down. 'Public servants that under this agreement face a gross reduction in pay of, say, 4 per cent could potentially see that increase to 7 per cent in the absence of an agreement,' he wrote, or rather his advisers did. The *Indo* splashed the warning across its front page. It looked like panic from Howlin. It was something like that.

In February when the union leaders agreed the deal – which saw pay, allowances, overtime and increments reduced by a varying array of degrees – their morbid assessment was that this was the best they could do in the circumstances. Seven weeks later, their members' answer was: Do better. On Tuesday, 16 April, word began to filter through to Howlin's officials. First it was indications; then unofficial word; then courtesy calls; and finally the official result. The mood in Government Buildings was black. SIPTU, as ever, was the crucial result. The country's largest union held the key: if it backed the deal, the votes it controlled on the public services' committee of the Irish Congress of Trade Unions (ICTU) would be enough to pass the deal, albeit by a tiny majority. That would create all sorts of problems for the union movement, as several unions, including those representing nurses, teachers and doctors, had already said they would refuse to be bound by a 'Yes' vote. But Howlin would have his deal and, crucially, Labour could implement the pay reductions while saying it was with the consent of the majority of unions. In the event, a low turnout among SIPTU workers chose to ignore union chief Jack O'Connor's typically agonized and watery endorsement. They narrowly voted to reject the deal. Croke Park II was dead.

Dead maybe, but not buried. Not yet, anyway.

Immediately, there was horror in Labour circles in government, and spinners struggled to even put out holding lines. Fine Gael filled the void. The savings would be made, the Taoiseach insisted. One way or the other. Labour pleaded with their colleagues not to do or say anything that would make retrieving the situation impossible. Fine Gael was deeply sceptical, but for the most part held off.

Though the coverage was muted, this was a moment of true crisis for Labour. Two weeks after the Meath by-election disaster, and following a slew of apparently unfavourable polls, few TDs would have been willing at that point to vote through a whopping 7 per cent pay cut on all public servants. Two years earlier, many of those same TDs had knocked on public servants' doors during the general election campaign and told them that if they wanted to keep the protections of the Croke Park Agreement, they had to vote Labour. Turning around now and saying 'Sorry, things have changed' was going to be problematic for many of them, to put it mildly.

One of the myths of Irish politics was that public servants voted for Labour. In fact, they were more likely to vote for Fianna Fáil – an allegiance that was only strengthened by the avalanche of pay increases and perks that came public servants' way during the Bertie Ahern era. When the Ahern years of bounty were followed by the Cowen–Lenihan regime that slapped two substantial pay cuts (one of them was the pension levy) on public servants, the ties between the public sector and the natural party of government were frayed and severed. In 2011 Labour made a straight play for public service votes and won a lot of them. Now its TDs were faced with the prospect of doing a U-turn and imposing a third pay cut on the same people whom they had promised to protect from Fine Gael's budget cutting agenda. 'No way could they get it through,' said one person familiar with the Parliamentary Labour Party at the time. 'Not a chance.'

If Labour lacked the political wherewithal to implement what was an agreed budget measure, that called the very survival of the coalition into question. Howlin did the only thing he could do: he played for time. Just wait, some officials cautioned. Don't do anything now. Just wait a bit. In war and in politics, delay can be a crucial, transformative tactic. The Labour leadership knew it was in a crisis, but also that consequences only truly began if they chose immediate confrontation – either with the unions or with their own TDs. So they delayed. 'It's only a crisis if we have the vote now,' said one of the key people involved.

Howlin, his secretary general Robert Watt, senior official Paul Reid and adviser Ronan O'Brien had been living with this for six months. They weren't ready to give up on it just yet. Within days, feelers had been put out to the unions. There might not have been a plan B, but both sides were willing to give plan A another go. Ireland's foremost industrial-relations fixer, Kieran Mulvey of the Labour Relations Commission, was contacted. Mulvey's report: All was not lost. Howlin held his nerve. A second round of negotiations tentatively got under way.

There were two great variables in any new process to reach a deal. The first was whether any concessions in the talks – necessarily limited, given the government's apparent determination to maintain its €300 million savings target – could persuade the thousands of public servants who had voted to reject the first deal to change their minds. The second was whether Labour was capable of making good on the threat to legislate for pay cuts if the renewed talks were not a success. Gilmore and Howlin's people set to work on both fronts. They also implored Fine Gael ministers: For God's sake, say nothing.

Both groups needed some time to assess their position. But they also began to realize that there were certain facts that would not change, however inconvenient they were. First, there was the government's budgetary situation and the commitments it had given to Ireland's lenders in the Troika – which was already expressing some concern about slippage in the much vaunted Irish appetite for reform. Union leaders were told that maintaining the budget numbers that the government had already pledged (not just to the Troika but, perhaps more importantly, to the financial markets that would be depended on to fund the country's borrowing requirements in the future) was not negotiable beyond cosmetic adjustments.

In addition, there was also a growing realization among the unions: an industrial-relations war with the government would produce no winners, and certainly not among their members. While Jack O'Connor's immediate reaction to the first ballot result was to warn the government against unilateral pay cuts on pain of industrial action, he knew that a wave of strikes could be disastrous for the trade union movement. In such encounters, public opinion is vital – because the state of public opinion is directly related to the strength of the government's position when the eventual negotiation comes.

It was an article of faith among trade union leaders that the public sector had been unfairly demonized in the media, and, while they had a point about the monotone of some coverage, they conveniently overlooked the piles of data that pointed to an irrefutable public sector advantage in salaries, conditions, pensions and job security. For many private sector workers, the defining image of a November 2009 public sector 'day of action' against threatened pay cuts was not a march on O'Connell Street demanding 'fairness', or picket lines of shivering nurses, it was lines of cars streaming northwards to Newry to do the Christmas shopping. Closing schools and other vital services would be unlikely to generate support for the public sector workers, and the union leaders knew it. They also knew that Howlin knew it. 'The underlying foundation of the whole thing was this: neither side wanted a strike,' said one participant.

Perhaps more importantly, the union chiefs began to realize that sinews were stiffening in the Parliamentary Labour Party. This too was a recognition of the facts of the situation – busting the budget meant busting the government. And if the polls said Labour's prospects looked shaky for a general election in 2016, that vista was positively rosy compared with what was likely to happen in 2013. There was no doubt that many TDs were unhappy with the things the government believed itself obliged to do. But once they started to contemplate it, withdrawing from the coalition did not appeal to many of them either. This was a harsh truth to face for Labour, but it has underpinned the entire middle phase of this government. Labour made a fateful decision when it entered government and signed up for years of austerity. It just has to make the best of it now.

Labour's thinking was communicated to the union leaderships in a series of frank conversations between Howlin and key officials in the Department of Public Expenditure. The coalition would go as far as it could to help the unions; but then it would do what it felt it had to do. The union chiefs came to believe that not only did the government intend to do what it said, but that it now had the political capacity to do so. The unions were also shown the legislation and taken through the way it would operate; it conferred huge powers on the government to tailor pay cuts in the most politically advantageous way. It was a much more potent threat. 'We told them we would do it in such a way as it was believed.'

The product of these emerging dynamics in the unions and in Labour rescued the Croke Park II deal, turning it into the Haddington Road Agreement (to the relief of the GAA authorities). Fine Gael was prepared to see some slippage on the €300 million target for 2013, but not on the essential thrust of the reductions in the pay bill. When unions signalled their acceptance of the deal in June, Howlin hailed their decision. His colleagues thought he should get the credit. He had backed the unions into a position where they had little choice but to agree. Faced with a political catastrophe in April, he had turned it into a stunning victory, setting himself up in a position of commanding authority for the budget process and reinforcing Labour's hand. It was a virtuoso piece of politics.

It is one of the great truisms of politics that what is claimed in public is often the direct opposite of what really happens in private. There are two political realities: the one presented to the public – where discussions are frank but friendly, where everyone supports the party leader and where the only poll that matters is the general election – and the one that takes place behind closed doors, where people fight bitterly, politicians scheme against their leaders, and parties fret constantly about how much the public likes or dislikes them. Nowhere is this truer than in the area of loyalty, party unity and personal relationships.

Since the beginning of the administration and before, relations between Eamon Gilmore and Joan Burton were simultaneously courteous in public and hostile in reality. There was no trust and little cooperation between them. Behind the imposing façades of Government Buildings and Leinster House, this had become an unmistakable and ever present part of everyday life in the government – Gilmore and the rebellious, independent deputy leader whom he couldn't control and who, he often believed, was undermining him and the government. There were numerous policy and budget battlegrounds between Burton and Howlin and Noonan, and the broader Fine Gael side of government. Some of the other Labour ministers thought she was a problem. But the war with Gilmore was constant, and personal.

The difficulties between the leader and the deputy leader of the Labour Party went back long before he had declined to appoint her to a finance ministry. There were differences of personality, party history, temperament and politics. She was old Labour; he was old Workers' Party. She was a lone woman in a man's world; he was — though no sexist — one of the boys. His office ran the party; she wanted to be acknowledged as deputy leader. She thought he was out of his depth politically and economically, and she thought she would do better; he believed she was running her own agenda — 'Team Joan' — to the detriment of the government and the Labour Party within it. His failure to appoint her to one of the finance jobs certainly wasn't the start of the problems between them, but it brought them to a new level of seriousness and antipathy. From then on, though they served in the same cabinet and ostensibly sought the same objectives, they were, by any meaningful definition, political rivals.

They clashed regularly, usually by proxy. Burton, or more usually her staff, had been savaged on several occasions by Gilmore's people for what they saw as her many transgressions. She had been warned at cabinet by both Gilmore and the Taoiseach (though her personal relations with Kenny were friendly) about budget leaks, and she had been told that speaking out about a deal on Ireland's bank debt — as she had on a few occasions before the fiscal treaty referendum — could put the entire effort to secure a deal at risk. In private, the two sides briefed against each other almost constantly. Fine Gael thought: Joan is Eamon's problem.

By the spring of 2013 Gilmore's people openly discussed the fact that Burton was seeking to take the Tánaiste's job. They scoffed when — in an interview with Miriam O'Callaghan on RTÉ radio along with her husband Pat Carroll — she repeatedly dodged the question on whether she would like to be Labour leader. It would have been easy to say, Eamon Gilmore is the leader and he has my full support. But she didn't. She said the public don't want to see politicians squabbling. Then Pat Carroll said the same thing. He referred to the constant behind-the-scenes war between Tony Blair and Gordon Brown and warned of the 'incredibly destructive effects' of such ongoing conflicts in a government. 'Joan is very conscious of that,' he added. It was the nearest Burton or those close to her ever came to a frank public admission of the difficulties between herself and Gilmore. 'Burton does not deny leader hopes,' reported the *Irish Times* of the conversation. Gilmore's people thought it was merely confirmation of something they knew already. 'She wants to be leader of the Labour Party,' one of them told me. They were right.

But Burton was doing so in a cautious and calculated way. She would not challenge Gilmore outright – not unless things got very much worse for the government and for Labour and even then probably not until after the local and European elections of 2014. There was lots of idle chat about a stalking horse, and there were even a few TDs who might have been prepared to volunteer for the role. But Burton did not have anything like the level of support among TDs necessary to launch a challenge; nor was disaffection with Gilmore's leadership sufficiently intense or widespread among TDs. Everyone could see that his political capital and capacity had been degraded by government, but that was a different thing from believing things would be better if he were dumped.

What Burton set out to do in the spring and summer of 2013 was part of a more sinuous and subtle strategy, but it was one with the same end – regicide – in mind. She agreed with analysis after the Meath by-election result – when several councillors were clamouring in the media for her to replace the leader, by means they did not specify – suggesting that a change of leader would amount to nothing more than a new leader doing the same things. So she set out to create a different and distinctive political space for herself, from where, if and when the time came, she could present a viable alternative for the party. After weeks and months of discussions among her closest circle, Burton began to ease herself away from the most unpopular aspects of government policy through a series of speeches, articles and interviews. It was never far enough away from government policy to provoke outright conflict, but it was far enough to send a message to Labour TDs, to the party organization, to the unions, to the public. And to Gilmore's allies, who watched her in anger, convinced treachery was afoot. 'Joan is trying to become leader of the Labour Party,' another said, 'and she doesn't care what the cost is.' One old hand was sanguine. 'Joan is positioning herself, of course she is. That's all she ever does. It'll come to nothing.' Others weren't so sure.

Three weeks after the Meath disaster, with tension and fear and uncertainty still bubbling in the Labour Party, Burton gave a speech to a conference of the St Vincent de Paul Society in Dublin. The symbolism was clear. The message was too. 'I believe,' Burton said in a speech that had been heavily trailed to the media in advance, 'that we have reached the limits of austerity.' The text of Burton's address carefully skirted the issue of whether she was taking exception to domestic economic policy or the wider European policy dispensa-tion. 'It is my strong conviction that the time is right to put in place a new economic strategy based on sustainable growth, investment and full employment.' It was a skilful feint, though the subtleties – as well she knew – would not gain as much amplification in the media as the basic message. 'End austerity now – Burton and Gilmore in serious rift' blazed the *Sunday Independent* headline. 'Her strong cri-tique,' the story said, 'will also be seized upon by a growing element within Labour which has been severely critical of the party leader-ship's emphasis on continued austerity.'

If reports of Burton's Vincent de Paul speech were enough to infu-riate Gilmore's people, they didn't calm down when they turned to the *Sunday Independent*'s magazine. Normally fronted by a young woman wearing very little, the magazine this weekend had a slightly older cover girl, wearing all her clothes. It was the minister for social protection. 'Joan stands firm as Gilmore's Labour crumbles around her' read the headline. The picture spread showed her relaxing at home in modest suburbia. Over the lengthy interview by the wry and observant Will Hanafin, the introduction ran, 'Joan Burton doesn't exactly say she wants to be leader of the Labour Party. Instead she tells you lots of little facts that lead you to conclude that she would be a better leader.' Actually, some of the facts weren't that lit-tle at all. Burton's positioning on policy might have been delicate, but the mood music was unmistakable.

Burton followed up her in-bed-with-the-*Sindo* act with a shame-lessly populist intervention in the growing public debate about the gigantic scale of corporate tax avoidance by means of offshore arrangements – some of which, it transpired, had been facilitated by the Irish government. Burton criticized rock band U2 for arranging some of its tax affairs through the Netherlands. It was, of course, irresistible for the media – Minister bashes Bono. It was also a criticism that was neither new, nor original, nor much refuted by the band's weak and constant rejoinder – that it was a 'global business which pays taxes globally'. The defence was repeated everywhere without anyone bothering to point out that it was a meaningless statement. The episode was initially a one-day media story, though it was inevitably interpreted in Government Buildings as evidence of Burton's plotting. If it was, it was pretty basic stuff. Burton's people chortled at the headlines. When it emerged months later that U2 had 'made known their displeasure' to the government after Burton's remarks, they were practically rolling around the floor.

A few weeks later Burton was again the cause of a spike in Gilmore's blood pressure. Along with four other European politicians, she published an article in the *Guardian* – and several other leading European newspapers – that was again critical of austerity policies and sought investment and stimulus in economically weaker states. Gilmore's people saw another act of distancing herself from government strategy and of moving towards a more populist stance – a further repositioning of herself by the deputy leader. Yet they could hardly disagree with the arguments Burton and her colleagues were making. 'Can you point to a single thing in it you disagree with?' asked Ed Brophy, her special adviser, when he was tackled. The mood in Government Buildings deteriorated further when they heard that German chancellor Angela Merkel had invited Burton to Berlin to discuss youth unemployment, a subject that the social protection minister had long been talking about. Gilmore had already asked the OECD to develop an action plan to tackle youth unemployment in Ireland. Burton was told she would be undermining Labour's allies in the German Social Democratic Party by fraternizing with Merkel in an election year. The meeting still went into her diary.

Whatever they thought were her deficiencies in the policy area, Gilmore's people acknowledged that Burton was good with the media – though they did not regard this skill as reflecting well on either party.

As the June bank holiday weekend heralded a period of fine weather that the country craved, they were reminded again of this facility. The front page of the *Mail on Sunday* blared: 'Burton: Work or I will cut your dole'. There are a few issues that are always sure to arouse the *Mail*'s front-page attention. House prices. Middle-class women drinking at home. Immigrants abusing the system. And welfare scroungers. For an announcement of a mild tweaking to welfare provisions that would reduce dole payments when recipients refused offers of work and training, Burton was rewarded with a lionizing editorial that gushed about her 'bold move on dole scroungers'. 'No previous minister had the stomach to do what Ms Burton is now preparing to do.' If the political double entendre was deliberate, it was rather good.

In fact, welfare reform (Fine Gael's phrase; Labour called it 'welfare cuts') was shaping up to become a bigger issue in the second half of the government's term. Burton was attempting to resist Fine Gael demands for huge reductions in the welfare budget, but she was also getting tough on 'activation measures' that pushed people off welfare and back into work. It was a 'twin track' strategy of holding out against the Fine Gael call for cuts, but pushing Labour well beyond its comfort zone on reforms. The technical complexities and political difficulties would go well beyond those allowed for by the *Mail*'s headline treatment of the subject, but one aspect of the issue especially appealed to Burton: she believed that Gilmore would have to back her on resisting the big cuts targeted for her department. If Burton was going to fight publicly against welfare cuts, it would be hugely problematic for the Labour leader not to support her. She began her public opposition of a proposed €440 million in cuts for the 2014 welfare budget in the early spring of 2013. Privately, she was telling people there was not a chance it could be done. By the summer, she was saying so publicly. She told a *Newstalk* interviewer it would be 'difficult, to be perfectly honest' and warned about the deflationary effects of cuts of the magnitude mandated. In Government Buildings, they kept their counsel. They figured they would be agreeing the welfare budget and just presenting it to Burton. The two camps were looking at the same issue, but politically they were on different planets.

Gilmore and his staff mostly resolved to ignore Burton's increasingly public efforts to assert herself as a strong presence in the budget debate. But they found it hard. In mid June, Gilmore spoke at a Labour Youth event in Cork, and used the occasion to lay down a marker with a speech calling for families to be given 'breathing room' from the 'relentless grind' of austerity in future budgets. It had been flagged by Labour spinners in advance as a significant speech, and everyone else was warned not to do or say anything that would detract from the impact of the message. But Burton was speaking before him, and, as ever, she had other ideas. The lead story in the following day's *Sunday Times* was 'Burton calls for minimum wage increase'. Gilmore's people had half expected it. Their attitude was: If she wants the leadership, she can come and try to take it off him. If she did, Gilmore planned to fight her for it.

'Who has done the most damage to Labour?' asked a senior figure in the administration, spreading his hands wide in interrogation, before answering his own question. 'Labour people have.'

The desertions from his parliamentary party wounded Gilmore and unsettled the party at every level. The old warhorse Willie Penrose had been the first to go, a man caught between the government's fiscal plight and the demanding local realities of Irish politics. It was a demonstration for the Labour organization, if one was needed, of how different government was from opposition. Dublin West TD Patrick Nulty was gone soon after winning a by-election in the autumn of 2011; Tommy Broughan, always an opponent of coalition, left then too, unwilling to support a budget that further slashed public spending in health, education, social welfare – all the things he believed Labour should be defending. Broughan was unbending in his adherence to his attitudes, which had taken on the rigidity of principles. The following autumn Róisín Shortall resigned in protest at Gilmore's failure to back her against James Reilly, provoking a reaction in the party that Broughan's departure had not. The stirrings of an alternative Labour view began: an organization called the Campaign for Labour Policies began to hold meetings. Another austerity budget a few months later prompted the exit of party chairman Colm Keaveney and Limerick senator James Heffernan. Keaveney's departure caused a political storm, and a furious backlash against him by Government Buildings. In April, MEP Nessa Childers announced she was resigning from the parliamentary party, saying she could no longer support a government that was 'actually hurting people'. Childers was long regarded as unreliable and even slightly eccentric, but her departure, though not a significant event – MEPs rarely have more than marginal impact on domestic politics – was unwelcome. Seven members of the parliamentary party had now gone. As every resignation put more pressure on the TDs who stuck with the government, insiders railed at the quitters. In public, they were depicted as flakes who just didn't have the bottle for the battle to save the country. 'Join the army, wear the boots,' growled one handler. In private they were variously lacerated by their former colleagues for being concerned only with saving their own necks, to the detriment of the party and the country. Those who abandoned the party or criticized its actions were accused of being bitter, attention-seeking, mendacious, disloyal, mentally unstable. But even Gilmore's staunchest loyalists admitted the stream of resignations hurt him. He couldn't go on losing them at this rate.

If the political scruples of Labour members were a constant headache for Gilmore, the misdeeds of Fine Gael ministers caused him the occasional migraine too. Health minister James Reilly's many mishaps were a constant worry. Labour insisted that it could not be expected to be the watchdog for Fine Gael ministers – the unspoken understanding was that Labour ministers were Gilmore's problem and Fine Gael ministers were Kenny's problem. But this was an operating procedure, not a rule. Labour knew that if Reilly was found to have committed a cardinal sin, like any other politician, he would have to resign. If he didn't resign, and if the offence was serious enough, Labour would have to insist he went. Conscious of the seriousness of such a move – Labour couldn't be rebuffed and stay in government – the bar was set pretty high. Reilly might have nudged the bar a few times, but he never dislodged it. Labour had no confidence and less trust in him. One staffer summed up the party's view of the health minister: 'He's a guy in a market in the East End of London who is trying to sell you a toaster. "Oi, mate! You wanna buy a TOASTAH? Look at this BEAUTY!"' Labour didn't want to buy Reilly's toaster, but they didn't want to call the police either, unless they had to.

With Alan Shatter, it was different. Labour didn't really understand Shatter (few did), and many of them didn't like him much. But they respected him, and they knew he was important to Kenny. So when Shatter landed himself in hot water by making comments on television about an encounter between independent TD Mick Wallace and the Garda, Labour regarded it as improper and unwise, but not a hanging offence. In truth, Shatter was hoist on his own petard. In the course of a *Prime Time* programme on RTÉ, he had thrown at Wallace an account of an incident in which the independent TD was subjected to nothing more than a bit of finger-wagging from a traffic garda. Shatter was attempting to discredit Wallace's entirely justified questioning about a largely underplayed scandal in which gardaí had cancelled penalty points for a series of well-known people. It was a typically aggressive gambit by Shatter, who was never content with defeating opponents – he seemed to want to destroy them. In any event Wallace's credibility – he was the Dáil's best-known tax cheat – was already pretty shaky. What soon became the issue was not whether Mick Wallace had been ticked off by a garda, but how Shatter had found out and how appropriate it had been for him to be throwing the information across a television studio. The *Daily Mail* did the research and unearthed what Shatter had said about Fianna Fáil's Willie O'Dea when he was forced to resign in 2010: O'Dea, Shatter had said then, 'publicly discussed, for his own electoral gain, confidential information furnished to him by a member of An Garda Síochána'. For this, Shatter said, O'Dea must resign. This was precisely what the justice minister had now done. 'Shatter's hypocrisy' boomed the *Mail*. Fianna Fáil put down a no-confidence motion.

'I'll tell you what,' said one senior Labour figure, 'it's easier than sticking by James Reilly.' But when another independent TD, Mattie McGrath, told the Dáil about an incident between Shatter and a garda with a breathalyser in which Shatter was alleged to have behaved superciliously and dismissively (nobody had any difficulty believing that), Labour became much more nervous. Shatter denied some of the detail, which included the deliciously incriminating 'Do you know who I am?' line, but confirmed an encounter had taken place. The controversy raged for weeks. The *Irish Independent* pursued the story with the sort of determination born of access to informed sources that always unnerves politicians. Labour and Fine Gael circled the wagons, and the justice minister survived the no-confidence motion. But that didn't make the story go away. The incident remains an unlit fuse under Shatter. If McGrath's – and the *Independent*'s – account of events is proven in the future, Shatter is surely finished. Labour remains deeply uneasy about it.

Coming into the summer of 2013, the anxiousness in Labour about its standing in the opinion polls had substantially abated, its nerves eased by the realization that once properly interrogated, the polls were not as bad as some people had thought they were, and that even if they were, Labour was pretty much stuck with the decision it had made to enter government in 2011. There was no going back now. The settled view of a very large majority of the parliamentary party was that pulling out of government in all but the most extreme circumstances was simply not an option. The voters were not anxious to see them, and they were certainly not pressing for an appointment with the voters. There is a deceptive simplicity to many political decisions.

And yet, in their hearts, many Labour people remain uneasy with the implementation of tough austerity policies. The psychodramas of the coalition government are largely Labour's. The leadership is hard-headed, as it must be, and makes decisions accordingly. The party, as a whole, buys the logic. But politics is sometimes an emotional business too. The tension between Labour's rational economic side and its emotional political side, reflected in the wider national debate on how we conduct our affairs in an age of international austerity, is a daily feature of life behind the public façade of politics.

Relations with the party's coalition partners are occasionally strained – and frequently hostile at the lower ends of the political food chain – but the commitment to see out the coalition programme at the top of government is as strong as when the two parties entered government in the first place. Ministers are becoming ever more restive about the dominating power of the Economic Management Council in the affairs of government, and the internal difficulties in Labour between the deputy leader and the leader seem likely to worsen, rather than abate. Fine Gael finds Labour's 'obsession' with its own political fortunes increasingly tiresome. As Labour determines to assert its identity more in government, this fault-line seems likely to widen. The two parties remain in agreement on the same broad strategy for the government. But the tactics to achieve it increasingly divide them.

Early in the summer, I had a lengthy conversation with one of the most senior people on the Labour side of the government machine, someone who knows Eamon Gilmore's mind intimately. We spoke about the effects on Labour of being in government, the current state of the party and its relationship with Fine Gael, and the future for Labour and for the coalition. Afterwards he walked me to the door of Government Buildings, while we chatted about the affairs of the week. The day's political chatter was of the usual crises of the moment, some of the coalition's own making, some not, some not really crises at all. I mentioned the 'government line' on an issue. He stopped at the door. 'There is no "government line",' he said. We stepped out and looked across the quadrangle of Government Buildings. The Taoiseach's office was to the right, the Tánaiste's to the left. Officials buzzed past us. The afternoon was bright and warm – after a long bleak winter and a spring that never seemed to arrive, summer was making a spirited effort to break through. He half turned to go back in, and then paused. 'There is no government message,' he repeated. 'There are two parties who are agreed on things that have to be done.'

Index